Who's On TIME?

Who's On TIME?

A Study of TIME's Covers From March 3, 1923 to January 3, 1977

by Donald J. Lehnus

OCEANA PUBLICATIONS, INC.
NEW YORK • LONDON • ROME

Library of Congress Cataloging in Publication Data

Lehnus, Donald J.   1934-
Who's on TIME?

Includes indexes.
1.   Biography—20th century.   I.   Title.
CT120.L35   920'.009'04   79-17330
ISBN 0-379-20684-6

TIME (Magazine)

Manufactured in the United States of America

TABLE OF CONTENTS

ADVERTENCE AND ACKNOWLEDGMENTS

The idea for this study; the research and analysis of the data; the organization and presentation of the information; and the conclusions drawn are entirely those of the author, who is solely responsible for the contents.

This author did not consult or use in any form or manner any employee, or anyone who is or ever was connected with TIME; nor did he consult or use any bibliothecal or archival material, or any other files or records that TIME may possess. This author is not now and has never been associated in any way with TIME—except as a reader and subscriber.

Much gratitude is owed to the librarians of the University of Puerto Rico Library (Río Piedras, P.R.) and the Martin Luther King Memorial Library (Washington, D.C.) for their assistance and suggestions in locating much of the biographical data necessary for this study. Also, special thanks must be given to the employees of the Computer Center of the University of Puerto Rico who keypunched the data and did the computer programing and printout of the analysis.

D.J.L.

FIFTEEN CENTS

TIME

The Weekly News-Magazine

VOL. 1, NO. 1

MARCH 3, 1923

JOSEPH G. CANNON, Appeared on the first cover of TIME. b. Guilford, North Carolina - 1836. d. 1926. A Representative from Illinois for twenty-three terms and Speaker of the House from 1903-11, declined renomination for Congress at the end of the Sixty-seventh Congress (March, 1923).

Who's On TIME?

CHAPTER 1
THE BEGINNING OF TIME

As early as 1921 the idea of a newsmagazine was conceived in the minds of two recent graduates of Yale University (Class of 1920), Henry Robinson Luce (1898-1967) and Briton Hadden (1898-1929). These two young men talked over many aspects of their future newsmagazine, and the possibilities and probabilities of its survival and later excelling all other such publications. They discussed such questions as:

> ... How differently would they treat the news in their magazine? How could news be more quickly told for busy readers? How could it be better organized? How could it be made more visually attractive? How could they maintain readers' interest in a weekly whose news would necessarily be far in arrears of daily papers with international wire-service facilities?
>
> They studied the newsmagazines they would have to buck, headed so decisively by the Literary Digest that they hardly had to consider the others. The Digest seemed to settle any doubts that "old news" was readily marketable. It was a national institution, circulation 1,200,000, fat with advertising, seen on every respectable fumed-oak table and assigned to high school and college students for its coverage of current events. Its "news service" was very nearly scot-free. It consisted of subscriptions to the more important American newspapers and a few published elsewhere in the world. The Digest frankly stole its news from these papers, usually quoting them directly. The victims seldom complained because the magazine gave them full credit and because by the time it used their property it was several days old—waste material by daily journalistic standards. In that sense the Digest ran the most profitable news junk shop in the world. But it performed a useful service, an advance over the breathless patchwork and discontinuity of the dailies and bringing vital issues into more leisurely focus. It gave two or more sides to contentious issues by quoting newspapers holding opposing opinions —important to a public that wished to be informed, but often done with tiresome verbosity.
>
> Luce and Hadden thought they could do better with Facts, the working title of their creation.[1]
>
> ... [They were not] satisfied with the title Facts, and Luce later said that it was he who hit on the title Time as he rode home on the subway in exhaustion late one night. Alas, the evidence trips him in a mendacity. A magazine named Time, edited by Edmund Yates, had been published in England from 1879 to 1890, with a distinctive logotype identical in its hand-lettered design with that taken by its American descendant, . . .[2]
>
> ... [Luce and Hadden] consulted Melville Stone, the recently retired head of the Associated Press, as to the propriety of lifting news from daily papers. Stone assured them that news was public property after a day or two of aging. . . . The trio slaved over a prospectus that buttered the upper-crust educators and financiers from whom they would solicit prestige and capital. It warned them that they riskd being unenlightened because until then "NO PUBLICATION HAS ADAPTED ITSELF TO THE TIME WHICH BUSY MEN ARE ABLE TO SPEND ON SIMPLY KEEPING INFORMED." Time would inform them swiftly

because of its condensation and systematic organization of the news.[3]

. . . The first issue of Time, after more than a year of preparation, was dated March 3, 1923.[4]

The purpose of Time, said the New York Herald Tribune in a two-paragraph notice hidden on page 7, "is to summarize the week's news in the shortest possible space." It compressed the world's events into twenty-eight pages, minus six pages of advertisements sold at give-away rates. Although this was a time of big news—the American quarrel over Prohibition, the French occupation of the Ruhr, the German protests, the turmoils of the League, the famine in Russia—Time's account of it all could be easily read in a half-hour.

It was of course not for people who really wanted to be informed. It was for people willing to spend a half-hour to avoid being entirely uninformed. The editors so well redeemed their promise of brevity that Time seemed the capsulized abridgment of a condensation. Yet, considering the youth of its founders and the hectic conditions of its production, it was a surprising achievement.[5]

At the time Luce and Hadden began publishing their newsmagazine they probably never dreamed that TIME would soon overtake the *Literary Digest* and later take it over. This was reported in an article in TIME under the heading, "*Digest* Digested," and stated:

After a life of 48 years, during which it achieved a unique place in U.S. journalism, the *Literary Digest* last week was taken over by TIME, thus ceasing to exist as a separate publication. First issue of the *Literary Digest* appeared on March 1, 1890. Its publishers, Isaac Kauffman Funk & Adam Willis Wagnalls, classmates at Wittenberg College (Springfield, Ohio) and ordained Lutheran ministers, conceived the magazine as "a repository of contemporaneous thought and research as presented in the periodical literature of the world." In 1905, this formula was extended to include newspaper comment on the news. . . . On February 24 it suspended publication.[6]

The cover of TIME's first issue on March 3, 1923, portrayed the U.S. Congressman, Joseph Gurney Cannon, who was retiring at the age of 86. About this choice James A. Linen wrote:

TIME's young founders, Henry R. Luce and Briton Hadden, had asked advertising agency friends for advice on the art layout for their first cover. During this consultation, they decided to use the portrait of a personality outstanding in the current news—a TIME tradition ever since.[7]

Because of his impending retirement from the U.S. House of Representatives after having served twenty-three terms, Cannon seemed the obvious choice for the cover. TIME's first cover story was entitled "Uncle Joe" and reads thusly in its entirety:

Joseph Gurney Cannon, grand old man of Congress, will retire from public life. At the age of 86, having served 23 terms in the House of Representatives, he feels that he has earned the right to spend the rest of his life in the quiet seclusion of Danville, Illinois. Uncle Joe is something more than a politician with an age-record.

He is the embodiment of a tradition, a political theory, a technique of party government and discipline that is fast perishing. He represents the Old Guard in the very flower of its maturity, in the palmy days of McKinley and Mark Hanna, when "a little group of wilful men" did more than make gestures of government; they actually ruled Congress, shrewdly, impregnably, and without too much rhetoric.

Uncle Joe in those days was Speaker of the House and supreme dictator of the Old Guard. Never did a man employ the office of Speaker with less regard for its theoretical impartiality. To Uncle Joe the Speakership was a gift from heaven, immaculately born into the Constitution by the will of the fathers for the divine purpose of perpetuating the dictatorship of the stand-patters in the Republican Party. And he followed the divine call with a resolute evangelism that was no mere voice crying in the wilderness, but a voice that forbade anybody else to cry out—out of turn.

On March 4 Uncle Joe will be gone and Henry Cabot Lodge alone will remain to carry on the banner of the ideal. To the American people, however, the senior Senator from Massachusetts must perforce seem a little too genteel, too cold, too Back Bay to serve as an adequate trustee for the Old Guard tradition. They will long for the homely democracy of Mr. Cannon, so often expressed by those homely democratic symbols—Uncle Joe's black cigar and thumping quid.[8]

TIME was quite popular from the very beginning and seems to have met a need of the American public for just such a newsmagazine, because in 1929 readers were asking for lifetime subscriptions. There were three letters published in the May 27, 1929, issue (page 4). Mr. Bigelow Green of Boston stated, "I should be interested to have you quote me a 'life' subscription to TIME . . . ," and George P. Jenks of Germantown, Pa., opined,

I think you fail to appreciate the calibre of most of your subscribers. Has it ever occurred to you that some of them would prefer to take out a life subscription at $100 now than be bothered every year about renewing? Think it over TIME. Meanwhile here's my check for $8 for another two years.

Also, Miss Dagmar Edwards of Brooklyn asked, "If you ever give out Life Subscription Blanks please don't forget me, as yours is the only magazine of its type that I have found I enjoy reading from cover to cover—reading many things which are not only good for me but entertaining." To these three letters the Editor responded: "Do other TIME subscribers want 'life' subscriptions? If there is sufficient interest to warrant establishing a life subscription rate, it shall be done forthwith."

In the June 10, 1929, issue there appeared more letters of the kind given above. The Editor's response in that same issue (page 8) was, "A Perpetual (that is, to the end of TIME) and Inheritable Subscription would cost little more than a life subscription. TIME's deceisions will await further comment from subscribers." In the following three issues (June 17, June 24 and July 1, 1929) there appeared more correspondence from readers on the subject and by this time TIME had made the decision not to offer a "life" subscription, but rather a "perpetual" subscription. The coupon that appeared in these three issues reads:

> In announcing a Perpetual TIME Subscription, the publishers believe their action is without precedent in Publishing history. Life Subscriptions there have been. But the thought of TIME's being limited to a single lifetime is incongruous. TIME is timeless and so, too, is TIME's Perpetual Subscription.
>
> Sixty dollars, payable at the expiration of your present subscription, will bring TIME to you during your lifetime—to your heir and his heir—to the end of TIME.
>
> Perpetual Subscriptions are transferable, inheritable, non-cancellable. Enter your Perpetual Subscription now—when your present subscription expires you will receive a bill for $60. Once paid, TIME will forever after bring to you and your descendants all the news of all the world—every week—to the end of TIME.

How many persons took advantage of this fantastic offer has not been ascertained by this writer, but according to James A. Linen in "A Letter from the Publisher" (Jan. 23, 1950, page 7) there were 189 ongoing perpetual subscriptions at that time. One may think that $60 was a very cheap price when today's annual subscription rate is $31 a year, but in the summer of 1929 wages were not high, nice apartments in Washington, D.C., were renting for $40 to $80 a month, and a new Pontiac Six was selling for $745. Grocery ads announced bread at 9¢ a loaf; a 24-pound bag of flour, 95¢; milk, 13¢ a quart; and six pounds of cabbage for 15¢. This outstanding offer was made for a very short time and then withdrawn forever, but the fact that readers were desirous of such an offer does prove TIME's positive impact on the American public during its early years.

Thus it can be seen that from the very early years TIME was very well received and its popularity seems not to have diminished over the years, but rather to have increased considerably. TIME replaced the old *Literary Digest*, and now it is TIME that is found in every respectable place and "assigned to high school and college students for its coverage of current events."

Notes: 1. Swanberg, W.A. *Luce and his empire.* New York: Scribner's, 1972, p. 50.
      2. Ibid., p. 53
      3. Ibid.
      4. Ibid., p. 56
      5. Ibid., p. 57
      6. TIME, May 23, 1938, p. 46.
      7. TIME, Apr. 30, 1956, p. 15.
      8. TIME, Mar. 3, 1923, p. 2.

CHAPTER 2
THE STUDY: ITS SCOPE,
METHODOLOGY AND TERMINOLOGY

Since that first issue of TIME with "Uncle Joe" Cannon on the cover many other persons and topics have been depicted to point out the person or topic of the week. TIME's subtitle is "the weekly newsmagazine" indicating that the purpose is to keep the American people informed about national and international news once a week. The cover illustration is used to indicate the important news story of the week. This has been explained by John A. Linen in editorials which appeared under the heading, "A letter from the publisher," in which he stated:

> Being on the cover of TIME can, in its way, be a recognition of position of fine achievement—but not necessarily. TIME's gallery of cover subjects, as varied as life itself, is composed of men and women well remembered and long forgotten. The criterion for being on the cover was, and has always been, that they were news.[9]

> Many ... [readers]have written to ask why TIME has on occasion "honored" the enemies of the U.S. by placing them on the cover. The answer: TIME's covers reflect the news.[10]

A starting point for this study was the publication *TIME faces in the news*, which reproduced in miniature form 2,812 TIME covers and on the back cover of which the editors wrote:

> For fifty years, the faces on TIME have been the faces of the world. The makers of peace and war, the prophets, merchants and creators, the rebels and kings, the heroes of the age or of the moment—they are the cast of TIME's cover characters. Occasionally, a cover picture will symbolize an event, a trend or an idea. But always the individual reappears. For TIME believes that history is made by men and women, no matter how strong the forces and movements that carry them along. TIME also believes that history has meaning, that the rush of events can be grasped, reported and interpreted in an organized pattern.[11]

In the light of these comments it can be assumed that the person or topic on each week's cover is the newsmaker of the week. An accumulation of these covers would therefore point out the persons and topics which have been the newsmakers of any given period.

This study covers the period from March 3, 1923, to January 3, 1977, a period of almost 54 years during which time 2,814 issues (regular and special) of TIME were published. These dates were chosen because the first issue of TIME was dated March 3, 1923, and as the study was first begun in March of 1977 it was decided to include the years 1923 to 1976. The first issue of 1977 was also included in order to incorporate the cover for the Man of the Year of 1976. This author is basing the study on the idea that IF each of TIME's covers portrays the "newsmaker" of the week (albeit a person or a topic)

THEN an analysis of a cumulation of 2,814 covers would point out the persons and topics that have been the "newsmakers" in the American news during this 54-year period. If each of TIME's covers does indeed depict the most newsworthy person (or persons) or topic of the week, then some very interesting questions arise, such as: (1) Who were the people that appeared the most times? (2) Which topics have most frequently been on the covers? (3) Is there any professional or occupational group that has dominated TIME's covers? (4) Since TIME is an American newsmagazine are foreigners often on its covers? (5) Are women, blacks or other such groups considered newsworthy enough to make TIME's covers very often? and (6) Are non-living persons ever represented on the covers? The following analysis of TIME's covers will answer these questions and many more about the persons and topics which have been selected to appear on the covers of this weekly newsmagazine.

The original published form of the cover of every issue was perused, except in a few cases where it was necessary to utilize microfilm copy. This perusal included a complete examination of the cover, and often required reading the cover story to determine who was on the cover. Sometimes it was necessary to compare cover figures with other sources in order to identify those whose likenesses were on the covers. The covers used were those of the standard U.S. edition. There are several editions of TIME each week and not all editions have the same cover, especially the foreign editions which often have different covers as well as different cover stories for the same issue published and distributed in the United States.

The person may have been represented by a photograph, drawing, painting, sculpture, caricature, or by any other means through which his (or her) likeness was either identifiable by this author or identified by TIME. On those covers where more than one person appeared NO importance was given to the fact that (1) certain persons were the primary topics while others were placed in a secondary or background position, and (2) often two or more persons were presented as the primary topics and of equal importance for the cover theme. Sometimes the person's appearance was just incidental to the topic of the cover, but this author made no attempt to determine which persons were on the covers by design and who by chance. The only determining factors used were that a likeness of the person did appear on the cover and the person was identifiable. Thusly any person who was represented in any form whatsoever and was identifiable was accorded full treatment in this study as a person appearing on a cover. Such covers were considered as "person" covers.

A "topical" cover is one on which no identified or identifiable person appears. Often models are used to illustrate a cover story; if they were identified then the cover was considered as a "person" cover, but on the other hand, if they were not identified or identifiable, it was considered as a "topical" cover.

No attempt was made to classify covers by topics when there were identified persons on them. Animals were consistently considered as "topics" even though they were identified by name.

Of the 2,814 covers analyzed in this study there were 2,613 which depicted 3,336 identified persons and 201 covers which were classified as "topical" because no identified or identifiable person appeared thereon. The number of persons on each cover ranges from one to twenty-seven, thus explaining why there are 723 more persons than there are "person" covers. Among these 3,336 "persons" there are many "individuals" who appeared more than once. In those cases where a person's likeness was reproduced two or more times on the same cover he was considered as "one person" on that cover, e.g., several photographs of Howard Hughes were used for the cover of the Jan. 24, 1972, issue, but Hughes was counted as appearing once on that cover; a photograph of Nixon was replicated ten times on the cover of Oct. 24, 1969—it was counted as a cover portraying a single person.

Even though the terms "person" and "individual" are synonymous they have been used with different meanings in this study. People who appeared more than once are considered as a "person" for each cover appearance, but as an "individual" when referred to by name, e.g., Richard Nixon appeared fifty-five times and this was counted as fifty-five persons appearing on the covers, but when referred to by name he is considered as a single individual. In his case he is an "individual" who accounts for 1.65 percent of all the "persons" on the 2,613 covers depicting identified people. Thusly there are 2,344 "individuals" who comprise the 3,336 "persons."

A file card was made for each identified person on all covers published from Mar. 3, 1923, to Jan. 3, 1977. Every time the same individual appeared a new file card was made. Each of these 3,336 cards contained the following information: (1) name, as currently known at the time of this study, (2) age at the time of his appearance on the cover, (3) birth and death dates, (4) profession, occupation or position at the time he "made" TIME's cover, (5) nationality, (6) date of the issue on which he appeared, and (7) other biographical data relevant to the person such as sex, race and reason for appearing on the cover when it could be determined. All biographical data were gathered from standard reference sources, viz., biographical dictionaries and directories, general and specialized encyclopedias, biographies, indexes, newspapers, periodicals, etc. Perhaps one of the most frequently consulted sources was the cover story from the issues of TIME. TIME was considered as a reliable reference source for biographical data and in many cases was the only source used when all necessary data were found in the "cover story."

The information from each of the 3,537 cards (3,336 "person" and 201 "topical" cards) was coded and keypunched for computer analysis. The results from the computer printout analysis formed the basis for most of the various items included in this study.

Notes: 9. TIME, June 22, 1959, p. 9.
      10. TIME, Oct. 20, 1952, p. 17.
      11. *TIME faces in the news: a gallery of 2810* [i.e., 2812] *TIME cover paintings and photographs.* New York: TIME, Inc., 1976.

CHAPTER 3
THE COVERS

The following tables point out the number of persons which have been portrayed on each cover. Table 1 shows the total number of persons which have appeared on the 2,814 covers; Tables 2-A to 2-F show the breakdown for each of the six periods into which this study was divided; and Table 3 is a summary of the foregoing ones. The inclusive dates for each of the six periods are:

1. Mar.3, 1923 - Dec. 28, 1931
2. Jan. 4, 1932 - Dec. 30, 1940
3. Jan. 6, 1941 - Dec. 26, 1949
4. Jan. 2, 1950 - Dec. 29, 1958
5. Jan. 5, 1959 - Dec. 29, 1967
6. Jan. 5, 1968 - Jan. 3, 1977

TABLE 1.—Number of Persons on Each Cover for the Six Periods, Mar. 3, 1923, to Jan. 3, 1977

2,334 covers with	1 person	=	2,334 persons
153 covers with	2 persons	=	306 persons
44 covers with	3 persons	=	132 persons
25 covers with	4 persons	=	100 persons
16 covers with	5 persons	=	80 persons
14 covers with	6 persons	=	84 persons
7 covers with	7 persons	=	49 persons
2 covers with	8 persons	=	16 persons
5 covers with	9 persons	=	45 persons
2 covers with	10 persons	=	20 persons
1 cover with	11 persons	=	11 persons
4 covers with	12 persons	=	48 persons
1 cover with	13 persons	=	13 persons
2 covers with	15 persons	=	30 persons
1 cover with	20 persons	=	20 persons
1 cover with	21 persons	=	21 persons
1 cover with	27 persons	=	27 persons

2,613 covers with . . . . 3,336 persons
  201 topical covers

2,814 covers

TABLE 2-A.—Number of Persons on Each Cover for Period 1, Mar. 3, 1923, to Dec. 28, 1931

437 covers with	1 person	=	437 persons
12 covers with	2 persons	=	24 persons
4 covers with	3 persons	=	12 persons
1 cover with	4 persons	=	4 persons
1 cover with	5 persons	=	5 persons
1 cover with	9 persons	=	9 persons

456 covers with . . . . 491 persons
  5 topical covers

461 covers

TABLE 2-B.—Number of Persons on Each Cover for Period 2,
Jan. 4, 1932, to Dec. 30, 1940

433 covers with	1 person	= 433 persons
19 covers with	2 persons	= 38 persons
3 covers with	3 persons	= 9 persons
4 covers with	4 persons	= 16 persons
2 covers with	5 persons	= 10 persons
2 covers with	6 persons	= 12 persons
1 cover with	7 persons	= 7 persons

464 covers with .... 525 persons
  6 topical covers

470 covers

TABLE 2-C.—Number of Persons on Each Cover for Period 3,
Jan. 6, 1941, to Dec. 26, 1949

437 covers with	1 person	= 437 persons
16 covers with	2 persons	= 32 persons
5 covers with	3 persons	= 15 persons
1 cover with	4 persons	= 4 persons
1 cover with	6 persons	= 6 persons

460 covers with .... 494 persons
  9 topical covers

469 covers

TABLE 2-D.—Number of Persons on Each Cover for Period 4,
Jan. 2, 1950, to Dec. 29, 1958

414 covers with	1 person	= 414 persons
22 covers with	2 persons	= 44 persons
7 covers with	3 persons	= 21 persons
2 covers with	4 persons	= 8 persons
1 cover with	7 persons	= 7 persons
1 cover with	10 persons	= 10 persons

447 covers with .... 504 persons
  23 topical covers

470 covers

TABLE 2-E.—Number of Persons on Each Cover for Period 5, Jan. 5, 1959, to Dec. 29, 1967

368 covers with	1 person	=	368 persons
35 covers with	2 persons	=	70 persons
7 covers with	3 persons	=	21 persons
4 covers with	4 persons	=	16 persons
4 covers with	5 persons	=	20 persons
6 covers with	6 persons	=	36 persons
2 covers with	7 persons	=	14 persons
2 covers with	9 persons	=	18 persons
1 cover with	10 persons	=	10 persons
1 cover with	11 persons	=	11 persons
2 covers with	12 persons	=	24 persons
1 cover with	15 persons	=	15 persons
1 cover with	20 persons	=	20 persons

434 covers with .... 643 persons
 38 topical covers

472 covers

TABLE 2-F.—Number of Persons on Each Cover for Period 6, Jan. 5, 1968, to Jan. 3, 1977

245 covers with	1 person	=	245 persons
49 covers with	2 persons	=	98 persons
18 covers with	3 persons	=	54 persons
13 covers with	4 persons	=	52 persons
9 covers with	5 persons	=	45 persons
5 covers with	6 persons	=	30 persons
3 covers with	7 persons	=	21 persons
2 covers with	8 persons	=	16 persons
2 covers with	9 persons	=	18 persons
2 covers with	12 persons	=	24 persons
1 cover with	13 persons	=	13 persons
1 cover with	15 persons	=	15 persons
1 cover with	21 persons	=	21 persons
1 cover with	27 persons	=	27 persons

352 covers with .... 679 persons
120 topical covers

472 covers

Tables 2-A to 2-F point out the fact that the trend has been (albeit by chance or by design) to include more persons on each cover and fewer covers with identified people. The number of topical covers increased steadily from the first period to the fifth, and then in the sixth period it zoomed upward dramatically by more than 200 percent over Period 5.

TABLE 3. — Summary of Tables 2-A — 2-F

	Total Number of Covers	Topical Covers	Covers with Persons	Total Number of Persons
Period 1	461 (16.39%)	5 (02.49%)	456 (17.45%)	491 (14.73%)
Period 2	470 (16.70%)	6 (02.98%)	464 (17.76%)	525 (15.75%)
Period 3	469 (16.67%)	9 (04.48%)	460 (17.60%)	494 (14.82%)
Period 4	470 (16.70%)	23 (11.44%)	447 (17.11%)	504 (15.12%)
Period 5	472 (16.77%)	38 (18.91%)	434 (16.61%)	643 (19.22%)
Period 6	472 (16.77%)	120 (59.70%)	352 (13.47%)	679 (20.36%)
Totals	2,814 (100.00%)	201 (100.00%)	2,613 (100.00%)	3,336 (100.00%)
Averages for Each of the Six Periods:	469 covers	33.5 topical covers	435.5 covers with persons	555.7 persons

Covers with persons	2,613	=	92.86%
Topical covers	201	=	7.14%
Total	2,814	=	100.00%

As can be seen from Table 3, TIME's covers are now depicting many more persons on each cover than during the earlier periods, and more topical covers are being published.

During Period 1 (1923-1931) there was an average of 1.08 persons per "person cover," while in Period 6 there was an average of 1.93 persons. The overall average for the six periods is 1.28 persons per "person cover."

For Period 1, TIME published only five topical covers, or 1.08 percent of the 461 covers for that period; in Period 6 there were 120 topical covers, or 25.4 percent of the 472 covers issued.

In short, the tendency has been to produce more covers with no identified or identifiable persons on them; when identified persons do appear it is much less likely that they will appear alone. Or, it could be said that TIME is issuing fewer covers with people, but still more people are appearing on its covers.

CHAPTER 4

NATIONALITY AND GEOGRAPHIC DISTRIBUTION

The 3,336 persons were grouped by nationality. Each was classified with the country of his residence or citizenship, depending on the country with which he is usually identified or with which he wishes to be identified. One such case was Vladimir Nabokov, who was considered an American, but his mother was treated as a Russian. Resident foreigners of the United States were consistently listed as foreign-born Americans.

Of the world's approximately 145 countries, seventy-six (or 52 percent) have been represented on the covers. Those countries that are currently divided, such as North and South Korea, Taiwan and Mainland China, East and West Germany, were all considered as single countries. All historical persons were classed with the country of their nationality or the one which they are usually associated. An exception was made for biblical personages which were treated as a separate category.

Latin America includes Mexico, Central and South America, Haiti, and the Spanish-speaking islands of the Caribbean. All of the "republics" of the Soviet Union were considered as a single European country. Israel, Iran, Iraq, Jordan, Lebanon, Saudi Arabia, Syria and Turkey compose the Near East (Palestinians were treated as though Palestine were a country and are included with those countries of the Near East); all other Asian countries, including the Philippines, form the Far East. The United States and Canada were considered apart from any continent.

Table 4 lists the countries in rank order according to the number of persons from each one (the subarrangement is alphabetical). Table 5 shows the number of persons from each continent for each of the six periods. Table 6 converts Table 5 into percentages for each of the six periods.

Americans make up more than two-thirds of all the persons on the covers. The next eleven countries form more than one-fifth of the total; in other words, the top twelve countries represent 90.25 percent of the 3,336 persons. The other sixty-four countries and the biblical personages constitute a mere 9.75 percent.

Among these top twelve countries are ten of the sixteen most populous countries of the world.[12] Also, nine of the same twelve countries are among the top ten in the world with the highest Gross National Product.[13] For the other three countries, China, Russia and Vietnam, there are no such statistics available.

In view of these two factors, population and the GNP, it is not surprising that these would be among the countries most often represented on the covers. It seems only normal that countries with a large population in addition to a high GNP would be the most important in world affairs. But, of course, there are exceptions; Brazil is a country with a high GNP (seventh in the world), and it also has a large population that ranks fifth among the world's most populous countries, but is only twenty-fifth in the list of countries in Table 4, thus proving that a high GNP and a large population are not the only factors which determine a country's importance in figuring in the world's news.

TABLE 4.—Number of Persons from Each Country

Country	No. of Persons	Percent
United States	2,294	68.80
Great Britain	193	5.80
Soviet Union	125	3.75
France	85	2.50
Germany	82	2.40
China	52	1.60
Italy	41	1.25
Japan	34	1.00
Canada	30	0.90
Spain	25	0.75
Vietnam	25	0.75
India	25	0.75
Egypt	16	0.48
Cuba	13	0.40
Greece	12	0.36
Mexico	12	0.36
Netherlands	12	0.36
Israel	11	0.33
Sweden	11	0.33
Romania	10	0.30
Argentina	9	0.27
Poland	9	0.27
Yugoslavia	9	0.27
Belgium	8	0.24
Brazil	8	0.24
Iran	8	0.24
Ireland	8	0.24
Norway	8	0.24
Austria	7	0.21
Czechoslovakia	7	0.21
Australia	6	0.18
Saudi Arabia	5	0.15
South Africa	5	0.15
Turkey	5	0.15
Denmark	4	0.12
Jordan	4	0.12
Philippines	4	0.12
Portugal	4	0.12
Thailand	4	0.12
Chile	3	0.09

TABLE 4.—Continued

Country	No. of Persons	Percent
Hungary	3	0.09
Indonesia	3	0.09
Morocco	3	0.09
Albania	2	0.06
Algeria	2	0.06
Bulgaria	2	0.06
Dominican Republic	2	0.06
Ethiopia	2	0.06
Finland	2	0.06
Guatemala	2	0.06
Iraq	2	0.06
Korea	2	0.06
Laos	2	0.06
Nigeria	2	0.06
Pakistan	2	0.06
Palestine	2	0.06
Peru	2	0.06
Puerto Rico	2	0.06
Rhodesia	2	0.06
Switzerland	2	0.06
Venezuela	2	0.06
Burma	1	0.03
Cambodia	1	0.03
Ghana	1	0.03
Guinea	1	0.03
Haiti	1	0.03
Kenya	1	0.03
Libya	1	0.03
Luxembourg	1	0.03
Malaysia	1	0.03
Nicaragua	1	0.03
Syria	1	0.03
Tanzania	1	0.03
Tibet	1	0.03
Tunisia	1	0.03
Zaire	1	0.03
Biblical personages	43	1.28
Totals	3,336	100.00

TABLE 5.—Geographic Numerical Distribution for Each of the Six Periods

Country or Continent	Period 1 (1923-31)	Period 2 (1932-40)	Period 3 (1941-49)	Period 4 (1950-58)	Period 5 (1959-67)	Period 6 (1968-76)	Total	Percent
United States	319	334	291	353	443	554	2,294	68.80
Canada	3	10	6	2	2	7	30	00.90
Latin America	8	7	10	13	15	4	57	01.70
Europe	138	135	145	85	108	61	672	20.13
Near East	3	1	7	9	5	13	38	01.14
Far East	13	22	28	23	46	25	157	04.70
Africa	4	2	1	10	11	11	39	01.17
Australia	1	3	1	0	1	0	6	00.18
Biblical	2	11	5	9	12	4	43	01.28
Totals	491	525	494	504	643	679	3,336	100.00

TABLE 6.—Geographic Percent Distribution for Each of the Six Periods

Country or Continent	Period 1 (1923-31)	Period 2 (1932-40)	Period 3 (1941-49)	Period 4 (1950-58)	Period 5 (1959-67)	Period 6 (1968-76)
United States	65.00%	63.60%	58.90%	70.00%	68.90%	81.60%
Canada	0.61	1.91	1.22	0.40	0.31	1.03
Latin America	1.62	1.33	2.02	2.60	2.33	0.59
Europe	28.10	25.70	29.35	16.86	16.80	8.98
Near East	0.61	0.20	1.42	1.80	0.77	1.92
Far East	2.64	4.20	5.67	4.56	7.15	3.68
Africa	0.81	0.39	0.20	1.98	1.71	1.62
Australia	0.21	0.57	0.20	0.00	0.16	0.00
Biblical	0.40	2.10	1.02	1.80	1.87	0.58
	100.00	100.00	100.00	100.00	100.00	100.00

Even though the number of persons from each area for most of the periods is somewhat evenly distributed throughout the fifty-four year period, there are a few exceptions which can most easily be seen in Table 6. Americans and those from the Near East have their highest representation during Period 6, obviously due to the Watergate affair and the Israeli-Palestinian problem. These two factors also will help explain why Europeans were much less represented during Period 6 than they were during the previous five. The Far East had the highest percentages in Periods 3 and 5, undoubtedly because of the Second World War and the war in Vietnam. Also, it must be remembered that India fought for and gained its independence in Period 3. Europe reached its highest percentage during Period 3 which includes the Second World War. Africa seems to have come much more into the news during the last three periods as 32 Africans (82 percent of the total) were on the covers during Periods 4, 5, and 6. For some reason one-third of all Canadians appeared on the covers during Period 2. In all periods Americans were the most represented group, Europeans were second, and thirdly those from the Far East. This order is not surprising and is what would be expected.

Notes: 12. The sixteen most populous countries in rank order are: China, USSR, USA, India, Indonesia, Japan, Brazil, Bangladesh, Germany, Pakistan, Nigeria, Mexico, Italy, United Kingdom, France and Vietnam.
13. The ten countries of the world with the highest GNP are: USA, United Kingdom, Japan, Germany, France, Italy, Canada, Brazil, India and Spain.

CHAPTER 5
PROFESSIONS

The profession and/or position of each person at the time of his portrayal was recorded along with other biographical data as they were researched. There were various persons who were classified in more than one profession, e.g., Dwight D. Eisenhower, who was classed as a politician, military person, president, and educator depending on what he was at the time of his appearance. Each historical figure was grouped with the profession for which he is best known. Biblical personages are included in religion. Table 7 lists the thirty major categories into which all persons were classed. Tables 8-A to 8-I analyze the top nine professions into more specific groups. Table 9 distributes the totals of each professional group according to the six periods into which this study was divided.

TABLE 7.—Professional Groups

Profession	Total Number	Percent
Politicians	1,592	47.7
Military	262	7.9
Business	248	7.5
Public entertainment	197	5.9
Sports	163	4.9
Religion	116	3.5
Music	115	3.5
Writers	90	2.7
Scientists	63	1.9
Educators	61	1.8
News media	59	1.7
Lawyers and judges	58	1.7
Medicine	37	1.1
Labor leaders	34	1.0
Artists	26	0.8
Astronauts	24	0.7
Civic leaders	23	0.7
Economists	22	0.6
Pilots	17	0.5
Architects	13	0.4
Dancers	13	0.4
Criminals	12	0.4
Fashion designers and models	11	0.3
Law enforcement and penologists	9	0.3
Engineers	7	0.2
Philosophers	7	0.2
Psychologists	7	0.2
Agriculturists	6	0.2
Sociologists	3	0.1
Miscellaneous	41	1.2
Total	3,336 persons	100.0

The above table does indeed show that the persons selected as the newsmakers of the week do come from a wide variety of professions and occupations. Considering that almost fifty percent are in politics, it can be safely assumed that politicians and statesmen are the big newsmakers.

The miscellaneous category includes such persons as a ship's captain, astrologer, cook, etc. Also included here are those persons used as models for a topic which cannot be categorized with any profession, such as William and Barbara Briard who were used as models for a cover story on old age (June 2, 1975).

Husbands and wives were classed with the profession of the spouse, but children who were not the topics of the covers were classed as miscellaneous. Parents were considered as miscellaneous when the subject cover was the child, such as the mother of Shirley Temple and Helene Nabokov, mother of Vladimir Nabokov. However, these cases are few and in no way skew the basic data.

Tables 8-A to 8-I break down the top nine professional groups to point out the specific numbers of persons in each subdivision of the group.

TABLE 8-A.—Politicians

	Number	Percent of American Politicians	Percent of All Politicians
Americans			
Presidents	99	10.80	6.22
Ex-Presidents	21	2.30	1.33
Vice-Presidents	35	3.80	2.20
Senators	169	18.40	10.61
Congressmen	62	6.75	3.90
Ambassadors	33	3.60	2.07
Secretaries of Departments	112	12.20	7.03
Governors	91	9.90	5.72
Mayors	27	2.95	1.70
First Ladies	17	1.86	1.06
Other family of presidents	13	1.42	0.81
Family members of other politicians	25	2.72	1.57
Miscellaneous	215	23.30	13.50
Totals	919	100.00	57.72
Foreigners			
Leaders, diplomats and politicians	551	81.87	34.62
Family members	8	1.20	0.50
Royalty	114	16.93	7.16
Totals	673	100.00	100.00

TABLE 8-B.—Military

	Number	Percent
American	159	60.68
Foreign	103	39.32
Total	262	100.00

TABLE 8-C.—Business

	Number	Percent
Automobile industry	45	18.0
Banking	25	10.0
Aerospace industry	20	8.0
Oil industry	16	6.4
Advertising	12	4.8
Railroads	12	4.8
Food industry	11	4.5
Stock market	10	4.0
Retail stores	9	3.6
Air Travel	9	3.6
Steel industry	8	3.3
Miscellaneous	71	29.0
Total	248	100.0

TABLE 8-D.—Public Entertainment

	Number	Percent
Actors	92	46.2
Actresses	87	44.2
Producers and directors of stage and screen	16	8.1
Circus	2	1.5
Total	197	100.0

TABLE 8-E.—Religion

	Number	Percent
Religious leaders, ministers, rabbis, and priests	55	46.5
Biblical personages	43	38.0
Popes	12	10.4
Miscellaneous	6	5.1
Total	116	100.0

TABLE 8-F.—Sports

	Number	Percent
Baseball	39	24.00
Football	37	22.70
Tennis	16	9.80
Ping-pong	12	7.40
Boxing	9	5.50
Golf	9	5.50
Horse racing	7	4.30
Track and field	5	3.05
Boating, canoeing	4	2.45
Hockey	4	2.45
Chess	3	1.84
Ice skating	3	1.84
Skiing	3	1.84
Swimming	3	1.84
Auto racing	2	1.22
Polo	2	1.22
Acrobatics, basketball, bullfighting, card playing, jai-alai (1 ea.)	5	3.05
Total	163	100.00

TABLE 8-G.—Music

	Number	Percent
Popular singers	43	37.4
Opera singers	21	18.3
Composers	20	17.4
Conductors	17	14.8
Instrumentalists	10	8.7
Opera managers	4	3.4
Total	115	100.0

TABLE 8-H.—Writers

	Number	Percent
Novelists	41	45.6
Playwrights	19	21.0
Poets	12	13.4
Historians	3	3.3
Miscellaneous	15	16.7
Total	90	100.0

TABLE 8-I.—Scientists

	Number	Percent
Physicists	26	41.0
Biologists	13	21.0
Chemists	8	12.7
Astronomers	4	6.3
Miscellaneous	12	19.0
Total	63	100.0

Among the American politicians it is interesting to note that the number of Senators is much greater than that of Congressmen. There are normally about four times as many Congressmen as there are Senators (in the Ninety-fifth Congress there were 435 Congressmen and 100 Senators). However, the representation of Congressmen on the covers has been almost in the reverse proportion, i.e., 167 Senators and only 62 Congressmen.

Of foreign politicians and statesmen one-sixth are members of royal families. Royalty seems always to be in the news.

At first glance it seems that foreign military persons constitute a high percentage of the total, but in actuality the percentage is quite similar to the overall average of foreigners who have been on the covers. In the overall figures Americans make up about 69 percent of the persons, while in the military group Americans are 61 percent.

In the group of businessmen it is not at all surprising that the automobile industry is the most represented. Second on the list is banking, but if one were to combine the aerospace and air travel industries this would form the second largest group.

The only group where women and men are about equally represented is in the public entertainment field. The number of actresses and actors is almost the same.

According to an article in the *U.S. News & World Report* (May 23, 1977, p. 63) the twelve leading spectator sports in rank order are: horse racing, auto racing, baseball, football, basketball, greyhound racing, wrestling, hockey, boxing, golf, soccer and tennis. Compare this list to that of Table 8-F and one can see the striking differences. On TIME's covers baseball and football players and their coaches make up almost one-half (46.3 percent) of all sports persons. Basketball, which is one of the top five spectator sports in the U.S., is the most outstanding difference in the two lists. In fact, only one basketball player was ever portrayed on a cover, viz., Oscar Robertson, who appeared on the Feb. 17, 1961, issue. Ping-pong seems to rank high on the covers, but it should be pointed out that those twelve were all on the same cover (Apr. 26, 1971).

The area of religion has an interesting makeup; biblical personages are 38 percent of this group and popes form 10 percent. In view of the frequency of the Nativity scene, and the leadership and importance in world events of the popes this does not seem unusual.

The music field seems to be about equally divided between the classical and the popular. This is especially evident when one considers that those classified as composers and instrumentalists will fall into both categories.

Almost one-half (45.6 percent) of all writers are novelists, but the three principal genres of the belles lettres are well represented and in about the same proportions that one would expect.

Physicists are very well represented on the covers; almost one-half (41 percent) of all the scientists fall into this group. This could be due to the development of the space sciences in which physics plays a very important role.

The figures in Table 9 distribute the professional groups as they appeared throughout the six periods into which this study was divided. There is a remarkable consistency in the distribution from period to period. Period 6 is usually larger because there were more persons during this period than in any other (cf. Table 3). TIME has always claimed that the cover subjects reflect the news. For a supporting fact of this statement notice the decrease in politicians and the marked increase in military persons in Period 3. This is easily explained by their dominance of world news due to the Second World War, thus offering further proof that TIME covers do reflect the news. Pilots declined considerably from Period 1 to Period 6, but then pilots are not the newsmakers today that they were in the early days of aviation. Also, note that the number of astronauts and pilots for the six periods is about equal.

An interesting distribution of lawyers and judges does appear. There are many more in Periods 1, 2, and 6, but the number for each of these three periods is about the same, whereas the number of these persons in Periods 3, 4, and 5 is quite inferior, but again this set of three is also quite consistent. Perhaps this can be accounted for by the fact that during the first two periods there were many government scandals and important court decisions in the U.S.; during Period 6 the Watergate affair affected much of the news and many lawyers and judges appeared on the covers as they were big newsmakers at that time.

At this point the reader should be reminded that the professional groupings and the period divisions were devised by the author and are in no way, means or manner based on any plan, design or intent (if such do really exist) of TIME.

Table 9 does prove that not only do TIME's covers portray persons of all fields of endeavor, but also that they have been extremely consistent throughout the years, and when there is a strong deviation it is due to the news events themselves which obviously dictate the subjects for TIME's covers.

TABLE 9.—Professional Groups Distributed According to the Six Periods

Profession	Period 1 (1923-31)	Period 2 (1932-40)	Period 3 (1941-49)	Period 4 (1950-58)	Period 5 (1959-67)	Period 6 (1968-76)	Total
Politicians	225	238	189	233	305	402	1,592
Military	16	27	132	38	24	25	262
Business	52	35	26	45	69	21	248
Public entertainment	19	34	31	37	32	44	197
Sports	29	27	18	25	18	46	163
Religion	16	19	16	24	30	11	116
Music	22	18	12	15	27	21	115
Writers	17	23	11	13	14	12	90
Scientists	12	10	5	11	24	1	63
Educators	10	15	4	12	16	4	61
News Media	14	15	9	9	5	7	59
Lawyers and judges	13	14	3	5	5	18	58
Medicine	8	9	4	3	9	4	37
Labor leaders	4	6	12	6	3	3	34
Artists	6	4	4	6	5	1	26
Astronauts	0	0	0	0	13	11	24
Civic leaders	6	5	0	1	6	5	23
Economists	0	3	1	0	9	9	22
Pilots	6	6	1	3	1	0	17
Architects	2	1	1	3	5	1	13
Dancers	0	0	1	1	5	6	13
Criminals	1	0	0	0	4	7	12
Fashion designers & models	1	1	2	3	1	3	11
Law enforcement & penologists	1	1	1	2	0	4	9
Engineers	3	0	2	1	1	0	7
Philosophers	1	1	2	1	2	0	7
Psychologists	1	1	1	2	0	2	7
Agriculturists	1	0	2	1	2	0	6
Sociologists	0	1	0	2	0	0	3
Miscellaneous	5	11	4	2	8	11	41
Total	491	525	494	504	643	679	3,336

TIME

The Weekly News-Magazine

VOL. I, NO. 22

ELEANORA DUSE
She set the Tiber on fire—
See Page 15

JULY 30, 1923

ELEANORA DUSE, First woman to appear on the cover of TIME. b. 1859. d. 1924. Italian actress who made her American debut in New York in 1893, known especially for interpretation of heroines of Dumas, Sardou, Ibsen, Sudermann, D'Annunzio and Maeterlinck.

CHAPTER 6
INDIVIDUALS: WOMEN AND MEN

Probably no one at all is surprised that the first person on a cover of TIME was a man. Men have so dominated the news since the beginning of history (as well as from the beginning of TIME) that only occasionally is a woman considered an important news figure. Even though women have been on the covers since the first year of publication, their representation has been far below that of men and, of course, much below what their proportion of the overall population might suggest.

The first woman to appear on a cover was an Italian actress, Eleanora Duse, who was on TIME's twenty-second cover (July 30, 1923). No other woman appeared in that first year of publication, but during the second year there were four females, viz., Mrs. Herbert Hoover, Queen Marie of Romania, Edith Cummings and Ethel Barrymore.

During fifty-four years of publication only 350 (a mere 10.5 percent) of the 3,336 persons have been women. It should not be forgotten that women do constitute a little more than fifty percent of the general population. These 350 women are represented by 295 individuals.

Table 10 shows the number of females in each of the six periods of this study. Only in the last period is there any significant change in the percentage of women, but even with this change females only account for fifteen percent of the total persons for that period. Table 11 is a geographic distribution of the 350 females. The percentage of American women is slightly higher than that of all Americans. Americans are 68.8 percent of the 3,336 persons on the covers, while American women are 74.3 percent of all women who have appeared. Table 12 lists how many times each of the 2,344 individuals have appeared on the covers.

TABLE 10.—Women and Men throughout the Six Periods

	No. of Women	Percent	No. of Men	Percent	Total
Period 1 (1923-31)	44	9	447	91	491
Period 2 (1932-40)	58	11	467	89	525
Period 3 (1941-49)	44	9	450	91	494
Period 4 (1950-58)	51	10	453	90	504
Period 5 (1959-67)	52	8	591	92	643
Period 6 (1968-76)	101	15	578	85	679
Total	350		2,986		3,336
Percents	10.5	+	89.5	=	100

TABLE 11.—Geographic Distribution of Women

Country or Continent	No. of Women	Percent
United States	260	74.30
Canada	7	2.00
Latin America	3	0.28
Europe	56	16.00
Far East	8	2.28
Near East	3	0.86
Africa	1	0.28
Australia	1	0.28
Biblical	11	3.14
Total	350	100.00

The data of Table 12 show that the percentage of women who never appear more than once is larger than that of men. Only 1.7 percent of all women appeared four or more times, while for men the percentage is 3.91.

TABLE 12.—Individuals (Women and Men) and the Number of Times Each Appeared

Women	Percent of Women	Men	Percent of Men	Total Individuals	Percent of All Individuals	No. of Times Each Appeared	Total No. of Persons
265	89.93	1,653	80.67	1,918	81.82	1	1,918
20	6.78	230	11.22	250	10.67	2	500
5	1.69	86	4.20	91	3.88	3	273
2	0.68	28	1.36	30	1.28	4	120
0	0.00	14	0.68	14	0.60	5	70
2	0.68	10	0.48	12	0.51	6	72
0	0.00	3	0.15	3	0.13	7	21
0	0.00	5	0.24	5	0.22	8	40
0	0.00	3	0.15	3	0.13	9	27
1	0.34	3	0.15	4	0.17	10	40
0	0.00	1	0.05	1	0.04	11	11
0	0.00	3	0.15	3	0.13	12	36
0	0.00	2	0.10	2	0.09	13	26
0	0.00	1	0.05	1	0.04	14	14
0	0.00	2	0.10	2	0.09	15	30
0	0.00	1	0.05	1	0.04	17	17
0	0.00	1	0.05	1	0.04	21	21
0	0.00	1		1	0.04	22	22
0	0.00	1	0.05	1	0.04	23	23
0	0.00	1	0.05	1	0.04	55	55
Total 295	100.00	2,049	100.00	2,344	100.00		3,336

The five women who make up this small percentage are the Virgin Mary, Queen Elizabeth II, Eleanor Roosevelt, Pat Nixon and Betty Ford. The Virgin Mary, the most frequently portrayed female, always appeared either in the Nativity scene or as background for some news figure, and for this reason probably cannot be considered as a real "newsmaker." Of the other four, only Eleanor Roosevelt was ever portrayed for what she did personally and not "ex officio" like the others. In other words, there seem to be no "big newsmakers among all the females who appeared repeatedly on TIME's covers, such as one might consider Douglas MacArthur or Henry Ford.

Not only is the number of females much less than that of men, but those who do appear seem to have much less opportunity to "make" a cover more than once.

CHAPTER 7
AGE: FROM INFANCY TO SENECTITUDE

The age of each person who appeared on a cover was recorded along with the other biographical data. The age of the person often appeared in the cover story and was used when available. When no age was given by TIME the year of birth was researched and the age calculated. The year of birth or age was determined for all but twenty-six individuals; however, enough biographical data was located to enable the author to approximate the age with sufficient accuracy.

Among the 3,336 persons there were 125 who were considered "historical figures," that is, those who were dead at least one year before an appearance on a cover. Some individuals appeared while alive and then again a few years after death, e.g., Marilyn Monroe; in this case she was regarded once as a living person and once as a "historical figure." The 125 (14 women and 111 men) historical figures were eliminated in the computation of average ages, thus leaving 3,211 persons whose ages were used to find the average ages of all persons on the covers. Biblical personages were treated as historical figures.

These 3,211 persons had an average age of 51 years at the time of their appearances on TIME. The 2,875 men had an average age slightly higher than the 336 women; for men it was 53 years and for women just 38. Politicians who make up almost one-half (47.7 percent) of all persons had an average age of 54 years, while dancers only averaged 27, and sports people 33 years. On the other extreme philosophers and psychologists averaged 65 years and the persons classed in religion averaged 62.

Of course, there were some very young people and others who were very old. Tables 13 and 14 list the eleven youngest and the eleven oldest. Exact birth dates were located for all but one of the youngest, and exact birth and death dates are given for the eleven oldest. Several of these twenty-two individuals appeared more than once, but the cover date given for each is that when the individual appeared at the youngest or the oldest age, and in some cases it is the only portrayal.

TABLE 13.—The Youngest Cover Figures

Age	Name	Birth Date	Date on Cover
2	Lindbergh, Charles A., Jr.	June 22, 1930	May 2, 1932
3	Queen Elizabeth II	Apr. 21, 1926	Apr. 29, 1929
3	Dionne Quintuplets (Annette, Cecile, Emilie, Marie and Yvonne)	May 28, 1934	May 31, 1937
6	Abbott, Matthew (son of Joe Abbott, POW in Vietnam)	1967	Feb. 19, 1973
6	Michael, King of Romania	Nov. 7, 1921	Aug. 1, 1927
8	Carter, Amy Lynn	Oct. 19, 1967	July 26, 1976
8	Temple, Shirley	Apr. 23, 1928	Apr. 27, 1936

The ages of those persons listed in the following tables prove that newsmakers have no age limits; they may be very old or very young.

TABLE 14.—The Oldest Cover Figures

Age	Name	Birth Date	Date on Cover	Death Date
96	Stagg, Amos Alonzo	Aug. 16, 1862	Oct. 20, 1958	Mar. 17, 1965
93	Moses, Anna Mary "Grandma"	Sept. 7, 1860	Dec. 28, 1953	Dec. 13, 1961
90	Depew, Chauncey Mitchell	Apr. 23, 1834	Dec. 1, 1924	Apr. 5, 1928
89	Scripps, Ellen Browning	Oct. 18, 1836	Feb. 22, 1926	Aug. 3, 1932
89	Rockefeller, John Davison	July 8, 1839	May 21, 1928	May 23, 1937
87	Cannon, Joseph Gurney	May 7, 1836	Mar. 3, 1923	Nov. 12, 1926
86	Hartford, George Ludlum	Nov. 7, 1864	Nov. 13, 1950	Sept. 23, 1957
86	Hindenburg, Paul von	Oct. 2, 1847	July 16, 1934	Aug. 2, 1934
85	Holmes, Oliver Wendell, Jr.	Mar. 8, 1841	Mar. 15, 1926	Mar. 6, 1935
85	Bridges, Robert Seymour	Oct. 23, 1844	Dec. 2, 1929	Apr. 21, 1930
84	Clemenceau, Georges	Sept. 28, 1841	Jan. 4, 1926	Nov. 24, 1929

CHAPTER 8

THE MOST FREQUENTLY PORTRAYED INDIVIDUALS

Of the 2,344 individuals who were portrayed on the covers there were only 85 (5 women and 80 men) who "made" it four or more times. Table 15 lists these individuals in rank order according to the number of appearances; in those cases where two or more individuals appeared the same number of times the subarrangement is alphabetical. The dates underneath the name indicate the first and last appearances during the period covered by the study. The number at the far right of the name under the heading "span of years" indicates the number of years during which the individual was portrayed, e.g., Joseph Stalin appeared seventeen times between 1930 and 1967, a span of 38 years from the first appearance to the last.

TABLE 15.—The Most Frequently Portrayed Individuals

No. of Times	Name and Dates of First and Last Appearances	Span of Years
55	Nixon, Richard Milhous, 1913- Aug. 25, 1952 - Sept. 16, 1974	23
23	Johnson, Lyndon Baines, 1908-1973 June 22, 1953 - Nov. 8, 1968	16
22	Ford, Gerald Rudolph, 1913- Jan. 15, 1973 - Nov. 8, 1976	4
21	Eisenhower, Dwight David, 1890-1969 Nov. 16, 1942 - Apr. 4, 1969	28
17	Stalin, Joseph, 1879-1953 June 9, 1930 - Nov. 10, 1967	38
15	Khrushchev, Nikita S., 1894-1971 Nov. 30, 1953 - Nov. 10, 1967	15
15	Kissinger, Henry Alfred, 1923- Feb. 14, 1969 - Nov. 17, 1975	7
14	Jesus Christ (five times as Baby Jesus and nine times as Jesus Christ) Dec. 17, 1928 - June 21, 1971	44
13	Brezhnev, Leonid I., 1906- Feb. 21, 1964 - Aug. 4, 1975	12
13	Gaulle, Charles de, 1890-1970 Aug. 4, 1941 - Nov. 29, 1968	28
12	Humphrey, Hubert H., 1911-1978 Jan. 17, 1949 - Mar. 8, 1976	28
12	Mao, Tse-tung, 1893-1976 Feb. 7, 1949 - Sept. 20, 1976	28
12	Rockefeller, Nelson Aldrich, 1907-1979 May 22, 1939 - May 17, 1976	38
11	Kennedy, John F., 1917-1963 Dec. 2, 1957 - June 21, 1963	7
10	Agnew, Spiro T., 1918- Aug. 16, 1968 - Oct. 8, 1973	6

TABLE 15—Continued

No. of Times	Name and Dates of First and Last Appearances	Span of Years
10	Carter, Jimmy, 1924- May 31, 1971 - Jan. 3, 1977	7
10	Chiang, Kai-shek, 1887-1975 Apr. 4, 1927 - Apr. 18, 1955	29
10	Mary, mother of Jesus Dec. 26, 1938 - Feb. 9, 1962	25
9	Kennedy, Robert Francis, 1925-1968 July 11, 1960 - June 14, 1968	9
9	Mussolini, Benito, 1883-1945 Aug. 6, 1923 - June 21, 1943	21
9	Truman, Harry S., 1884-1972 Mar. 8, 1943 - Aug. 13, 1956	14
8	Chou, En-lai, 1898-1976 June 18, 1951 - Feb. 3, 1975	25
8	Churchill, Winston, 1874-1965 Apr. 14, 1923 - Nov. 5, 1951	29
8	Franco, Francisco, 1892-1975 Aug. 24, 1936 - Nov. 3, 1975	40
8	MacArthur, Douglas, 1880-1964 Mar. 25, 1935 - Apr. 30, 1951	17
8	Roosevelt, Franklin D., 1882-1945 May 26, 1923 - Jan. 22, 1945	23
7	Hirohito, Emperor of Japan, 1901- Nov. 19, 1928 - Oct. 4, 1971	44
7	Reagan, Ronald, 1911- Oct. 7, 1966 - June 21, 1976	11
7	Stevenson, Adlai Ewing, 1900-1965 Jan. 28, 1952 - Dec. 14, 1962	11
6	Dewey, Thomas Edmund, 1902-1971 Feb. 1, 1937 - Nov. 1, 1948	12
6	Eden, Anthony, 1897-1977 April 8, 1935 - Nov. 19, 1956	22
6	Elizabeth II, Queen of Great Britain, 1926- Apr. 29, 1929 - May 3, 1976	48
6	Goldwater, Barry M., 1909- June 23, 1961 - Sept. 25, 1964	4
6	Hitler, Adolf, 1889-1945 Dec. 21, 1931 - May 7, 1945	15
6	Kennedy, Edward Moore, 1932- July 11, 1960 - Jan. 15, 1973	14
6	Lewis, John Llewellyn, 1880-1969 June 4, 1923 - Dec. 16, 1946	24
6	Marshall, George C., 1880-1959 July 29, 1940 - Jan. 5, 1948	9
6	Nasser, Gamal Abdel, 1918-1970 Sept. 26, 1955 - Oct. 12, 1970	16

TABLE 15—Continued

No. of Times	Name and Dates of First and Last Appearances	Span of Years
6	Nehru, Jawaharlal, 1889-1964 Aug. 24, 1942 - Nov. 30, 1962	21
6	Nixon, Patricia, 1912- Feb. 29, 1960 - Oct. 7, 1974	15
6	Sadat, Anwar, 1918- May 17, 1971 - Aug. 25, 1975	5
5	Albert, Carl Bert, 1909- Jan. 15, 1965 - Jan. 27, 1975	11
5	Baldwin, Stanley, 1867-1947 Aug. 10, 1925 - June 17, 1935	11
5	Balthasar, wise man of the Three Magi Dec. 26, 1938 - Dec. 30, 1974	37
5	Castro, Fidel, 1927- Jan. 26, 1959 - June 13, 1969	11
5	Ford, Henry, 1863-1947 July 27, 1925 - Feb. 4, 1946	22
5	Gandhi, Mahatma, 1869-1948 Mar. 31, 1930 - May 11, 1953	24
5	George V, King of Great Britain, 1865-1936 Apr. 7, 1924 - May 6, 1935	12
5	Ho, Chi Minh, 1890-1969 Nov. 22, 1954 - May 12, 1975	22
5	Kosygin, Aleksei N., 1904- Oct. 23, 1964 - Apr. 1, 1974	11
5	Thieu, Nguyen Van, 1923- Sept. 15, 1967 - Apr. 7, 1975	9
5	Tito, Josip Broz, 1892- Oct. 9, 1944 - June 13, 1969	26
5	Wallace, Henry Agard, 1888-1965 Apr. 10, 1933 - Aug. 9, 1948	16
5	Warren, Earl, 1891-1971 Jan. 31, 1944 - Jan. 27, 1961	18
5	Washington, George, 1732-1799 Oct. 18, 1948 - Special Bicentennial Issue, 1976	29
4	Bradley, Omar Nelson, 1893- May 1, 1944 - July 24, 1950	7
4	Conant, James Bryant, 1893-1978 Feb. 5, 1934 - Sept. 14, 1959	26
4	Connally, John Bowden, 1917- Jan. 17, 1964 - May 17, 1976	13
4	Dean, John Wesley, 1939- Apr. 30, 1973 - July 9, 1973	1
4	Dulles, John Foster, 1888-1959 Aug. 13, 1951 - Apr. 16, 1956	6
4	Ford, Betty, 1918- Dec. 17, 1973 - Jan. 5, 1976	4

TABLE 15—Continued

No. of Times	Name and Dates of First and Last Appearances	Span of Years
4	Ford, Henry II, 1917- Feb. 4, 1946 - July 20, 1970	25
4	Gaspar, wise man of the Three Magi Dec. 26, 1938 - Dec. 30, 1974	37
4	George VI, King of Great Britain, 1895-1952 Jan. 12, 1925 - Mar. 6, 1944	20
4	Hindenburg, Paul von, 1847-1934 Mar. 22, 1926 - July 14, 1941	16
4	Hoover, Herbert Clark, 1874-1964 Nov. 16, 1925 - Dec. 18, 1939	15
4	Hoover, J. Edgar, 1895-1972 Aug. 5, 1935 - Dec. 22, 1975	41
4	Hughes, Howard, 1906-1976 July 19, 1948 - Dec. 13, 1976	29
4	John XXIII, Pope, 1881-1963 Nov. 10, 1958 - June 7, 1963	6
4	Joseph, husband of the Virgin Mary Dec. 26, 1938 - Dec. 28, 1959	22
4	Lodge, Henry Cabot, 1902- Dec. 17, 1951 - May 15, 1964	14
4	McGovern, George Stanley, 1922- May 8, 1972 - Oct. 2, 1972	1
4	Martin, Joseph William, 1884-1968 Apr. 11, 1938 - Aug. 9, 1954	17
4	Melchior, wise man of the Three Magi Dec. 26, 1938 - Dec. 30, 1974	37
4	Mills, Wilbur Daigh, 1910- Feb. 2, 1959 - Jan. 15, 1973	15
4	Mitchell, John Newton, 1913- June 8, 1970 - July 23, 1973	4
4	Molotov, Viacheslav M., 1890- July 15, 1940 - Apr. 20, 1953	14
4	O'Neill, Eugene Gladstone, 1888-1953 Mar. 17, 1924 - Oct. 21, 1946	23
4	Romney, George W., 1907- Apr. 6, 1959 - Apr. 14, 1967	9
4	Roosevelt, Eleanor, 1884-1962 Nov. 20, 1933 - Apr. 7, 1952	20
4	Taft, Robert Alphonso, 1889-1953 Jan. 29, 1940 - June 2, 1952	13
4	Trotsky, Leon, 1877-1940 May 18, 1925 - Jan. 25, 1937	13
4	Wallace, George Corley, 1919- Sept. 27, 1963 - Mar. 8, 1976	14
4	Wilson, Charles Erwin, 1890-1961 Jan. 24, 1949 - June 4, 1956	8
4	Wilson, Harold, 1916- Oct. 11, 1963 - Nov. 24, 1967	5

The preceding list of individuals in Table 15 points out that there are 29 of the 85 (or 1.24 percent of the 2,344 individuals analyzed) who appeared seven or more times. These 29 individuals account for 10.85 percent of all persons who have been on TIME's covers. Among this group there will surely be found the important newsmakers of the past 54 years.

In order to determine who some of these important newsmakers might be some other method besides just the number of times on the covers should be examined. The list of individuals in Table 15 was carefully scrutinized and it was discovered that after removing all the historical figures and biblical personages that there were sixteen who appeared ten or more times; there were seventeen who were portrayed for a span of 25 years or more. These two groups were used as a basis for Table 16-A. For this table the sixteen who appeared ten or more times were listed in rank order in Column A. Column B lists in rank order the seventeen individuals who appeared over the longest spans of time. Then to determine the individuals for Column C the number of times on the covers for all 85 individuals was multiplied by the number of the span of years during which each appeared. This method was used to attempt to determine the most important newsmakers of the period, 1923-1976, and can be stated in terms of a formula, $I = f \times t$, that is, importance as a newsmaker is equal to the frequency (i.e., the number of times on the covers) when multiplied by the length of time (i.e., the span of years during which the individual was portrayed on the covers). After applying this formula the top sixteen were chosen and listed in rank order in Column C. The number at the right of each name in this column is the "score" which results from multiplying the two basic factors, frequency and time.

It should be noted that there are only 27 different names in all three columns. There are seven who appear in all three columns, viz., Chiang Kai-shek, Dwight D. Eisenhower, Charles de Gaulle, Hubert H. Humphrey, Mao Tse-tung, Nelson A. Rockefeller and Joseph Stalin. There are eight who appear in two columns, viz., Chou En-lai, Winston Churchill, Queen Elizabeth II, Francisco Franco, Emperor Hirohito, Lyndon B. Johnson, Nikita S. Khrushchev, and Richard M. Nixon. The other twelve individuals just appeared in one column. There can be little doubt that these fifteen individuals whose names are in at least two of the three columns are among the most important newmakers of the fifty-four year period covered by this study.

Table 16-B is an extension of Column C of Table 16-A. It contains the names of sixteen persons who resulted with a "score" of 100 or more when the number of times on the covers was multiplied by the span of years, and who did not fall into the top sixteen.

TABLE 16-A.—Important Newsmakers

Column A Name and Number of Times on Covers		Column B Name and Span of Years on Covers		Column C Name and Span of Years Multiplied by Times on Covers	
Nixon, Richard M.	(55)	Queen Elizabeth II	(48)	Nixon, Richard M.	(1,265)
Johnson, Lyndon B.	(23)	Emperor Hirohito	(44)	Stalin, Joseph	(646)
Ford, Gerald R.	(22)	Hoover, J. Edgar	(41)	Eisenhower, Dwight D.	(588)
Eisenhower, Dwight D.	(21)	Franco, Francisco	(40)	Rockefeller, Nelson A.	(456)
Stalin, Joseph	(17)	Rockefeller, Nelson A.	(38)	Johnson, Lyndon B.	(368)
Khrushchev, Nikita S.	(15)	Stalin, Joseph	(38)	Gaulle, Charles de	(364)
Kissinger, Henry	(15)	Chiang, Kai-shek	(29)	Humphrey, Hubert H.	(336)
Brezhnev, Leonid I.	(13)	Churchill, Winston	(29)	Mao, Tse-tung	(336)
Gaulle, Charles de	(13)	Hughes, Howard	(29)	Franco, Francisco	(320)
Humphrey, Hubert H.	(12)	Eisenhower, Dwight D.	(28)	Emperor Hirohito	(308)
Mao, Tse-tung	(12)	Gaulle, Charles de	(28)	Chiang, Kai-shek	(290)
Rockefeller, Nelson A.	(12)	Humphrey, Hubert A.	(28)	Queen Elizabeth II	(288)
Kennedy, John F.	(11)	Mao, Tse-tung	(28)	Churchill, Winston	(288)
Agnew, Spiro T.	(10)	Conant, James B.	(26)	Khrushchev, Nikita S.	(232)
Carter, Jimmy	(10)	Tito, Josip Broz	(26)	Chou, En-lai	(225)
Chiang, Kai-shek	(10)	Chou, En-lai	(25)	Mussolini, Benito	(200)
		Ford, Henry II	(25)		(189)

TABLE 16-B.—Other Important Newsmakers

Name	"Score"
Roosevelt, Franklin D.	(184)
Hoover, J. Edgar	(164)
Brezhnev, Leonid I.	(156)
Lewis, John L.	(144)
MacArthur, Douglas	(136)
Eden, Anthony	(132)
Tito, Josip Broz	(130)
Nehru, Jawaharlal	(126)
Truman, Harry S	(126)
Gandhi, Mahatma	(120)
Hughes, Howard	(116)
Ford, Henry	(110)
Ho, Chi Minh	(110)
Kissinger, Henry A.	(105)
Conant, James B.	(104)
Ford, Henry II	(100)

There can be little doubt that the 32 individuals who are listed in Column C of Table 16-A and in Table 16-B are among the very most important newsmakers in the past 54 years. Of the 36 individuals listed in Tables 16-A and 16-B only seven are not politicians, viz., James B. Conant, Henry Ford, Henry Ford II, J. Edgar Hoover, Howard Hughes, John L. Lewis and Douglas MacArthur. These seven individuals only appear in Column B of Table 16-A and/or in Table 16-B. Only those involved directly with politics resulted in Columns A and C of Table 16-A. Queen Elizabeth II is the only female in Tables 16-A and 16-B.

An accurate means by which to measure "importance" is indeed very difficult to devise, but no one can deny the importance of the aforementioned 32 individuals who came out with the highest "score" when the formula, $I = f \times t$, was applied. These are undoubtedly the "biggest" newsmakers of the 85 individuals listed in Table 15.

FIFTEEN CENTS

January 2, 1928

TIME

The Weekly Newsmagazine

THE MAN OF THE YEAR
He defeated fame
(See HEROES)

Volume XI

Number 1

Publication and Circulation Offices, Penton Building, Cleveland. Editorial and Advertising Offices, 25 West 45th Street, New York City.

CHARLES A. LINDBERGH, First "Man of the Year" b. Detroit, Michigan - 1902. d. 1974.
Made the first solo nonstop transatlantic flight, from Roosevelt Field, New York, to Le Bourget
Air Field, Paris (1927) in his monoplane The Spirit of St. Louis.

CHAPTER 9
MAN OF THE YEAR

Since 1928 TIME's editors have been choosing annually a subject to illustrate the first January issue of each year who is designated "Man of the Year."

TIME's choice of the Man of the Year seems, in retrospect, an obvious extension of . . . [the]practice of singling out a man each week to put on . . . [the] cover. But not until TIME was nearly five years old did it occur to the editors to proclaim a hero it described as "the most cherished citizen since Theodore Roosevelt" as Man of the Year.[14]

. . . [This choice] was announced in the issue of Jan. 2, 1928. He was Charles Augustus Lindbergh, who eight months before had soloed the Atlantic in 33½ hours. Since then, the annual choice by TIME's editors has become a journalistic tradition.[15]

Picking the Man of the Year for TIME's first January cover has become such a tradition with TIME's readers that you might be amused to learn that the whole thing began because the first week of January 1928 was so dull.[16]

The front pages of many U.S. newspapers carried a reproduction of a handwritten note from President Calvin Coolidge addressed to the American people. "Christmas," announced the President solemnly, "is not a time or a season but a state of mind." The rest of the news that final week of 1927 was scarcely more exciting. Warren Gamaliel Harding and his wife Florence were reburied in a marble tomb in Marion, Ohio. Mussolini was forced to revalue the Italian lira. Salvage work on the submarine S-4, sunk off Provincetown, was delayed by winter storms.

The editors of a fledgling newsmagazine called TIME were hard put to select an individual who so dominated the week's stories that he deserved a place on the magazine's cover. "Forget the man of the week," someone finally suggested. "Let's select a Man of the Year." That choice was easy. Charles A. Lindbergh, first man to fly solo across the Atlantic, was clearly the hero of 1927. Thus, almost by accident, Lindbergh became TIME's first Man of the Year.[17]

The Man of the Year idea caught on with a bang and, somewhat surprised, . . . [the editors] decided to make it an annual event. The choice is in no way an accolade, nor a Nobel Prize for doing good. Nor is it a moral judgment. (Al Capone was runner-up in riotous, bootleg 1928.) The two criteria are always these: who had the biggest rise in fame; and who did the most to change the news for better (like Stalin in 1942) or for worse (like Stalin in 1939, when his flop to Hitler's side unleashed . . . [the] worldwide war).[18]

In 1951 the following statements were made about the selection of the Man of the Year:

One man's story can never sum up the news of any one year—but often, one man's personal history leaves an indelible mark on the news of that year. And that man—having had the greatest rise to, or fall from, fame; having done the most to change the news for better or for worse—can be called the "Man of the Year."

. . . ...The man whose story will, in the opinion of the Editors, best reflect the spirit of the dreadful, wonderful weeks and months of the year just past.

He may be a statesman whose efforts have brought us closer to a working peace...or perhaps one whose actions have led us in the other direction.

He may be a scientist...or a mystic. He may be a peacemaker...or a trouble maker. He may be a spiritual leader...a military leader...or a powerful politician.

He need not be, from a purely American point of view, an admirable person. He may even be an enemy—as was Hitler in 1938, or Stalin in 1939...for these men, too, changed the course of history.

The Man of the Year is, suitably, a symbol of his time...whether the best of times, the worst of times, an age of reason, an age of wickedness, an age of longing, an age of hope.[19]

This was summed up subsequently by James A. Linen when he wrote:

As most readers know, TIME's choice is based not on a popularity poll but on a single criterion: Who did the most in the year to affect the news for good or ill?[20]

TIME's selection for the Man of the Year for the fifty years, 1927 to 1976, covered by this study has not always been a single person, nor has it always been a man. Four times topics have been chosen instead of a specific individual (or individuals). Only four times have women been selected. The first female was Wallis Warfield Simpson (later the Duchess of Windsor) who was designated "Woman of the Year" for 1936; Mei-ling Chiang appeared with her husband, the Generalissimo Chiang the following year. They were called the "Couple of the Year," and this is the only time that a couple was chosen for this honor. In 1952 Queen Elizabeth II was "Woman of the Year." For 1975 TIME selected twelve women as the "Women of the Year." All others have been males.

The following table shows the number of persons selected for each of the fifty covers.

TABLE 17.—Man of the Year Covers

41 covers with	1 person	= 41 persons
2 covers with	2 persons (1937, 1972)	= 4 persons
1 cover with	3 persons (1968)	= 3 persons
1 cover with	12 persons (1975)	= 12 persons
1 cover with	15 persons (1960)	= 15 persons
4 covers with	topics (1950, 1956, 1966, and 1969)	= 0 persons
50 covers with	. . . .	75 persons

This group of 75 persons is made up of 15 women and 60 men, that is, 20 and 80 percent respectively. It may seem at first glance that the percentage of female "Persons of the Year" is higher than the overall average, but when stated in terms of covers it is obvious that this is not true. There have been only three covers exclusively dedicated to women, one cover with a woman and a man, and 46 covers devoted to males. [Note: this author has preferred to use the non-sexist term, "Person of the Year," even though TIME has yet to do so.]

The average age of the Person of the Year is 57 years, compared to 51 for the average of all persons on the covers. The male Person of the Year averages 60 years and the female 43 years; these figures are both higher than the overall averages of 53 for men and 38 for women. This is not surprising as one must be much more outstanding in the news to be honored as TIME's Person of the Year.

The following tables group the Persons of the Year by profession and nationality.

TABLE 18.—Professions of the Person of the Year

Professions and Positions	Women	Men	Total	Percent
U.S. Presidents and Presidents-elect	0	12	12	16.00
U.S. Secretaries of Departments	1	3	4	5.33
Other U.S. Politicians	2	3	5	6.68
Wives of politicians	3	0	3	4.00
Royalty	1	2	3	4.00
Foreign Heads of State and politicians	0	13	13	17.33
Scientists (on same cover)	0	15	15	20.00
U.S. military	1	3	4	5.33
Astronauts (on same cover)	0	3	3	4.00
Industrialists	0	2	2	2.67
Jurists	1	1	2	2.67
Religion	1	1	2	2.67
Civil Rights	1	1	2	2.67
Educator	1	0	1	1.33
News Media	1	0	1	1.33
Tennis player	1	0	1	1.33
Labor leader	1	0	1	1.33
Pilot	0	1	1	1.33
Total	15	60	75	100.00

TABLE 19.—Nationality of the Person of the Year

Country	Number	Percent
United States	57	76.00
Germany	3	4.00
Great Britain	3	4.00
Soviet Union	3	4.00
China	2	2.67
France	2	2.67
Ethiopia	1	1.33
India	1	1.33
Iran	1	1.33
Italy	1	1.33
Saudi Arabia	1	1.33
Total	75	100.00

Table 18 again proves the importance of politicians and statesmen in the news; forty (53.34 percent) of all Persons of the Year have been in politics, and only thirty-five (46.66 percent) in other endeavors. In Table 19 it is obvious that Americans most often are chosen as Persons of the Year, as only 24 percent are foreigners. Only two foreign women have been chosen as Person of the Year, Queen Elizabeth II and Mei-ling Chiang; all other women are Americans.

The following list contains the names of all individuals who have been designated as Person of the Year. At the right of each name appears the year for which that individual was selected.

TABLE 20.—Persons of the Year

Name	Year
1. Adenauer, Konrad, 1876-1967	1953
2. Anders, William Alison, 1933-	1968
3. Beadle, George Wells, 1903-	1960
4. Borman, Frank, 1928-	1968
5. Brandt, Willy, 1913-	1970
6. Brownmiller, Susan, 1936-	1975
7. Byerly, Kathleen, 1944-	1975
8. Byrnes, James Francis, 1879-1972	1946
9. Carter, Jimmy, 1924-	1976
10. Cheek, Alison, 1928-	1975
11. Chiang, Kai-shek, 1886-1975	1937
12. Chiang, Mei-ling, 1897-	1937

TABLE 20.—Continued

Name	Year
13. Chrysler, Walter Percy, 1875-1940	1928
14. Churchill, Winston, 1874-1965	1940, 1949
15. Conway, Jill Ker, 1935-	1975
16. Curtice, Harlow Herbert, 1893-1962	1955
17. Draper, Charles Stark, 1901-	1960
18. Dulles, John Foster, 1888-1959	1954
19. Eisenhower, Dwight David, 1890-1969	1944, 1959
20. Elizabeth II, 1926-	1952
21. Enders, John Franklin, 1897-	1960
22. Faisal Ibn Abdul-Aziz, 1905-1975	1974
23. Ford, Betty, 1918-	1975
24. Gandhi, Mahatma, 1869-1948	1930
25. Gaulle, Charles de, 1890-1970	1958
26. Glaser, Donald Arthur, 1926-	1960
27. Grasso, Ella, 1919-	1975
28. Haile Selassie, 1891-1975	1935
29. Hills, Carla, 1934-	1975
30. Hitler, Adolf, 1889-1945	1938
31. John XXIII, Pope, 1881-1963	1962
32. Johnson, Hugh Samuel, 1882-1942	1933
33. Johnson, Lyndon Baines, 1908-1973	1964, 1967
34. Jordan, Barbara, 1936-	1975
35. Kennedy, John Fitzgerald, 1917-1963	1961
36. Khrushchev, Nikita S., 1894-1971	1957
37. King, Billie Jean, 1943-	1975
38. King, Martin Luther, Jr., 1929-1968	1963
39. Kissinger, Henry, 1923-	1972
40. Laval, Pierre, 1883-1945	1931
41. Lederberg, Joshua, 1925-	1960
42. Libby, Willard, 1908-	1960
43. Lindbergh, Charles A., 1902-1974	1927
44. Lovell, James A., 1928-	1968
45. Marshall, George Catlett, 1880-1959	1943, 1947
46. Mossadeq, Mohamed, 1879-1967	1951
47. Nixon, Richard Milhous, 1913-	1971, 1972
48. Pauling, Linus Paul, 1901-	1960
49. Purcell, Edward Mills, 1912-	1960
50. Rabi, Isidor Isaac, 1898-	1960
51. Roosevelt, Franklin Delano, 1882-1945	1932, 1934 1941
52. Schockley, William, 1911-	1960
53. Segre, Emilio Gino, 1905-	1960
54. Sharp, Susie Marshall, 1907-	1975
55. Simpson, Wallis Warfield, 1896- "Duchess of Windsor"	1936

TABLE 20.—Continued

Name	Year
56. Sirica, John Joseph, 1904-	1973
57. Stalin, Joseph, 1879-1953	1939, 1942
58. Sutton, Carol, 1933	1975
59. Teller, Edward, 1908-	1960
60. Townes, Charles Hard, 1915-	1960
61. Truman, Harry S, 1884-1972	1945, 1948
62. Van Allen, James Alfred, 1914-	1960
63. Westmoreland, William Childs, 1914-	1965
64. Woodward, Robert Burns, 1917-	1960
65. Wyatt, Addie, 1925-	1975
66. Young, Owen D., 1874-1962	1929
67. Topic—G.I. Joe	1950
68. Topic—Hungarian Patriot	1956
69. Topic—Twenty-five and under	1966
70. Topic—The Middle Americans	1969

Twenty (30.3 percent) of the above sixty-six individuals who were selected as Person of the Year are among the eighty-five who also appeared on the covers four or more times. Thirteen of these same twenty appeared eight or more times on the covers. Thus it can be said that the Person of the Year is one who is likely to be in the news frequently, but those frequently in the news are not necessarily those who qualify to be selected as the person "who did the most in the year to affect the news for good or ill" and thusly selected as the Person of the Year.

Notes: 14. TIME, Jan. 4, 1963, p. 11.
15. TIME, Dec. 7, 1959, p. 14.
16. TIME, Jan. 4, 1943, p. 13.
17. TIME, Dec. 20, 1968, p. 9.
18. TIME, Jan. 1, 1945, p. 9.
19. TIME, Dec. 31, 1951, p. 3.
20. TIME, Dec. 30, 1957, p. 8.

CHAPTER 10
AMERICAN PRESIDENTS, VICE-PRESIDENTS
AND FIRST LADIES

Presidents, vice-presidents and first ladies are often in the news and consequently frequently appear on the covers of TIME. The following lists include all the individuals who have been presidents, vice-presidents and first ladies of the United States, and who at one time or another have appeared on TIME's covers. The three groups are listed separately and are in chronological order from Washington to Carter. The total number of appearances is given in parentheses after the name, followed by the position(s) held; the number written next to the position indicates how many times the individual appeared while holding that office. At the right of each position are dates of the first and last appearance when that individual was depicted while in that particular position.

TABLE 21.—American Presidents

Name	Dates
Washington, George (5) Ex-President	Oct. 18, 1948 - Special Bicentennial Issue, 1976
Jefferson, Thomas (1) Ex-President	Special 1776 Issue, 1976
Madison, James (1) Ex-President	Aug. 6, 1973
Monroe, James (1) Ex-President	Sept. 21, 1962
Lincoln, Abraham (2) Ex-President	Sept. 28, 1959 - May 10, 1963
Cleveland, Grover (2) Ex-President	May 28, 1945 - Feb. 23, 1976
Roosevelt, Theodore (2) Ex-President	Sept. 7, 1942 - Mar. 3, 1958
Wilson, Woodrow (1) Ex-President	Nov. 12, 1923
Harding, Warren G. (1) President	Mar. 10, 1923
Coolidge, Calvin (1) President	Jan. 16, 1928
Hoover, Herbert (4) Secretary of Commerce (2) Ex-President (2) President (0)	Nov. 16, 1925 - Mar. 26, 1928 Oct. 14, 1935 - Dec. 18, 1939

TABLE 21.—Continued

Name	Dates
Roosevelt, Franklin D. (8)	
Lawyer (1)	May 26, 1923
Governor of New York (1)	Feb. 1, 1932
President-elect (1)	Jan. 2, 1933
President (5)	Jan. 7, 1935 - Jan. 22, 1945
Truman, Harry S (9)	
Senator (1)	Mar. 8, 1943
Vice-Presidential candidate (1)	Nov. 4, 1944
President (6)	Apr. 23, 1945 - Apr. 23, 1951
Ex-President (1)	Aug. 13, 1956
Eisenhower, Dwight D. (21)	
Military person (6)	Nov. 16, 1942 - Feb. 12, 1951
Educator (1)	June 16, 1952
Presidential candidate (1)	Nov. 3, 1952
President-elect (1)	Nov. 10, 1952
President (10)	July 4, 1955 - Aug. 15, 1960
Ex-President (2)	July 21, 1961 - Apr. 4, 1969
Kennedy, John F. (11)	
Senator (2)	Dec. 2, 1957 - Nov. 24, 1958
Presidential candidate (3)	July 11, 1960 - Nov. 7, 1960
President-elect (1)	Nov. 16, 1960
President (5)	Jan. 27, 1961 - June 21, 1963
Johnson, Lyndon B. (23)	
Senator (4)	June 22, 1953 - Apr. 25, 1960
Vice-Presidential candidate (2)	July 18, 1960 - Aug. 15, 1960
Vice-President (1)	Jan. 27, 1961
President (16)	Nov. 29, 1963 - Nov. 8, 1968
Nixon, Richard M. (55)	
Senator (2)	Aug. 25, 1952 - Nov. 10, 1952
Vice-President (10)	Jan. 18, 1954 - Oct. 31, 1960
Lawyer and political candidate (6)	July 21, 1961 - Nov. 15, 1968
President (36)	Jan. 24, 1969 - July 22, 1974
Ex-President (1)	Sept. 16, 1974
Ford, Gerald R. (22)	
Congressman (1)	Jan. 15, 1973
Vice-President-elect (1)	Oct. 22, 1973
Vice-President (1)	Dec. 17, 1973
President (19)	Aug. 19, 1974 - Nov. 8, 1976
Carter, Jimmy (10)	
Governor of Georgia (1)	May 31, 1971
Presidential candidate (6)	Mar. 8, 1976 - Nov. 8, 1976
President-elect (3)	Nov. 15, 1976 - Jan. 3, 1977

TABLE 22.—American Vice-Presidents

Name	Dates
Coolidge, Calvin*	
Dawes, Charles G. (2)	
Vice-President	Dec. 14, 1925 - June 11, 1928
Curtis, Charles (3)	
Senator (2)	Dec. 20, 1926 - June 18, 1928
Vice-President (1)	Dec. 5, 1932
Garner, John N. (3)	
Congressman (1)	Dec. 7, 1931
Vice-President (2)	June 3, 1935 - Mar. 20, 1939
Wallace, Henry A. (5)	
Secretary of Agriculture (3)	Apr. 10, 1933 - Sept. 23, 1940
Vice-President (0)	
Secretary of Commerce (1)	Sept. 30, 1946
Magazine editor (1)	Aug. 9, 1948
Truman, Harry S*	
Barkley, Alben W. (2)	
Senator (1)	Aug. 23, 1937
Vice-President (1)	July 28, 1952
Nixon, Richard M.*	
Johnson, Lyndon B.*	
Humphrey, Hubert H. (12)	
Senator (4)	Jan. 17, 1949 - Sept. 4, 1964
Vice-President (7)	Apr. 1, 1966 - Sept. 6, 1968
Senator (1)	Mar. 8, 1976
Agnew, Spiro T. (10)	
Governor of Maryland (2)	Aug. 16, 1968 - Sept. 20, 1968
Vice-President (8)	Nov. 14, 1969 - Oct. 8, 1973
Ford, Gerald R.*	
Rockefeller, Nelson A. (12)	
Public official (2)	May 22, 1939 - Oct. 6, 1958
Governor of New York (8)	Aug. 1, 1960 - July 26, 1968
Vice-President (2)	Sept. 2, 1974 - May 17, 1976
Mondale, Walter F. (3)	
Senator (2)	Jan. 15, 1973 - July 26, 1976
Vice-President-elect (1)	Dec. 20, 1976

*Note: Those Vice-Presidents marked with an asterisk were also
    Presidents and the dates of the covers on which they
    appeared are listed in the preceding table.

TABLE 23.—First Ladies

Name	Dates
Coolidge, Grace (1)	
First Lady	Sept. 17, 1928
Hoover, Lou Henry (2)	
Wife of Secretary of Commerce (1)	Apr. 21, 1924
First Lady (1)	May 13, 1929
Roosevelt, Eleanor (4)	
First Lady (3)	Nov. 20, 1933 - Apr. 17, 1939
Delegate to the U.N. (1)	Apr. 7, 1952
Truman, Bess (0)	
Eisenhower, Mamie Doud (1)	
First Lady	Jan. 19, 1953
Kennedy, Jacqueline (3)	
First Lady (2)	July 11, 1960 - Jan. 20, 1961
Mrs. Onassis (1)	Oct. 25, 1968
Johnson, Lady Bird (1)	
First Lady	Aug. 28, 1964
Nixon, Patricia (6)	
Wife of Vice-President (1)	Feb. 29, 1960
First Lady (5)	Mar. 6, 1972 - Oct. 7, 1974
Ford, Betty (4)	
Wife of Vice-President (1)	Dec. 17, 1973
First Lady (3)	Oct. 7, 1974 - Jan. 5, 1976

The foregoing tables verify that presidents, vice-presidents, and the first ladies do appear recurrently on TIME's covers. Since the first issue of TIME every president but one, Herbert Hoover, appeared on TIME during his presidency. Hoover did appear four times, but never during his term in office as President. (Jimmy Carter and Walter Mondale are included here even though they had not officially taken office during the period covered by this study.)

Like the presidents, all vice-presidents have been on TIME, but not all were on during their vice-presidencies. Those who never made TIME's covers during their vice-presidencies are Calvin Coolidge, Henry Wallace and Harry Truman; however, these three did appear at other times in other capacities.

The only first ladies who never were portrayed on a cover were Florence Harding and Bess Truman. All others did appear while they were in the White House. It is interesting to note that Pat Nixon was on a cover dated February 29; TIME has only published two issues dated with this bissextile day. The other person who appeared on a February

29 cover was William Henry Murray (1869-1956) who was governor of Oklahoma when he was portrayed in 1932.

Table 24 indicates the number of issues published during the period of each presidency since TIME's inception in 1923 until the first issue of 1977, that is, March 3, 1923, to January 3, 1977, inclusively. This figure is followed by the number of times that each president appeared on the cover during his presidency. From these data it is obvious that the most recent presidents have a much higher percentage of appearances on TIME's covers than did the earlier ones. The percentage for Harding is skewed due to the fact that he was president for two full years (Mar. 4, 1921, to Mar. 3, 1923) before the first issue of TIME was published. It should be pointed out again that Herbert Hoover is the only president who never was depicted on a cover during his presidency, but his wife did appear as the First Lady on the May 13, 1929, issue. Of the 2,814 covers analyzed there were exactly 99 that portrayed the President in office, or 3.5 percent of all covers. The list is given in reverse chronological order, which coincidentally is in rank order from the highest to the lowest percentage, except, of course, for Hoover and Harding.

TABLE 24.—Number and Percentage of Covers Portraying the President

President	No. of Issues	No. of Cover Appearances	Percent
Ford, G. R.	128	19	14.85
Nixon, R. M.	289	36	12.45
Johnson, L. B.	270	16	5.93
Kennedy, J. F.	149	5	3.36
Eisenhower, D. D.	418	10	2.40
Truman, H. S.	406	6	1.48
Roosevelt, F.D.	632	5	0.80
Hoover, H. C.	209	0	0.00
Coolidge, C.	291	1	0.34
Harding, W. G.	22	1	4.50
Total	2,814 covers	99 presidential portrayals	

The above table presents information that makes one wonder if the most recent presidents are more important newsmakers than the earlier ones, or if TIME's criteria have changed.

CHAPTER 11
HISTORICAL FIGURES AND BIBLICAL PERSONAGES

Even though the great majority of those who appear on the covers are living persons, from time to time people from the past are portrayed. Historical figures who continue to be in the news are usually those who have left their mark on history, albeit for better or for worse. The following lists contain the names of the 129 persons who appeared on covers at least one year after death and 15 who appeared immediately after death or while on their deathbeds. These 144 persons (14 women and 130 men) are composed of 89 individuals (5 women and 84 men). The reader should be reminded that some of these individuals were used as principal cover subjects, some served as background material for others, and several were used as symbols signifying a topic or theme.

Table 25 contains the names of 30 individuals who appeared on a TIME cover at least one year after death and who never appeared on a cover while alive. As it resulted all were dead at least five years before they ever appeared; most were dead for many more years than this. Included with name of the individual are the years of birth and death and the dates of the issues of TIME on which he was depicted.

TABLE 25.—Historical Figures Who Never Appeared while Alive

1. Aristotle, 384-322 B.C.
   (Nov. 24, 1961)

2. Bach, Johann Sebastian, 1685-1750
   (Dec. 27, 1968)

3. Buddha, ca. 563-483 B.C.
   (Aug. 30, 1954, and Dec. 11, 1964)

4. Cleveland, Grover, 1837-1908
   (May 28, 1945, and Feb. 23, 1976)

5. Confucius, ca. 551-479 B.C.
   (May 26, 1947)

6. Fitzgerald, John Francis, 1863-1950
   (July 11, 1960)

7. Hamilton, Alexander, 1757-1804
   (Nov. 23, 1959; Sept. 10, 1965; and Aug. 6, 1973)

8. Harvard, John, 1607-1638
   (Mar. 1, 1954, and April 18, 1969)

9. Homer, fl. ca. 1000 B.C.
   (Nov. 24, 1961)

10. Irving, Washington, 1783-1859
    (Oct. 2, 1944)

TABLE 25.—Continued

11. Jefferson, Thomas, 1743-1826
    (Special 1776 Issue, 1976)

12. Joan of Arc, 1412-1431
    (Aug. 4, 1941)

13. Keynes, John Maynard, 1883-1946
    (Dec. 31, 1965)

14. Lee, Robert E., 1807-1870
    (Oct. 18, 1948)

15. Lenin, Nikolai, 1870-1924
    (Sept. 13, 1963; Apr. 24, 1964; and Nov. 10, 1967)

16. Lincoln, Abraham, 1809-1865
    (Sept. 28, 1959, and May 10, 1963)

17. Louis XIV, King of France, 1638-1715
    (Feb. 8, 1963)

18. Luther, Martin, 1483-1546
    (Mar. 24, 1967)

19. Marx, Karl, 1818-1883
    (Feb. 23, 1948, and Sept. 13, 1963)

20. Monroe, James, 1758-1831
    (Sept. 21, 1962)

21. Nabokov, Helene R., 1876-1937
    (May 23, 1969)

22. Napoleon Bonaparte, 1769-1821
    (July 14, 1941, and Dec. 22, 1952)

23. Rijn, Titus van, 1642?-1668
    (June 4, 1965)

24. Roosevelt, Theodore, 1858-1919
    (Sept. 7, 1942, and Mar. 3, 1958)

25. Ruth, George Herman "Babe," 1895-1948
    (Apr. 26, 2976)

26. Shakespeare, William, 1564-1616
    (July 4, 1960)

27. Smith, Adam, 1723-1790
    (July 14, 1975)

28. Washington, George, 1732-1799
    (Oct. 18, 1948; July 6, 1953; Dec. 14, 1970; Aug 6, 1973; and the
    Special Bicentennial Issue, 1976)

29. Wesley, John, 1703-1791
    (May 8, 1964)

30. White, Harry Dexter, 1892-1948
    (Nov. 23, 1953)

The one cover which depicted the most identifiable individuals was that of Aug. 6, 1973, which contained twenty-seven individuals. For this cover TIME used the painting, *The Signing of the Constitution*, by Howard Chandler Christy (1873-1952), which is in the House wing of the Capitol in Washington. Christy included forty men in the painting; TIME used only the middle section, eliminating five men from the right hand side of the painting and eight from the left.[21] The twenty-five individuals who are listed below all appeared just once when they were portrayed on this cover. The other two individuals who were in the portion of the painting used for the cover were George Washington and Alexander Hamilton, but as they were also on other covers they are listed in the preceding table and excluded here.

The forty men in Christy's painting can be accounted for easily by quoting from David Whitney's book on the Constitution in which he explained:

> . . . The delegates reached agreement on the Constitution [on Monday, September 17, 1787]. Thirty-eight delegates signed the document, and the name of a thirty-ninth who was absent, John Dickinson, was signed by proxy. William Jackson, the secretary of the Convention, signed the Constitution to attest the signatures of the delegates, but he generally is not counted among the signers of the Constitution because he was not an official delegate from any state.[22]

TABLE 26.—Signers of the U.S. Constitution

1. Bedford, Gunning, 1747-1812
2. Blair, John, 1732-1800
3. Blount, William, 1749-1800
4. Breasley, David, 1745-1790
5. Broom, Jacob, 1752-1810
6. Butler, Pierce, 1744-1822
7. Clymer, George, 1739-1813
8. Dickinson, John, 1732-1808
9. Fitzsimmons, Thomas, 1741-1811
10. Franklin, Benjamin, 1706-1790
11. Gilman, Nicholas, 1755-1814
12. Ingersoll, Jared, 1722-1781
13. Jackson, William, 1759-1828
14. Johnson, William Samuel, 1727-1819
15. Langdon, John, 1741-1819
16. Livingston, William, 1723-1790
17. McHenry, James, 1753-1816
18. Madison, James, 1751-1836

TABLE 26.—Continued

---

    19. Mifflin, Thomas, 1744-1800
    20. Morris, Gouveneur, 1752-1816
    21. Paterson, William, 1745-1806
    22. Pinckney, Charles C., 1746-1825
    23. Sherman, Roger, 1721-1793
    24. Spaight, Richard Dobbs, 1758-1802
    25. Williamson, Hugh, 1735-1819

Eight different biblical personages have appeared on the covers of TIME. Various Nativity scenes have been used five times; the Madonna and Child appeared four times. All but one of these were covers related to the Christmas season. The various Christmas covers account for most of the appearances of biblical personages. Jesus Christ appeared on fourteen covers, ten of which were Christmas covers. Of these ten covers he appeared nine times as Baby Jesus and once as Jesus Christ. The other four times he also appeared as Jesus Christ. The Virgin Mary was depicted ten times, nine times with Baby Jesus and once as background for Mother Mary Columba (Apr. 11, 1955). Joseph and the Three Magi (Balthazar, Gaspar and Malchior) only appeared on Christmas covers related to the Nativity scene. Eve was depicted on a cover (Oct. 25, 1954) with the evangelist, Billy Graham. Saint Paul was on the cover of the April 18, 1960, issue in a reproduction of a painting which is attributed to Lippo Memmi of the fourteenth century. The number of times and the inclusive dates of appearances for Jesus Christ, the Virgin Mary, Joseph and the Three Magi are listed in Table 15, The Most Frequently Portrayed Individuals. These eight individuals are the only biblical personages who have been on TIME's covers.

Table 27 lists the names of fourteen individuals who appeared on covers at the time of death or shortly thereafter. Three of these had never been on a cover previously. It seems that TIME follows a policy, albeit written or unwritten, of not portraying individuals on its covers at the time of the person's death, but there are a few exceptions made occasionally. These fourteen men were all depicted within one year after death; some immediately thereafter and others seemed to have been on their deathbeds when the cover was published. Eleven of the fourteen appeared within two weeks after death. James William Good appeared five months after dying; Lee Harvey Oswald almost ten months after his assassination. Howard Hughes did appear on a cover immediately after death, and then again eight months later.

TABLE 27.—Individuals Who Appeared within One Year after Death

Name	Birth and Death Dates	Date on Cover after Death	Date on First (or Only) Cover while Alive
1. Allende, Salvador	July 26, 1908 - Sept. 11, 1973	Sept. 24, 1973	Oct. 19, 1970
2. Carlson, Paul Earle	1928 - Nov. 24, 1969	Dec. 4, 1964	None
3. Eisenhower, Dwight D.	Oct. 14, 1890 - Mar. 28, 1969	Apr. 4, 1969	Nov. 16, 1942
4. Faisal ibn Abdul Aziz King of Saudi Arabia	1905 - Mar. 25, 1975	Apr. 7, 1975	Nov. 19, 1973
5. Hitler, Adolf	Apr. 20, 1889 - Apr. 30, 1945	May 7, 1945	Dec. 21, 1931
6. Hughes, Howard Robard	Dec. 24, 1906 - Apr. 5, 1976	Apr. 19, and Dec. 13, 1976	July 19, 1948
7. Good, James William	Sept. 24, 1866 - Apr. 11, 1929	Sept. 2, 1929	Sept. 24, 1928
8. John XXIII, Pope	Nov. 25, 1881 - June 3, 1963	June 7, 1963	Nov. 10, 1958
9. Kennedy, Robert F.	Nov. 20, 1925 - June 6, 1968	June 14, 1968	July 11, 1960
10. Luce, Henry Robinson	Apr. 3, 1898 - Feb. 28, 1967	Mar. 10, 1967	None
11. Mao, Tse-tung	Dec. 26, 1893 - Sept. 9, 1976	Sept. 20, 1976	Feb. 7, 1949
12. Nasser, Gamal Abdel	Jan. 15, 1918 - Sept. 28, 1970	Oct. 12, 1970	Sept. 26, 1955
13. Oswald, Lee Harvey	Oct. 18, 1939 - Nov. 24, 1963	Oct. 2, 1964	None
14. Vandenberg, Arthur H.	Mar. 22, 1884 - Apr. 18, 1951	Dec. 17, 1951	Oct. 2, 1939

TABLE 28.—Individuals Who Appeared while Alive and Re-appeared More than One Year after Death

Name	Birth Date	First Time on a Cover	Death Date	Last Time on a Cover
1. Cannon, Joseph G.	May 7, 1836	Mar. 3, 1923	Nov. 12, 1926	Jan. 15, 1973
2. Faulkner, William C.	Sept. 25, 1897	Jan. 23, 1939	July 6, 1962	July 17, 1964
3. Freud, Sigmund	May 6, 1856	Oct. 27, 1924	Sept. 9, 1939	Apr. 23, 1956
4. Gandhi, Mahatma	Oct. 2, 1869	Mar. 31, 1930	Jan. 30, 1948	May 11, 1953
5. Hindenburg, Paul von	Oct. 2, 1847	Mar. 26, 1926	Aug. 2, 1934	July 14, 1941
6. Ho, Chi Minh	May 19, 1890	Nov. 22, 1954	Sept. 3, 1969	May 12, 1975
7. Hoover, J. Edgar	Jan. 1, 1895	Aug. 5, 1935	May 2, 1972	Dec. 22, 1975
8. Lodge, Henry Cabot	May 12, 1850	Jan. 21, 1924	Nov. 9, 1924	Dec. 17, 1951
9. Monroe, Marilyn	June 1, 1926	May 14, 1956	Aug. 5, 1962	July 16, 1973
10. Reuter, Ernst	July 29, 1889	Sept. 18, 1950	Sept. 29, 1953	May 25, 1959
11. Shaw, George Bernard	July 26, 1856	Dec. 24, 1923	Nov. 2, 1950	July 23, 1956
12. Stalin, Joseph	Dec. 21, 1879	June 9, 1930	Mar. 5, 1953	Nov. 10, 1967

Among all of the 2,344 individuals included in this study there are only twelve who were on a cover at least once while alive and then re-appeared later after having been dead for more than a year. Table 28 gives the names of these twelve individuals, the birth date, the date of the first cover on which each appeared, date of death, and the date of the cover on which each re-appeared a year or more after death. None re-appeared less than two years after death and one individual even has a 47-year span between the date of death and that of the cover on which he later re-appeared; this was Joseph G. Cannon, who was on TIME's first cover. His second and last appearance was on a cover that contained a reproduction of TIME's first cover. However, the average length of time for the re-appearance after death is twelve years. Marilyn Monroe is the only woman who qualified for inclusion in this group. It is surprising that of these twelve individuals only five are Americans. In Table 27 it is almost the other way around, only six are not Americans.

The 89 individuals who were considered as historical figures and biblical personages only make up 3.8 percent of the 2,344 individuals under study. When one takes into consideration the multiple appearances of these 89 individuals there are then 144 persons who were dead at the time of being depicted on TIME. These 144 persons are only 4.3 percent of the 3,336 persons who have been on the covers. This does point out that TIME's covers are definitely for the living newsmakers and that the people of the past are only occasionally used as cover subjects, and often this is done in conjunction with live individuals.

Notes: 21. *World Book Encyclopedia*, s.v. United States Constitution (vol. 20, pp. 126-127). Chicago: Field Enterprises Educational Corp., 1972.
22. Whitney, David C. *Founders of freedom in America: lives of the men who signed the Constitution of the United States and so helped to establish the United States of America.* Chicago: J.G. Ferguson Publishing Co., 1965, p. 32.

CHAPTER 12

MINORITY GROUPS IN AMERICAN SOCIETY

The 2,294 Americans who have appeared on the covers can be divided into various categories according to national origin or racial ascendency. For the purpose of this study the 2,294 Americans were divided into five groups as shown in Table 29.

TABLE 29.— Americans Grouped by Origin or Racial Ascendency

Group	Number	Percent
White Americans	2,229	97.17
Native born 2,052 (89.45%)		
Foreign born 177 (07.72%)		
Black Americans	57	02.48
Native born 56 (02.44%)		
Foreign born 1 (00.04%)		
Spanish-surnamed Americans	4	00.18
Japanese-Americans	3	00.13
Native born 2 (00.09%)		
Foreign born 1 (00.04%)		
American Indians	1	00.04
Total	2,294	100.00

The following table gives in round numbers the various racial groups in the United States which made up the 1970 census.[23] These figures are used to point out the percentage of each group in the general population and how each group fared in being portrayed on the covers.

TABLE 30.—Population of the United States

Group	Total Population	% of Total Pop.	No. on Covers	% of Each Group on Covers
White Americans	167,000,000	81.85	2,229	0.00134
Black Americans	23,000,000	11.27	57	0.00025
Spanish-surnamed Americans	11,050,000	05.42	4	0.00004
Japanese-Americans	600,000	00.30	3	0.00050
American Indians	800,000	00.40	1	0.00013
Chinese-Americans	450,000	00.22	0	0.00000
Others	1,100,000	00.54	0	0.00000
Total	204,000,000	100.00	2,294	

Tables 29 and 30 indicate that there have been 65 persons on TIME's covers who represent four minority groups. Table 31 distributes these 65 persons according to the six periods covered by this study to show how the trend has changed from Period 1 to Period 6. Of the 65 persons from the minority groups 48 (74 percent) appeared on the covers since 1959.

TABLE 31.—Distribution of Minority Groups for the Six Periods

	Black Americans	Spanish-surnamed Americans	Japanese-Americans	American Indians	Total	Percent
Period 1 (1923-31)	0	0	0	1	1	01.54
Period 2 (1932-40)	2	1	0	0	3	04.62
Period 3 (1941-49)	4	0	0	0	4	06.15
Period 4 (1950-58)	7	0	2	0	9	13.85
Period 5 (1959-67)	22	1	1	0	24	36.92
Period 6 (1968-76)	22	2	0	0	24	36.92
Total	57	4	3	1	65	100.00

White Americans have appeared in a much greater number than their percentage of the total population. It should be pointed out that in the census and other population statistics the Spanish-surnamed are included in the group of white Americans, but here they have been treated separately. No minority group is represented in the proportion as its composition of the population. White Americans make up 81.85 percent of the population and account for 97.17 percent of the Americans on TIME. Blacks and Japanese-Americans are the only groups who have any kind of representation in proportion to their numbers in the total population. More than eleven million Spanish-surnamed live in the United States, yet only four have been on the covers of TIME; and the first Chinese-American has yet to appear.

Table 29 shows that there have been 179 foreign-born Americans on the covers; they compose 7.8 percent of all American persons. The censuses of the United States from 1920 to 1970 show that there has been an average of 8.4 percent of foreign born Americans in these six censuses.[24] This is almost a perfect correlation between the total population and the persons covered in this study. In other words, from the foreign born Americans come some very prominent persons, thus proving that among the immigrants to this country there are newsmakers who indeed do contribute to the society. No other group, except for the white Americans, has appeared on TIME's covers in the same proportion as their percentage of the overall population.

Since there have been so few individuals on the covers representing the minority groups they are all listed in Tables 32 and 34. Table 32 is a list of the Spanish-surnamed, Japanese-Americans and the American Indian. Table 34 gives the names of the American blacks.

TABLE 32.—Minority Individuals (Excluding Blacks)

	Date on Cover
Spanish-surnamed	
Chavez, Cesar	July 4, 1969
Labor union organizer, born in Yuma, Arizona, Mar. 31, 1927	
Gomez, Vernon	July 9, 1934
Baseball player, born in Rodeo, California Nov. 26, 1909	
Lopez, Trini	May 21, 1965
Singer, born in Dallas, Texas, May 15, 1937	
Trevino, Lee	July 19, 1971
Golfer, born in Dallas, Texas, Dec. 1, 1939	
Japanese-Americans	
Suzuki, Pat	Dec. 22, 1958
Singer and actress, born in Cressey, California, in 1930(?)	
Umeki, Miyoshi	Dec. 22, 1958
Singer and actress, born in Japan, in 1929, but has lived most of her life in the United States	
Yamasaki, Minoru	Jan. 18, 1963
Architect, born in Seattle, Washington, Dec. 1, 1912	
American Indian	
Rogers, Will	July 19, 1926
Humorist and actor, born in Oklahoma, Nov. 4, 1879, died in Alaska, Aug. 15, 1935	

Will Rogers is included in Table 32 as he is the only person that this author could determine who was even part Indian.

> Will Rogers was born on November 4, 1879, in the Indian Territory [near Oolagah in what is now the state of Oklahoma] twelve miles from a post office. . . . Will was nine-thirty seconds Indian; that is, a trifle more than one-quarter. He always said that he was a quarter-Indian, which was close enough for all practical purposes.[25]

Blacks form the largest racial minority in the United States and they are the most represented minority on TIME's covers. Fifty-seven times blacks have appeared on the covers. The first one to be so honored was Richard Berry Harrison, an actor famous for his role of "De Lawd" in both the stage production and the film version of Marc Connelley's play, *The Green Pastures.* "His parents were slaves who fled to freedom in Canada. He and five sisters and brothers were born in London, Ontario. . . ."[26] "With visions of becoming a great actor, the young Harrison migrated to Detroit, determined to study and hopeful that the opportunity to act in a theater in the big city would materialize."[27] "For Richard Berry Harrison, life up to his 65th year was woefully thin."[28] Then on February 26, 1930, at the age of 65 his role in the premiere of *The Green Pastures* assured him a place in the history of the American theater. He had just given his 1,652nd performance when he was chosen for TIME's cover of Mar. 4, 1935.

This milestone did not go unnoticed by TIME's readers. Two weeks later in the *Letters* section of the Mar. 18, 1935, issue on page 10, William A. Clem of West Mansfield, Massachusetts, wrote:

> Your account of *The Green Pastures* in your March 4 issue is indeed a masterpiece. One point, however, I would like to have cleared up. Is Richard B. Harrison the first Negro to ... appear on the cover of TIME?

The editor's answer was, "Yes." In that same issue another reader, Thomas C. Jervay, the Managing Editor of the *Cape Fear Journal,* Wilmington, N.C., remarked, "Hats off to TIME for reproducing the very excellent photo of 'De Lawd' and on the cover at that!"

A little less than three years later the second black was depicted on a cover. He was Walter Francis White, who at that time was the Executive Secretary of the National Association for the Advancement of Colored People. TIME's cover story stated that he was:

> . . . The most potent leader of his race in the U.S. Son of a fair-skinned Georgia postman and his fair-skinned wife. Walter White is blond and palefaced. He himself does not know how much Negro blood runs in his veins; Harvard's far-ranging Anthropologist Earnest Alfred Hooton computes it at 1/64. But despite a skin that last week fooled fellow guests at Washington's Hay-Adams House, Walter White has always regarded himself as a Negro.[29]

Fifty-seven blacks have appeared on the covers. These 57 persons are made up of 51 different individuals. Of the 57 persons there are 44 males and 13 females, or 77 and 23 percent respectively. Females account for only 10.5 percent of all persons on the covers, but among American blacks the percentage of women is much higher. Also, the average age is much lower for blacks than it is for the entire group of 3,211 persons of this study. The average age for blacks is 35; for males it is 36 and for females it is only 31. For all persons in the study the average age is 51, and that for males is 53 and for females it is 38.

The following table shows the different professional and occupational groups into which the 57 blacks are classified. More than one-half (52.5 percent) are in sports and music.

TABLE 33.—Professions of American Blacks

Profession		Number	Percent
Politicians		6	10.50
Senators	2		
Congressmen	2		
Secretary of HUD	1		
Mayor	1		
Military		1	01.75
Sports		20	35.00
Football	6		
Baseball	5		
Boxing	5		
Basketball	1		
Ping-pong	1		
Tennis	1		
Track	1		
Civil rights leaders		7	12.25
Labor leader		1	01.75
Lawyers and judges		3	05.25
Music		10	17.50
Singers	7		
Instrumentalists	3		
Actors		3	05.25
Novelist		1	01.75
Others		5	09.00
		57	100.00

Table 34 lists the 51 black individuals who have appeared on the covers a total of 57 times, thus accounting for the 57 blacks on TIME. Each is listed with his birth and death dates and the dates of the covers on which he appeared.

TABLE 34.—The Fifty-one Blacks Who Have Been on TIME

Names	Date on Cover
1. Ali, Muhammad, 1942-	Mar. 22, 1963 and Mar. 8, 1971
2. Anderson, Marian, 1902-	Dec. 30, 1946
3. Armstrong, Louis, 1900-1971	Feb. 21, 1949
4. Baldwin, James, 1924-	May 17, 1963
5. Ballard, Florence, 1944-	May 21, 1965
6. Belafonte, Harry, 1927-	Mar. 2, 1959
7. Blue, Vida, 1949-	Aug. 23, 1971
8. Braithwaite, George, 1935-	Apr. 26, 1971
9. Brooke, Edward, 1919-	Nov. 18, 1966 and Feb. 17, 1967
10. Brown, Clide, 1942-	May 26, 1967
11. Brown, James N. (Jimmy), 1936-	Nov. 26, 1965
12. Campanella, Roy, 1921-	Aug. 8, 1955
13. Davis, J. Mason, 1936-	June 17, 1974
14. Davis, Jay, 1963-	June 17, 1974
15. Davis, June, 1942-	June 17, 1974
16. Davis, Karen, 1958-	June 17, 1974
17. Ellington, Duke, 1899-1974	Aug. 20, 1956
18. Flack, Roberta, 1940-	Feb. 12, 1973
19. Foxx, Redd, 1922-	Sept. 25, 1972
20. Franklin, Aretha, 1942-	June 28, 1968
21. Frazier, Joe, 1944-	Mar. 8, 1971
22. Gibson, Althea, 1927-	Aug. 26, 1957
23. Greene, Joe, 1946-	Dec. 8, 1975
24. Greenwood, L.C., 1946-	Dec. 8, 1975
25. Harrison, Richard Berry, 1864-1935	Mar. 4, 1935
26. Holms, Ernie, 1948-	Dec. 8, 1975
27. Jackson, Jesse, 1941-	Apr. 6, 1970
28. Jackson, Reggie, 1946-	June 3, 1974
29. Johnson, Rafer, 1935-	Aug. 29, 1960
30. Jordan, Barbara, 1936-	Jan. 5, 1976 and Dec. 20, 1976
31. King, Martin Luther, 1929-1968	Feb. 18, 1957, Jan. 3, 1964 and Mar. 19, 1965
32. Louis, Joe, 1914-	Sept. 29, 1941
33. Marshall, Thurgood, 1908-	Sept. 19, 1955 and July 22, 1974
34. Mays, Willie, 1931-	July 26, 1954
35. Monk, Thelonius, 1918-	Feb. 28, 1964
36. Price, Leontyne, 1927-	Mar. 10, 1961
37. Robertson, Oscar, 1938-	Feb. 17, 1961
38. Robinson, Jackie, 1919-1972	Sept. 22, 1947

TABLE 34.—Continued

Names	Date on Cover
39. Robinson, Sugar Ray, 1920-	June 25, 1951
40. Ross, Diana, 1944-	May 21, 1965
41. Smith, Guy, 1945-	Sept. 29, 1967
42. Smith, John William, 1935-	July 21, 1967
43. Stokes, Carl, 1927-	Nov. 17, 1967
44. Weaver, Robert C., 1907-	Mar. 4, 1966
45. White, Dwight, 1949-	Dec. 8, 1975
46. White, Walter Francis, 1893-1955	Jan. 24, 1938
47. Wilkins, Roy, 1901	Aug. 30, 1963
48. Wilson, Flip, 1933-	Jan. 31, 1972
49. Wilson, Mary, 1944-	May 21, 1965
50. Wyatt, Addie, 1924-	Jan. 5, 1976
51. Young, Whitney, 1921-	Aug. 11, 1967

Even though the minorities have not been as well represented on the covers as have white Americans, there has been a definite increase in the past fifty years. Perhaps in another decade or two their representation on TIME will be in accordance with their proportion of the general population. For some reason the Spanish-surnamed minority has appeared the least in comparison with the vast number that does exist. Blacks seem to have made more advances than any other group. It will be interesting to see what the next few years will bring about, as other minority groups come forward to take their rightful place in American society.

Notes: 23. *Statistical abstract of the United States.* 97th annual edition. Washington: Bureau of the Census, 1976, pp. 31 and 35.
24. Ibid., p. 34.
25. Croy, Homer, *Our Will Rogers.* New York: Duell, Sloan and Pearce, 1953, p. 3.
26. TIME, Mar. 4, 1935, p. 38.
27. Robinson, Wilhemina S. *Historical negro biographies.* New York: Publishers Company, Inc., 1968. p. 199.
28. TIME, Mar. 4, 1935, p. 38.
29. TIME, Jan. 24, 1938, p. 9.

CHAPTER 13
ROYALTY

Members of royal families from all parts of the world are often in the news and have been frequently used as cover subjects from the beginning of TIME. The first was King Fuad I of Egypt who appeared on TIME's ninth issue (Apr. 28, 1923). In 1924 King George V of Great Britain, Queen Marie of Romania, and Spain's King Alfonso XIII were depicted on TIME. Throughout the years sixty-four members of the world's royalty have appeared a total of 114 times.

Table 35 lists those members of royalty that have been on the covers. The number in parentheses indicates the number of times each individual appeared when he was on more than once. The dates under each name are those of the portrayals on the covers when the individual appeared once or twice; if the individual appeared more than twice the dates are those of the first and last portrayal. The arrangement is by continent and subarranged alphabetically by country; under the name of each country the order is alphabetical by name of the individual. The dates after each name are those of birth and death.

TABLE 35.—The World's Royalty

EUROPE

Belgium

Albert I, king, 1875-1934
Aug. 6, 1928

Baudouin I, king, 1930-
July 30, 1951

Leopold III, king, 1901-   (3)
Nov. 22, 1937 - July 18, 1949

Mary Liliane de Rethy, consort of Leopold III, 1911-
July 18, 1949

Bulgaria

Boris III, king, 1894-1943
Jan. 20, 1941

Denmark

Anne-Marie Dagmar Ingrid, princess, 1945-
July 3, 1964

Christian X, king, 1870-1947   (2)
May 17, 1937 - Jan. 2, 1939

Margrethe II, queen, 1940-
May 3, 1976

France

Louis XIV, king, 1638-1715
Feb. 8, 1963

TABLE 35.—Continued

Germany

Wilhelm II, emperor, 1859-1941
June 28, 1926

Great Britain

Charles, prince of Wales, 1949-
June 27, 1969

Edward, duke of Windsor, 1894-1972   (2)
Aug. 8, 1927 - Apr. 1, 1929

Elizabeth II, queen, 1926-   (6)
Apr. 29, 1929 - May 3, 1976

Elizabeth Bowes-Lyon, consort of George VI, 1900-   (2)
Aug. 11, 1930 - Oct. 9, 1939

George V, king, 1865-1936   (5)
Apr. 7, 1924 - May 6, 1935

George VI, king, 1895-1952   (4)
Jan. 12, 1925 - Mar. 6, 1944

George, duke of Kent, 1902-
Aug. 8, 1927

Henry, duke of Gloucester, 1900-1974
Aug. 8, 1927

Margaret Rose, princess, 1930-   (2)
June 13, 1949 - Nov. 7, 1955

Mary of Teck, consort of George V, 1867-1953   (3)
May 30, 1927 - Oct. 27, 1930

Philip, consort of Elizabeth II, 1921-
Oct. 21, 1957

Greece

Constantine, king, 1940-
Apr. 28, 1967

Frederika, consort of Paul I, 1917-
Oct. 26, 1953

George II, king, 1890-1947   (2)
Nov. 4, 1940 - Feb. 24, 1947

Italy

Vittorio Emmanuel III, king, 1869-1947
June 15, 1925

Netherlands

Bernhard, consort of Juliana, 1911-
May 3, 1976

Juliana, queen, 1909-   (2)
Sept. 6, 1948 - May 3, 1976

Wilhelmina, queen, 1880-1962   (3)
Aug. 12, 1935 - May 13, 1946

Norway

Haakon VII, king, 1872-1957   (3)
May 3, 1926 - Jan. 2, 1939

TABLE 35.—Continued

Norway (Continued)
   Olaf V, king, 1903-
   Mar. 25, 1929

Romania
   Carol II, king, 1893-1953
   Nov. 13, 1939

   Marie, consort of Ferdinand I, 1875-1931
   Aug. 4, 1924

   Michael, king, 1921-
   Aug. 1, 1927

Spain
   Alfonso XIII, king, 1886-1941   (3)
   Dec. 22, 1924 - Apr. 6, 1931

   Juan Carlos, king, 1938-   (2)
   Nov. 3, 1975 - May 3, 1976

   Juan de Borbon y Battenberg, prince, 1913-
   June 22, 1962

Sweden
   Carl XVI Gustaf, king, 1946-
   May 3, 1976

   Gustaf V, king, 1858-1950
   Jan. 2, 1939 - Apr. 29, 1940   (3)

   Gustaf VI, king, 1882-1973
   May 31, 1943

   Martha, princess, 1901-1954
   Mar. 25, 1929

Yugoslavia
   Alexander, king, 1888-1934
   Feb. 11, 1929

   Paul, prince, 1893-1976
   Dec. 12, 1938

AFRICA

Egypt
   Farouk I, 1920-1965   (2)
   Aug. 9, 1937 - Sept. 10, 1951

   Fuad I, king, 1868-1936
   Apr. 28, 1923

Ethiopia
   Haile Selassie, emperor, 1891-1975   (2)
   Nov. 3, 1930 - Jan. 6, 1936

Morocco
   Aisha Lalla, princess, 1930-
   Nov. 11, 1957

   Mohammed V, king, 1911-1961
   Apr. 22, 1957

TABLE 35.—Continued

NEAR EAST

Iran

Mohammed Reza Pahlevi, shah, 1919-   (3)
Dec. 17, 1945 - Nov. 4, 1974

Reza Shah Pahlevi, shah, 1877-1944   (3)
July 2, 1934 - Sept. 8, 1941

Jordan

Abdullah ibn Hussein, king, 1882-1951
May 24, 1948

Hussein, king, 1936-   (3)
Apr. 2, 1956 - July 14, 1967

Saudi Arabia

Abdul Aziz ibn Saud, king, 1880-1953
Mar. 5, 1945

Saud ibn Abdul Aziz, king, 1902-1969
Jan. 28, 1957

Faisal ibn Abdul Aziz, king, 1905-1975   (3)
Nov. 19, 1973 - Apr. 7, 1975

FAR EAST

Cambodia

Sihanouk, prince, 1922-
Apr. 3, 1964

China

Pu-yi, Henry (Hsuan Tung), emperor, 1906-1967   (2)
Mar. 5, 1934 - Feb. 24, 1936

India

Osman Ali Khan, Nizam of Hyderabad, 1886-1967
Feb. 22, 1937

Japan

Hirohito, emperor, 1909-   (7)
Nov. 19, 1928 - Oct. 4, 1971

Konoye, prince, 1891-1945   (2)
July 26, 1937 - July 22, 1940

Shoda, Michiko, wife of Prince Akihito, 1935-
Mar. 23, 1959

Laos

Savang Vatthana, king, 1907-
Mar. 17, 1961

Thailand

Phumiphol Adulet, king, 1927-   (2)
(also known as Bhumibol Adulyadej and Rama IX)
Apr. 3, 1950 - May 27, 1966

Prajadhipok, king, 1893-1941
Apr. 20, 1931

TABLE 35.—Continued

Thailand (Continued)

Sirikit, consort of Phumiphol Adulet, 1932-
May 27, 1966

Table 36 shows the geographic distribution of royalty for each of the six periods. More than one-half (54.64 percent) of all royal appearances occurred in the first two periods, i.e., between 1923 and 1940, and less than one-half (47.36 percent) in the next 36 years. Great Britain is listed separately from continental Europe to reveal the dominance (importance?) in the American news when compared to the thirteen countries which are represented in the column of continental Europe. But this is understandable when one considers our cultural heritage and language.

All reigning monarchs have not appeared on TIME. The most notable absence is that of King Edward VIII of Great Britain; he was on two covers as the Prince of Wales, but never as Edward VIII or the Duke of Windsor.

Members of the world's royal families have been well represented on the covers because they are often in the news. However, the data in Table 36 prove that their importance has decreased greatly since 1940, which is due in part to their diminishing numbers.

TABLE 36.—Geographic Distribution of the World's Royalty for the Six Periods

	Great Britain	Continental Europe	Africa	Near East	Far East	Total	Percent
Period 1 (1923-31)	13	13	2	0	2	30	26.32
Period 2 (1932-40)	5	13	2	2	8	30	26.32
Period 3 (1941-49)	3	7	0	4	2	16	14.04
Period 4 (1950-58)	4	2	3	3	1	13	11.40
Period 5 (1959-67)	1	4	0	2	5	12	10.52
Period 6 (1968-76)	2	6	0	4	1	13	11.40
Total	28	45	7	15	19	114	100.00

CHAPTER 14

WORKS OF ART

Many, if not most, of TIME's covers are reproductions of works of art, but almost all are commissioned by TIME for its covers. Very few wree not created for TIME, that is, they were produced for artistic reasons with no intention of appearing on a cover. This section of the study only deals with those works of art which were *not* produced for TIME. They have been divided into four categories, viz., art works used for Christmas covers; paintings; statues and sculptures; and national symbols. Architectural works have been excluded except for the U.S. Capitol, the Washington Monument and the White House.

Besides the works mentioned in the following tables others appeared coincidentally in the background of other covers, but were not identifiable or were by unidentified artists, e.g., the lynching scene on the cover with Walter Francis White (Jan. 24, 1938) and the unsigned portrait of a man who is believed to be a New England merchant ship captain which hangs in the dining room of John F. Kennedy's house at Hyannis Port and is in the background of the cover announcing Kennedy's presidential election (Nov. 16, 1960).

There are 29 different works listed in the following tables which have been depicted a total of 57 times. The most frequently depicted is the U.S. Capitol, which has appeared on 16 covers.

The art works used for Christmas covers include paintings which range from a 15th century *Madonna and Child* to the secular 20th century painting of *The Night before Christmas*, crèche figures from the 18th century, a stained glass window, and a very modern tapestry. In Table 37 the title of each work is followed by the name of the artist, his birth and death dates (when ascertainable), and the date of the cover on which each work appeared. They are arranged chronologically by the cover date.

TABLE 37.—Works of Art Used for Christmas Covers

1. *The Nativity,* painting by Jean Charlot, 1898-
   (Dec. 26. 1938)
2. *The Nativity,* painting by Gerard David, 1460-1523
   (Dec. 24, 1945)
3. *Madonna and Child,* painting by Alesso Baldovinetti, 1425-1499
   (Dec. 29, 1947)
4. *The Night before Christmas,* painting by Arthur Rackham, 1867-1939
   (Dec. 27, 1948)
5. *The Gift,* painting by Fred Meyer, 1922-
   (Dec. 25, 1950)

6. *Madonna and Child,* stained glass window in the Chartres Cathedral
(Dec. 24, 1951)

7. *Virgin and Child,* painting by Fra Angelico (Giovanni Angelico da Fiesole), 1387-1455
(Dec. 26, 1955)

8. *Nativity Scene,* an 18th century crèche which is one of the famous Neapolitan "presepios" that delighted King Charles III of Naples and his queen. Also, this was TIME's first gatefold cover.
(Dec. 28, 1959)

9. *Christ in Glory,* tapestry by Graham Sutherland, 1903-
(Dec. 25, 1964)

10. *The Three Magi,* sculptured terra cotta and wood figures, part of the 18th century Neapolitan crèche at the Metropolitan Museum of Art.
(Dec. 30, 1974)

There are ten paintings which are not related to Christmas and have appeared on the covers for a variety of reasons. Eight of these were used as cover subjects, and two were used in conjunction with a person. The order is chronological by the date of the cover on which they appeared.

TABLE 38.—Paintings

1. *George Washington,* by Gilbert Stuart, 1755-1828.
   On page seven of the July 6, 1953, issue of TIME James A. Linen wrote: "I am very excited about this week's TIME cover and cover story. It is a departure from TIME's normal practice of putting living men on the cover. But in this case, the 177th anniversary of the Declaration of Independence, we thought an exception was a good idea."

2. *St. Paul,* a tempera on wood painting attributed to Lippo Memmi, fl. 1317-1347, of the school of Simone Martini, of whom Lippo Memmi was a pupil as well as his brother-in-law.
   The cover story for the April 18, 1960, issue dealt with missionaries of all faiths in all parts of the world and included much information on St. Paul, the first missionary.

3. *Persian miniature,* by an unknown artist of the Safavid Dynasty, 1501-1734.
   This miniature was copied into the background of the painting of the Shah of Iran when he appeared on the cover of the September 12, 1960, issue.

4. *The Cry,* by Edvard Munch, 1863-1944.
   This painting illustrated the cover for a story in the "Medicine" section which had to do with the psychological aspects of guilt and anxiety, which was in the March 31, 1961, issue.

5. *Aristotle Contemplating the Bust of Homer,* by Rembrandt van Rijn, 1606-1669.
   In 1961 the Metropolitan Museum of Art paid $2,300,000 for this painting, which at that time was the highest known price ever paid for a painting anywhere. It was reproduced on the November 24, 1961, cover of TIME.

6. *James Monroe,* by Gilbert Stuart, 1755-1828.
   This is TIME's second cover depicting a painting by Gilbert Stuart, the famous early American portrait painter; it was used as the cover for a story on the Monroe Doctrine and Cuba which was in the issue of September 21, 1962.

7. *Siesta,* by John Koch, 1909-
   This painting of a bedroom scene was used to illustrate the cover story, Sex in the U.S.: mores and morals, in the "Modern Living" section and was about the sexual revolution and changing attitudes toward sex. It appeared on the TIME cover of January 24, 1964.

8. *Titus,* by Rembrandt van Rijn, 1606-1669
   TIME's second cover with a Rembrandt painting was used for the issue of June 4, 1965. It appeared with Norton Winfred Simon, head of Hunt Foods & Industries, Inc. (Hunt's Catsup), who had just purchased this painting of Rembrandt's son, Titus, in London for $2,234,400.

9. *Martin Luther,* by Lucas Cranach the Elder, 1472-1553.
   In the issue of March 24, 1967, the cover story treated Protestantism today and its history and development. As would be most befitting for such a topic, Luther appeared on the cover.

10. *The Signing of the Constitution,* by Howard Chandler Christy, 1873-1952.
    During the Watergate affair of the Nixon administration there was much talk about presidential power and the interpretation of the Constitution. This painting was used on the cover of the August 6, 1973, issue for the cover story dealing with the battle of presidential power. (For more information on this painting see the text preceding Table 26 in Chapter 11, Historical Figures and Biblical Personages.)

As far as this author was able to determine only six sculptures and statues were used on TIME's covers. These include the four mentioned in Table 39 and the Statue of Liberty and the Statue of Freedom which are listed in Table 40, National Symbols.

TABLE 39.—Statues and Sculptures

1. *Christ of the Andes,* by Mateo Alonso, 1878-
   After the November election of 1928 President-elect Herbert Hoover traveled to South America. During his visit to Chile he went to the Upsallata Pass high in the Andes between Chile and Argentina, where this heroic size statue is located. This statue, which is cast from bronze of old cannons left at the time of Argentinian independence, was unveiled on March 13, 1904, to commemorate international peace between Chile and Argentina. TIME used a photograph of this statue to illustrate the cover story on Hoover's trip to South America in the December 17, 1928, issue.

2. *John Harvard,* by Daniel Chester French, 1850-1931.
   The first time this statue appeared on TIME's cover of March 1, 1954, it was placed in the background of the portrayal of Harvard's president, Nathan Marsh Pusey. The second time it was used was on April 18, 1969, for the cover story on the student strike at Harvard and the disruptive situations at other American universities.

3. *Alexander Hamilton,* by James Earle Fraser, 1876-1953.
   This statue of the first Secretary of the Treasury, located at the Treasury Building in Washington was used as background for the cover which depicted the Secretary of the Treasury, Robert B. Anderson, on the issue of November 23, 1959.

4. *The Thinker,* by Auguste Rodin, 1840-1917.
   The cover story of April 7, 1961, was about arms, diplomacy and the military power of the United States. The cover portrayed the Secretary of Defense, Robert S. McNamara; this statue; a rocket; and other military weapons.

The perusal of the covers of TIME revealed that there are five national symbols which have appeared occasionally. These five are included here as they can easily be considered as works of art. They are the Liberty Bell, the Statue of Liberty, the White House, the Washington Monument, and the Capitol, which is considered as the most symbolic and representative building of our government. None of these symbols has ever been the cover subject, but rather always used with people who are the topics of the covers. Table 40 lists these five symbols, the artist or designer, the dates when they were used on the covers, and the names and positions of the individuals who were the objects of the cover stories. The order under each of the symbols is chronological by the date of the cover.

TABLE 40.—National Symbols

Symbol and Artist or Designer	Date of Cover	Person(s) on Cover
1. Liberty Bell, originally cast by Thomas Lister in London in 1752, and later recast twice in Philadelphia in 1753 by John Pass and Charles Stow, Jr.	July 4, 1955	President Dwight D. Eisenhower
2. Statue of Liberty, by Frederic Bartholdi, 1834-1904	Nov. 10, 1952	President-elect Dwight D. Eisenhower and Vice-President-elect Richard M. Nixon
	Sept. 28, 1959	Premier Nikita S. Khrushchev and Abraham Lincoln
	Jan. 18, 1960	Topical cover entitled: Getting to work: trials of U.S. commuters
3. White House, designed by James Hoban, 1762-1831	Aug. 12, 1946	George E. Allen, Director of the Reconstruction Finance Corporation
	Aug. 22, 1955	Carmine DeSapio, leader of the New York County Democratic Committee (known as Tammany Hall)
	Jan. 23, 1956	Budget Director Rowland R. Hughes
	Jan. 20, 1961	First Lady Jacqueline Kennedy
	May 18, 1970	Unidentified student protesting against the U.S. involvement in Vietnam
	May 28, 1973	Watergate affair defendants: John Dean, John Ehrlichman, Harry Haldeman, E. Howard Hunt, G. Gordon Liddy and James McCord
4. Washington Monument, designed by Robert Mills, 1781-1855	Mar. 14, 1949	Washington's hostess, Perle Mesta
	Oct. 13, 1952	Senator John Williams
	Mar. 17, 1958	Senator Lyndon B. Johnson
	Feb. 15, 1960	Newspaper columnist James B. Reston
	Dec. 6, 1963	Secretary of State Dean Rusk

TABLE 40.—Continued

Symbol and Artist or Designer	Date of Cover	Person(s) on Cover
	Nov. 21, 1969	Counterattack on dissent over the Vietnam war. News analysts: Walter Cronkite, David Brinkley, Chester Huntley and Frank Reynolds; President Richard Nixon; Vice-President Spiro T. Agnew; and Dean Burch, Chairman of the Federal Communications Commission
5. Capitol Building, original plan by William Thornton, 1759-1828; the dome, Senate and House wings desinged by Thomas Ustick Walter, 1804-1887; Statue of Freedom on the dome by Thomas Crawford, 1813-1857	Sept. 22, 1941	Japan's Ambassador to the United States, Kichisaburo Nomura
	Mar. 8, 1943	Senator Harry S Truman
	Nov. 18, 1946	Congressman Joseph Martin
	May 12, 1947	Senator Arthur Vandenberg
	Nov. 1, 1948	Presidential candidates Harry S Truman and Thomas E. Dewey
	Dec. 13, 1948	Newspaper columnist Drew Pearson
	Apr. 25, 1955	Senator Walter George
	Jan. 23, 1956	Budget Director Rowland R. Hughes
	May 27, 1957	Senator John McClellan
	Aug. 12, 1957	Senator Richard Russell
	Sept. 5, 1960	Senator Margaret Chase Smith and Senatorial candidate Lucia Marie Cormier
	Jan. 11, 1963	Congressman Wilbur D. Mills
	Oct. 26, 1970	President Richard M. Nixon, Vice-President Spiro T. Agnew, and thirteen Senatorial candidates
	Nov. 16, 1970	Senators William Brock, James Buckley, Adlai Stevenson and John Tunney
	Jan. 29, 1973	Richard M. Nixon's second presidential inauguration
	Jan. 5, 1976	Congresswoman Barbara Jordan

The classes of persons who have been portrayed with the national symbols are very few. Politicians, statesmen, and others with political positions account for the majority of all of those used with national symbols. Of the total number of 68 persons who have been shown with the national symbols, there are 60 (88.24 percent) who fall into the area of politics. The other eight are composed of four news analysts, two newspaper columnists, society hostess Perle Mesta, and an unidentified student. Senators and Congressmen are the most often portrayed politicians with these symbols. These are only shown with the Capitol and the Washington Monument. The Capitol and the Washington Monument have been portrayed 22 times; ten times with Senators and three times with Congressmen. It is interesting to note that no president has ever appeared with the White House.

The following table indicates how recent the national symbols have been used on the covers of TIME.

TABLE 41.—The Use of National Symbols during the Six Periods

	Capitol	Washington Monument	White House	Statue of Liberty	Liberty Bell	Total
Period 1 (1923-31)	0	0	0	0	0	0
Period 2 (1932-40)	0	0	0	0	0	0
Period 3 (1941-49)	6	1	1	0	0	8
Period 4 (1950-58)	4	2	2	1	1	10
Period 5 (1959-67)	2	2	1	2	0	7
Period 6 (1968-76)	4	1	2	0	0	7
Total	16	6	6	3	1	32

The *first* person, as well as the *only* foreigner, to be shown on a cover with the Capitol was the Japanese Ambassador, Kichisaburo Nomura. He was sent to Washington in 1940 and during the following year until December 7, he made a sincere effort to improve Japanese-American relations in order to avoid involving the United States in Japan's territorial expansion in Asia. The only other foreigner to ever appear with one of our national symbols was Nikita Khrushchev who was depicted with the Statue of Liberty, Abraham Lincoln and other symbols of American life and freedom. The following appeared in James A. Linen's "A letter from the publisher":

> The peasant face of Nikita Khrushchev . . . [looms] on this week's [Sept. 28, 1959] cover against a symbolic background of the

> U.S. . . . [containing] tall Iowa corn; a white-painted New England
> church; buildings under construction in U.S. cities; an Army
> Redstone missile; a gate at Brown University in Providence, R.I.; a
> new U.S. automobile; the presence of the guiding spirit of
> Abraham Lincoln.[30]

For some reason Linen did not mention the other very important
symbol in the cover painting, the Statue of Liberty. This is indubitably
one of the most symbolic of all of TIME's covers.

Works of art, as they were described at the beginning of this section,
have not been on many covers; and one-third of them were used as
Christmas covers. Those classed as national symbols have been the
most frequently used and probably will continue to be so. The other
works listed in Tables 38 and 39 have been portrayed because they
were "newsmakers" per se, such as Rembrandt's *Aristotle Contemplating the Bust of Homer,* or were used as background symbols for
other topics, such as Rodin's *The Thinker* or as symbols representing
the idea of the cover story, as the statue of John Harvard was used for
the student strike at Harvard; and Christy's *The Signing of the
Constitution,* was reproduced to represent the question of Constitu-
tional interpretation during the Watergate affair.

Note: 30. TIME, Sept. 28, 1959, p. 7.

CHAPTER 15
ANIMALS AND SYMBOLISM

Quite a variety of animals have appeared on at least 462 (16.4 percent) of TIME's covers. Many were used as part of the cover design; others were the cover subjects and often used with people; and some were just on the covers incidentally. The first cover with an animal was the July 12, 1926, issue depicting Benito Mussolini with a lion. A basset hound puppy was the subject of the first cover devoted exclusively to an animal; this was the issue of Feb. 27, 1928. Since 1926 many animals have appeared in numerous forms, viz., cover subjects; background material; minuscule design and decoration; symbols of political parties, such as the elephant and donkey; national emblems or symbols, such as the eagle, rooster and bear; and even as indicators of stock market activity when the bear and/or the bull appear.

Each different kind of animal was counted only once per cover even if it appeared more than once on the same cover, e.g., the May 10, 1937, issue had four horses on its cover, but it was counted as a "horse cover." The cover of the Aug. 24, 1953, issue contained two birds and a bee; it was considered as a "bird cover" and a "bee cover." All animals were taken into consideration, be they represented by photographs, drawings, characters from the comics, e.g., Mickey Mouse; or any other form.

Many persons in the news were depicted in the company of a live animal, such as Geraldine Farrar with a little dog (Dec. 5, 1927); Arthur Cutten with a bull (Dec. 10, 1928); and Clyde Beatty with a lion (Mar. 29, 1937). However, no person has ever been shown with a domestic cat. The house (or domestic) cat has been a very popular pet with man since about 3500 B.C., but still the cat has only appeared twice on TIME's covers (Dec. 27, 1954, and Mar. 19, 1956). Both of these times it only appeared as a small drawn figure almost hidden in the background. Could it be that people in the news or the designers of TIME's covers are ailurophobic? More than likely it's just fate or coincidence.

Table 42 lists the different kinds of animals in six categories. At the end of four of these six categories appears the word "others." In some cases this signifies that there were so many kinds of animals that only appeared once that it was considered unnecessary to mention them all; in other cases, there were some animals which were not identifiable, e.g., birds were used on many covers, but often they were only identifiable as birds; in other cases, there were "bugs" which were not identifiable as any specific kind of insect. The fact that there are 483 animals on 462 covers is because several covers contain more than one kind of animal.

TABLE 42.—Animals on TIME with the Number of Covers on Which Each Appeared

Domestic Animals		Wild Animals		Birds		Insects		Aquatic Animals		Mythological Animals	
Horses	37	Lions	38	Eagles	111	Ants	1	Fish	16	Dragons	8
Cattle	24	Elephants	36	Doves	6	Bees	1	Octopuses	3	Unicorns	4
Donkeys	23	Bears	16	Roosters	6	Butterflies	1	Crabs	2	Dogs	3
Dogs	19	Snakes	12	Ducks	4	Crickets	1	Snails	2	Phoenix	1
Pigs	8	Tigers	6	Cardinals	2	Others	4	Dolphin	1	Others	2
Camels	4	Deer	4	Chickens	2			Sea elephant	1		
Sheep	3	Kangaroos	4	Hawks	2			Seahorse	1		
Cats	2	Giraffes	2	Owls	2			Seal	1		
Goats	2	Gorillas	2	Others	34			Starfish	1		
Mule	1	Monkeys	2								
		Moose	2								
		Others	13								
Total	123		137		169		8		28		18

= 483

Table 43 lists those animals which appeared on eight or more covers. The eagle accounts for 23 percent of all animals on the covers, but this is easily accountable when one remembers that the eagle is the symbol for the United States. Lions rank very high because the lion is often used to symbolize Great Britain and also as a symbol of royalty of many countries. Elephants and donkeys stand for the two major American political parties. Horses and dogs appear very often because they seem to be among the most common domestic animals; also horse racing is the most popular spectator sport in the United States. TIME has published four covers on which the cover subject was a specific racehorse (see Chapter 16, Topical Covers).

TABLE 43.—Animals Depicted on Eight or More Covers

Animal	Number	Percent
Eagles	111	23.00
Lions	38	7.86
Horses	37	7.66
Elephants	36	7.45
Cattle	24	4.97
Donkeys	23	4.76
Dogs	19	3.93
Bears	16	3.32
Fish	15	3.10
Snakes	12	2.48
Dragons	8	1.66
Pigs	8	1.66
Others	136	28.15
Total	483	100.00

Animals were quite frequently used as symbols in the design of the covers. Basically there are two kinds of symbols; a symbol can be either an object that stands for another object, such as the use of the eagle to represent the United States or the kangaroo symbolizing Australia as depicted on the Apr. 24, 1944, cover. Perhaps the best example of a cover in which animals represent specific countries is that of July 25, 1955, which portrays Russia's Premier Nikolai Bulganin and in the background is a table with a samovar around which are seated a bear, an eagle, a cock and a lion representing the Soviet Union, the United States, France and Great Britain. Also, a symbol can be an object which stands for an idea, such as the snail which represents slowness and was used in this way on the covers dated Oct. 14, 1957 (The U.S. repairman), and Jan. 18, 1960 (Getting to work: the trials of U.S. commuters). Another such symbol is the phoenix representing resurrection, which appeared with Japan's Prime Minister, Nobusuke

Kishi (Jan. 25, 1960). Animals are not the only symbols that have been depicted on TIME's covers, but they are the most frequently used.

Some of the other symbols and objects that have been used on the covers are listed in Table 44. They are given in order of frequency with the dates of the first and last covers on which each appeared.

TABLE 44.—Other Symbols and Objects on TIME

Symbol	No. of Covers	Dates
Automobiles	93	May 2, 1938 - Mar. 15, 1976
Airplanes	76	Sept. 2, 1929 - July 5, 1976
Boats and ships	73	Sept. 15, 1930 - July 5, 1976
Flowers	65	Feb. 15, 1926 - Apr. 12, 1976
Food	41	Apr. 13, 1942 - Sept. 17, 1973
Musical instruments	36	Feb. 16, 1931 - Oct. 27, 1975
Rockets and missiles	22	Dec. 8, 1952 - Aug. 15, 1969
Trains	18	Sept. 23, 1935 - July 26, 1963
Helicopters	13	Sept. 6, 1943 - May 26, 1975
Motorcycles	5	Sept. 25, 1944 - June 28, 1976
Bicycles	3	Sept. 13, 1954 - Oct. 19, 1959

The list of objects in Table 44 shows that modes of transportation are the most commonly used, either as symbols or as part of the cover design. There are 445 covers with the above objects and 281 (63 percent) are modes of transportation. Food has been depicted frequently and the types of food cover a wide range, including an ice cream cone (Sept. 7, 1953), bananas (June 28, 1954), carrots (Apr. 13, 1942, and May 19, 1952), and eggs (Mar. 9, 1959). Some examples of the musical instruments are: organs (Jan. 2, 1939, and July 11, 1949, drums (Nov. 19, 1945, and Oct. 27, 1952), violins (Dec. 19, 1949, and Dec. 7 , 1962), guitar (July 7, 1967), and other covers with pianos, trumpets, tubas, and other musical instruments. Flowers appear in many varieties and forms, some of these are roses (Aug. 24, 1953, and June 16, 1958), sunflowers and lilies (Oct. 13, 1975), a memorial wreath (Aug. 31, 1962), a lei (May 19, 1961), and a wedding bouquet (Sept. 29, 1967).

Even though many different kinds of symbols have appeared on the covers, the most frequently employed are animals. One reason for this is that animals are very important to man and play significant roles in his existence for many reasons; therefore, they have always been quite symbolic in expressing ideas and subjects.

CHAPTER 16
TOPICAL COVERS

Topical covers were defined earlier as those which portray no identified or indentifiable person. During the 54-year period covered by this study there have been 201 covers which fall into this category. No attempt was made to classify all the 2,814 covers into categories according to the topic of the cover story. The following groups of covers are only those which did not depict any identifiable person. Table 3 pointed out that the 201 topical covers make up 7.14 percent of the 2,814 covers. In Period 6 there were 120 topical covers published; this is 60 percent of all the topical covers which appeared during the entire 54-year period. Since 1923 there has been an ever-increasing number of covers without identifiable persons. It will be interesting to see if this trend continues in the future.

The topical covers were divided into eight discrete groups, viz., American life and society; International and foreign issues; Science and technology; The economy and business; Religion and the occult; Entertainment and the arts; Geography, travel and flags; and Dogs and horses. Each of these groups contains subdivisions which further categorize the topical covers. The following pages list the topical covers with their titles (or a descriptive phrase) and the dates of the issues; each subdivision is arranged chronologically.

I. AMERICAN LIFE AND SOCIETY

1. People (19 covers)

The American people	Nov. 5, 1928
Common citizens	Nov. 7, 1932
U.S. taxpayer	Mar. 10, 1952
U.S. commuters	Jan. 18, 1960
Suburban wife	June 20, 1960
Harlem	July 31, 1964
Today's teenagers	Jan. 29, 1965
Young Americans, twenty-five and under	Jan. 6, 1967
The hippies	July 7, 1967
Black vs. Jew	Jan. 31, 1969
The middle Americans	Jan. 5, 1970
Generation Gap	Aug. 17, 1970
Blue collar power	Nov. 9, 1970
U.S. family	Dec. 28, 1970
Suburbia	Mar. 15, 1971
The graduate, 1971	May 24, 1971
The American woman	Mar. 20, 1972

Americans on the move   Mar. 15, 1976
America's birthday issue   July 5, 1976

2. Social Conditions, Problems and Attitudes (15 covers)

Sex in the U.S.: mores & morals Jan. 24, 1964
Poverty in America   May 17, 1968
Sex explosion   July 11, 1969
The homosexual in America   Oct. 31, 1969
American Indian   Feb. 9, 1970
Postal breakdown   Mar. 30, 1970
The urban guerrillas   Nov. 2, 1970
U.S. prisons   Jan. 18, 1971
The welfare maze   Feb. 8, 1971
The bitter lessons of Attica [prison riots]Sept. 27, 1971
Sex and the teenager   Aug. 21, 1972
Alcoholism   Apr. 22, 1974
The porno plague   Apr. 5, 1976
The West Point scandal   June 7, 1976
Gambling goes legit   Dec. 6, 1976

3. Race Problems (6 covers)

Paratroopers at Little Rock   Oct. 7, 1957
The Los Angeles riot   Aug. 20, 1965
Twelfth Street, Detroit   Aug. 4, 1967
Retreat from integration   Mar. 9, 1970
Battle over busing   Nov. 15, 1971
Busing battle   Sept. 22, 1975

4. Political Campaigns and Conventions (5 covers)

Convention time, USA   July 14, 1952
A national disgrace: the $400,000,000
 election   Oct. 23, 1972
Inside Convention City   July 19, 1976
The plight of the G.O.P.   Aug. 23, 1976
Campaign kickoff   Sept. 13, 1976

5. Responsibility of Public Officials (4 covers)

Nixon's jury: the people   Nov. 12, 1973
The telltale tape   Jan. 28, 1974
The press: fair or foul   July 8, 1974
Leadership in America   July 15, 1974

6. Crime (5 covers)

The gun in America   June 21, 1968
Law and order   Oct. 4, 1968

The Mafia v. America	Aug. 22, 1969
Gang war	Apr. 24, 1972
Crime	June 30, 1975

7. Drugs (3 covers)

Drugs and the young	Sept. 26, 1969
Heroin hits the young	Mar. 16, 1970
Global was on heroin	Sept. 4, 1972

8. Military (4 covers)

G. I. Joe	Jan. 1, 1951
The Pentagon	July 2, 1951
The military under attack	Apr. 11, 1969
Pentagon papers	June 28, 1971

II. INTERNATIONAL AND FOREIGN ISSUES

1. Vietnam War (17 covers)

The turning point in Viet Nam	Oct. 22, 1965
Inside the Viet Cong	Aug. 25, 1967
Under fire at Con Thien	Oct. 6, 1967
Peace marchers	Oct. 27, 1967
Starting to go home	June 20, 1969
Moratorium: at war with war	Oct. 17, 1969
The new war	May 11, 1970
Protest!	May 18, 1970
The cooling of America	Feb. 22, 1971
Viet Nam: the big test	Apr. 17, 1972
Nixon strikes back	May 22, 1972
Shape of peace	Nov. 6, 1972
After the bombs, what peace?	Jan. 8, 1973
Indochina, how much longer?	Mar. 24, 1975
The last retreat	Mar. 31, 1975
Collapse in Viet Nam	Apr. 14, 1975
Hanoi's triumph	May 5, 1975

2. Middle East Problem (7 covers)

Middle East in turmoil	June 22, 1970
Pirates in the sky	Sept. 21, 1970
The Arab guerrillas	Sept. 28, 1970
Murder in Munich	Sept. 18, 1972
War in the Middle East	Oct. 15, 1973
Mid-East massacres	May 27, 1974
Mid-East in agony	Apr. 12, 1976

3. Foreign Political and National Problems   (7 covers)

French strikers	June 22, 1936
Hungarian freedom fighter	Jan. 7, 1957
The Berlin wall	Aug. 31, 1962
Invasion of Czechoslovakia	Aug. 30, 1968
Pakistan's agony	Aug. 2, 1971
The new spy	Oct. 11, 1971
Masked IRA fighter	Jan. 10, 1972

4. War Weapons (5 covers)

H-bomb over the Pacific	Apr. 12, 1954
The missile	Jan. 30, 1956
U.S. atomic arsenal	Aug. 23, 1963
The great missile debate	Mar. 14, 1969
The world arms trade	Mar. 3, 1975

III. SCIENCE AND TECHNOLOGY

1. Aerospace (9 covers)

Space pioneer	Dec. 8, 1952
Space exploration	Jan. 19, 1959
Rush hour in space	June 6, 1960
Gemini rendezvous	Dec. 24, 1965
Race for the moon	Dec. 6, 1968
To the moon	July 18, 1969
After the SST	Apr. 5, 1971
Looking for life out there	Dec. 13, 1971
Space spectacular	July 21, 1975

2. Medicine and Health (7 covers)

Guilt & anxiety	Mar. 31, 1961
The pill	Apr. 7, 1967
What's wrong with U.S. medicine	Feb. 21, 1969
The new genetics	Apr. 19, 1971
Eating may not be good for you	Dec. 18, 1972
Inside the brain	Jan. 14, 1974
Disease detectives	Aug. 16, 1976

3. Energy Crisis, Pollution and Population (7 covers)

The population explosion	Jan. 11, 1960
Water: worldwide use & misuse	Oct. 1, 1965
The biggest blackout	Nov. 19, 1965
The polluted air	Jan. 27, 1967
Nixon's energy cuts	Dec. 3, 1973
The big car	Dec. 31, 1973
Rebates and smaller cars	Feb. 10, 1975

4. Miscellaneous (13 covers)

Mark III [computers]	Jan. 23, 1950
Amateur photographer	Nov. 2, 1953
Do-it-yourself	Aug. 2, 1954
Roadbuilders	June 24, 1957
The U.S. repairman	Oct. 14, 1957
The telephone man	Feb. 23, 1959
New products	Sept. 19, 1960
Computer in society	Apr. 2, 1965
Communications explosion	May 14, 1965
Inefficiency in America	Mar. 23, 1970
Forecast: earthquake	Sept. 1, 1975
The bugs are coming	July 12, 1976
Stars: where life begins	Dec. 27, 1976

IV. THE ECONOMY AND BUSINESS

1. Inflation and Recession (7 covers)

Is the U.S. going broke?	Mar. 13, 1972
Food prices	Apr. 9, 1973
World inflation	Apr. 8, 1974
Economy: the big headache	Sept. 9, 1974
The big raise: labor & inflation	Nov. 25, 1974
Recession's greetings	Dec. 9, 1974
Voting your pocketbook	Nov. 1, 1976

2. Wall Street (6 covers)

Young Wall Street bull	June 14, 1948
Wall Street bull	June 5, 1950
The bull market	Jan. 10, 1955
Wall Street bull	Mar. 24, 1958
Wall Street bull	Dec. 29, 1958
Bear v. bull on Wall Street	June 1, 1962

3. Private Companies (2 covers)

Coca-Cola	May 15, 1950
McDonald's	Sept. 17, 1973

V. RELIGION AND THE OCCULT

1. General (7 covers)

The Dead Sea scrolls	Apr. 15, 1957
Is God dead?	Apr. 8, 1966
Is God coming back to life?	Dec. 26, 1969
The do-gooders	Dec. 27, 1971
The occult revival	June 19, 1972
The psychics	Mar. 4, 1974
U.S. Catholicism	May 24, 1976

2. Christmas (4 covers)

The night before Christmas	Dec. 27, 1948
Christmas shopping	Dec. 15, 1961
The child's world—Christmas 1973	Dec. 24, 1973
U.S. shopping surge	Dec. 1, 1975

VI. ENTERTAINMENT AND THE ARTS

1. Entertainment, Leisure and the Arts (9 covers)

Circus animals	Apr. 18, 1932
3-D [movies]	June 8, 1953
Music in the air	Dec. 23, 1957
Camping	July 14, 1961
International cinema	Sept. 20, 1963
TV commercials	July 12, 1968
Japan shows off at Expo '70	Mar. 2, 1970
Sesame Street: TV's gift to children	Nov. 23, 1970
Super shark: "Jaws" on film	June 23, 1975

2. Sports (5 covers)

Football public	Nov. 17, 1930
Football	Nov. 13, 1933
Football's public	Nov. 11, 1935
The New York Mets	Sept. 5, 1969
Sex & tennis	Sept. 6, 1976

3. Cartoons and Comic Strip Characters (3 covers)

Willie, by Bill Mauldin	June 18, 1945
Peanuts, by Bill Schulz	Apr. 9, 1965
Doonesbury, by Garry B. Trudeau	Feb. 9, 1976

VII. GEOGRAPHY, TRAVEL AND FLAGS

1. Foreign places (10 covers)

(10 covers) Paris	Sept. 4, 1944
Jerusalem	Aug. 26, 1946
India	Oct. 27, 1947
Hong Kong	Nov. 21, 1960
The faraway places	May 19, 1961
Great Britain	Jan. 25, 1963
London	Apr. 15, 1966
Biafra	Jan. 26, 1970
Bangladesh	Dec. 20, 1971
Europe	Mar. 12, 1973

2. United States (4 covers)

California	Nov. 7, 1969
Alaska	July 27, 1970

Travel '76, rediscovering America   June 28, 1976
The South today   Sept. 27, 1976

3. Flags (4 covers)

American flag   July 6, 1942
The big three [flags of the U.S., Great
   Britain and U.S.S.R.]   May 14, 1945
Japanese flag   Aug. 20, 1945
Fight over the [U.S.] flag: patriots and
   put-ons   July 6, 1970

VIII. DOGS AND HORSES

1. Dogs (3 covers)

Baby basset hound   Feb. 27, 1928
Pointer Mary Blue   Mar. 3, 1930
The American pet   Dec. 23, 1974

2. Horses (4 covers)

Billy Barton   Mar. 18, 1929
Cavalcade   Aug. 20, 1934
Native Dancer   May 31, 1954
Secretariat   June 11, 1973

Table 45 lists the different topics and subtopics into which the 201 topical covers were classified. At the right of each subject and its subdivisions is the number of covers which were classified in that group. The total number of covers that fall into each of the eight categories is accompanied by the percentage of the 201 covers which it represents. Table 46 points out the subjects of the topical covers according to the six periods into which this study was divided.

TABLE 45.—Classification of Topical Covers

Subjects	Number	Percent
1. American Life and Society	61	30.35
People	19	
Social conditions, problems and attitudes	15	
Race problems	6	
Political campaigns and conventions...............	5	
Responsibility of public officials.	4	
Crime......................	5	
Drugs......................	3	
Military	4	

TABLE 45.—Continued

Subjects	Number	Percent
2. International and Foreign Issues	36	17.91
Vietnam war.................. 17		
Middle East problem 7		
Foreign political and national		
problems 7		
War weapons 5		
3. Science and Technology	36	17.91
Aerospace 9		
Medicine and health 7		
Energy crisis, pollution and		
population 7		
Miscellaneous 13		
4. The Economy and Business	15	7.46
Inflation and recession 7		
Wall Street 6		
Private companies 2		
5. Religion and the Occult	11	5.47
General 7		
Christmas 4		
6. Entertainment and the Arts	17	8.46
Entertainment, leisure, and		
the arts 9		
Sports 5		
Cartoons and comic strip		
characters 3		
7. Geography, Travel and Flags	18	8.96
Foreign places 10		
United States 4		
Flags 4		
8. Dogs and Horses	7	3.48
Dogs 3		
Horses...................... 4		
Total	201	100.00

TABLE 46.—Distribution of Topical Covers for the Six Periods

	Period 1 (1923-31)	Period 2 (1932-40)	Period 3 (1941-49)	Period 4 (1950-58)	Period 5 (1959-67)	Period 6 (1968-76)	Total
American Life and Society	1	1	0	5	9	45	61
International and Foreign Issues	0	1	0	3	6	26	36
Science and Technology	0	0	0	6	13	17	36
The Economy and Business	0	0	1	5	1	8	15
Religion and the Occult	0	0	1	1	2	7	11
Entertainment and the Arts	2	2	1	2	3	7	17
Geography, Travel and Flags	0	0	6	0	4	8	18
Dogs and Horses	2	2	0	1	0	2	7
Total	5	6	9	23	38	120	201

Over 30 percent of all topical covers fall into the group dealing with American life and society. The largest subgroups are those dealing with the American people (nineteen covers) and the war in Vietnam (seventeen covers). The was in Vietnam is the only event in the entire history of TIME that had so many cover stories that were illustrated by covers that contained no identifiable individuals. The other three major news events of the fifty-four year period were the Second World War, the Korean conflict and the Watergate affair. These three were more often illustrated by covers depicting identifiable persons than was the war in Vietnam. There were forty-four covers which dealt with this war and seventeen of them depicted no identifiable individuals.

Science and technology has been one of the areas most often illustrated by topical covers.

Table 46 emphasizes the heavy concentration of topical covers during Period 6. There were 120 topical covers published during this period which account for 60 percent of all topical covers for the 54 years covered by this study, and 45 (37.5 percent) of these had to do with "American life and society." In the area of "Science and technology" 30 (83 percent) topical covers were issued during Periods 5 and 6; the other 6 covers came out in Period 4 and account for the other 17 percent.

The only subject areas in which the number of topical covers has anything approximating consistency throughout the six periods are "Entertainment and the Arts" and "Dogs and Horses." Topical covers of all the other subject areas are heavily concentrated in Periods 5 and 6.

In the area of "The economy and business" there are two covers representing private companies, viz., Coca-Cola (May 15, 1950) and McDonald's (Sept. 17, 1973). These are the only covers that portray no person and are devoted exclusively to a private enterprise. There have been other covers with logotypes, trademarks, products, or other symbols representing private companies as a conspicuous part of the cover design, excluding, of course, a mere mention of a corporate name in connection with that of a person appearing on the cover. The most outstanding of these are listed below with the dates of the covers on which they appeared.

TABLE 47.—Private Enterprises on the Covers

Names	Dates
A & P (Great Atlantic & Pacific Tea Company)	Nov. 13, 1950
American Express Company	Apr. 9, 1956
Borden Company (Elsie the Cow)	Oct. 12, 1962

TABLE 47—Continued

Names	Dates
Budweiser	July 11, 1955
Campbell's Soups	Oct. 12, 1962
Chicago Tribune	May 20, 1974
Chrysler	Dec. 28, 1962
Esso	Dec. 29, 1967
Exxon	Feb. 18, 1974
Ford Motor Company	Dec. 29, 1967
G D (General Dynamics Corporation)	Jan. 20, 1958
GE (General Electric)	Nov. 2, 1953
GM (General Motors)	Dec. 29, 1967
General Motors (emblems of Buick, Cadillac, Chevrolet, Oldsmobile and Pontiac)	Jan. 24, 1949
Holiday Inn	June 12, 1972
IBM (International Business Machines)	Dec. 29, 1967
IT&T (International Telephone and Telegraph)	Sept. 8, 1967
Kansas City Times	May 20, 1974
Kodak (Eastman Kodak Company)	Nov. 2, 1953 Dec. 29, 1967
New York Times	May 8, 1950 June 28, 1971 Aug. 30, 1971 May 20, 1974
Omaha World Herald	May 20, 1974
Pan American World Airways	Jan. 19, 1970
Plain Dealer	May 20, 1974
Polaroid	June 26, 1972
RCA (Radio Corporation of America)	July 23, 1951
Sony	May 10, 1971
TIME	Jan. 15, 1973
United Airlines	Apr. 21, 1947
Washington Post	May 20, 1974

Even though topical covers have appeared with much more frequency in the past ten years than ever before, the individual still predominates in TIME's selection of the "newsmaker of the week."

CHAPTER 17
TWENTIETH CENTURY NOTABLES

Who are the most eminent personalities of the twentieth century? The answer to this question will be as varied as the number of persons who attempt to answer it. To find some of these varied answers one may simply consult the subject catalog of a library under the heading: BIOGRAPHY—20TH CENTURY.

Many collective biographies have been compiled in which the authors have attempted to select the most outstanding personalities. One may ask: Outstanding or important in terms of what? Again, the authors' answers will vary because each will define the terms "outstanding" or "important" in his own way and with his own parameters. After consulting many of these collective biographies containing persons whom each author termed "most important" or some other similar phrase, it was discovered that the authors often do not mention the method of selection or the criteria used for choosing those whom they consider to be the most prominent. Another very conspicuous lacuna in most of these collections of biographical sketches is that the authors fail to give their definitions of "outstanding," "great," or "important."

TIME claims that the individual (or individuals) on each cover is the "newsmaker of the week." This study has analyzed those "newsmakers of the week," and with defined terms and parameters this author discovered a group of "twentieth century notables." (See Chapter 8, The Most Frequently Portrayed Individuals.)

Is there any correlation between TIME's cover figures and those included in books which attempt to list the "greats" of the twentieth century? James A. Linen was curious about this and in his "A letter from the publisher" (Aug. 4, 1952, p. 7) he mentioned the following comparison that he had made:

> In a new book called *The 100 Most Important People in the World Today*, Author Donald Robinson has selected 100 people who, he feels, "have had the greatest impact upon our civilization in the last 15 years," and those who "may have the greatest impact in the next 10 years." I was interested in seeing how many of his choices had appeared on TIME's covers (in the past 29 years). There were 60.

After he made the above comparison, seven more of Robinson's "100 most important people"[31] did appear on the covers of TIME in the ensuing years. so as it resulted there were 67 of the 100 individuals who finally made TIME's covers.

Robinson defines his "important people" as:

> ... the men and women who have been making our history and who are likely to make more of it for us; the people *now alive*, of all

nationalities and occupations, who have had the greatest impact upon our civilization in the last 15 years (from 1937 through 1951) and/or may have the greatest impact in the next ten years, a 25-year span that may well be the most significant in many centuries.[32]

His selection was done by polling others on their opinions, and then making a selection from the results of these polls.

In 1970 Robinson published a second work entitled, *The 100 Most Important People in the World Today*.[33] For this publication he used the same method of polling to obtain the opinions of others in order to choose those persons that he described as:

. . . the 100 living men and women, of all nationalities and occupations, who have had the greatest influence on our civilization for good or for evil, during the past five years, or who may have the greatest impact during the next five years. These are the men and women who have done the most (or may do the most) to make our political world, our economy, our climate of public opinion from 1965 to 1975. They've produced the most significant scientific, medical, and educational advances, the principal religious and philosophical dicta, the outstanding literature, and the contributions to the fine arts that will identify this age.[34]

Louis Untermeyer published a collection of biographies of persons that he termed "makers of the modern world."[35] He stated in his foreword: "The selection of the ninety-two personalities was determined partly by what seemed to me the imperatives, partly by preference."[36] This is not convincing as a scientific method of selection because it is totally subjective.

In 1977 the *New York Times* published a collection of biographies from its back issues which was entitled, "Great lives of the century."[37] The only comment on its selection was given in the blurb on the front book jacket flap which stated:

From the pages of *The New York Times* comes this gallery of portraits of personalities who have left their stamp on contemporary history. Printed as they originally appeared in *The Times* (in column from with accompanying headlines), the articles present with authentic *Times* style and authority vivid word portraits of over 100 [i.e. 104] famous figures from the worlds of science, entertainment, the arts, sports, politics, and government.

Not a single clue is offered as to the method of selection; one can only assume that it was completely subjective.

Dale Carnegie published a collection of "highlights in the lives of forty [i.e., 41] famous people" in 1944.[38] This publication contains no introduction, foreword or other prefatory matter that might suggest how he arrived at the forty-one persons included therein.

The five works just mentioned all seem to consist of biographies completely chosen by subjectiveness. Not one used any method that would even approximate a scientific one. The weekly selection made by TIME for its cover may also be subjective, but it is a selection made each and every week that is based on the events and circumstances of the preceding seven days. Also, TIME's choices have been made by many individuals over the past fifty-four years. The purpose of the cover subject is to point out the "newsmaker of the week," albeit a person or a topic.

How did the five aforementioned collections of biographies compare to TIME's cover subjects? The following table shows the percentage of the biographees that appeared on the covers at least once. The base number of biographees in each work is the number of persons who were living at one time or another during the publishing history of TIME. All persons who died before March 3, 1923, have been eliminated from the count.

TABLE 48.—Comparison of Biographical Works with TIME's Covers

Work	No. of Biographees	No. Who Were on TIME's Covers	Percent
Robinson, 1937-1951	100	67	67
Robinson, 1965-1975	100	49	49
Untermeyer	61	35	53
New York Times	100	76	76
Carnegie	39	32	82
Total	400	259	65

The publication with the highest percentage is that of the *New York Times* and the lowest is Donald Robinson's book which covered the period from 1965 to 1975. There are 264 of the 400 biographees who appear in only one of the above five works; 41 persons are included in two works; 14 are in three publications; three individuals are listed in four; and no one is included in all five publications. Those who were included in four of the above works are: Winston Churchill, Charles de Gaulle and Joseph Stalin. The fourteen persons who appeared in the three works are listed below; the number at the right of the name indicates the number of times that person was on a TIME cover.

Einstein, Albert	3
Eisenhower, Dwight D.	21
Faulkner, William	2
Hemingway, Ernest	2
MacArthur, Douglas	8
Malraux, André	2
Mao, Tse-tung	12
Picasso, Pablo	2
Russell, Bertrand	0

Sartre, Jean-Paul	0
Schweitzer, Albert	1
Shaw, George Bernard	2
Stravinsky, Igor	1
Wright, Orville	1

Among the seventeen persons who were included in either three or four of the above works there is not a single female. Only seven of the seventeen are Americans, and two of these are foreign born: Albert Einstein and Igor Stravinsky. There are 85 individuals who appeared four or more times on the covers of TIME, yet only six of these are among the seventeen persons who were included in at least three of the five works under discussion. The author invites the reader to compare these seventeen prominent persons with those listed in Table 16-A and 16-B in Chapter 8.

Attempting again to answer the question, "Who are the most eminent personalities of the twentieth century?," one might examine the selection made by the United States Postal Service of those individuals chosen to be honored on postage stamps. To be portrayed on a United States postage stamp is indeed a great honor. The requirements for being thusly honored are quite rigorous and the competition is very keen; hundred of suggestions for the subjects of new stamps are received each by the U.S. Postal Service. The current "Standards for Stamp Selection" for determining those individuals to be portrayed or honored on U.S. postage stamps are:

1. Living Persons

No living person shall be honored by portrayal on any United States postage stamp. A person may be portrayed on a postage stamp ten years after his or her death.

2. Significant Anniversaries

All postage stamps, including commemoratives, honoring individuals will be issued preferably on significant anniversaries of their births. The exceptions are memorial stamps and regular issues honoring recently deceased presidents. A former president may be honored with a stamp on his first birthdate following his death.[39]

Most of the persons who have been on U.S. postage stamps are historical figures from the past and had no opportunity to appear on a TIME cover. However, there are 82 individuals who have appeared on U.S. postage stamps who were living at one time or another during TIME's publishing history and died after March 3, 1923. Fifty-eight (71 percent) of these 82 individuals have been portrayed or honored on U.S. stamps. This is indeed a very high percentage. Of the 85 individuals who were portrayed on TIME's covers four or more times there are 36 who qualify to be portrayed or honored according to the standards given above. Twenty-two of those 36 individuals have been on U.S. postage stamps; this is 61 percent. An analysis of the 14 individuals who were never on a stamp shows that eight are foreigners and among them are Adolf Hitler, Benito Mussolini, Joseph Stalin, Leon Trotsky and Paul von Hindenburg; these probably have very remote chances of ever being on U.S. postage stamps. If the percentage were calculated after removing just these five individuals it would be 71 percent, exactly the same as that which resulted from figuring the percentage of those who have been on stamps and were alive when TIME began publishing.

Any selection of "important people" or "notables" should be based on some scientific method or at least one that approximates such a method. (For the description of a completely objective method of selecting eminent persons in a specific field of endeavor please see the author's publication, *Milestones in cataloging.*[40]) The 2,814 covers have provided a basis for a more objective approach to the selection of the "greats" of the past fifty-four years. Surely other methods which may even be more objective in their selection of eminent persons can be devised.

The foregoing discussion and comparisons of TIME's cover subjects with persons selected for collective biographies and for portrayal on U.S. postage stamps have pointed out that TIME does indeed do very well in its selection of the "newsmaker of the week."

Notes: 31. Robinson, Donald B. *The 100 most important people in the world today.* New York: Pocket Books, Inc., 1952, 427 p.
32. Ibid., pp. xi-xii.
33. Robinson, Donald B. *The 100 most important people in the world today.* New York: G.P. Putnam's Sons, 1970. 384 p.
34. Ibid., p.20.
35. Untermeyer, Louis, *Makers of the modern world: the lives of ninety-two writers, artists, scientists, statesmen, inventors, philosophers, composers, and other creators who formed the pattern of our century.* New York: Simon and Schuster, 1955. 809 p.
36. Ibid., p. vii.
37. *Great lives of the century,* as reported by The New York Times. Edited by Arleen Keylin. New York: Arno Press, 1977, 305 p.
38. Carnegie, Dale. *Biographical roundup: highlights in the lives of forty famous people.* New York: Greenburg, Publisher, 1944. 233 p.
39. United States Postal Service. *Stamp selection: who and why.* Washington: Government Printing Office, 1977, p. 9
40. Lehnus, Donald J. *Milestones in cataloging: famous catalogers and their writings, 1835-1969.* Littleton, Colorado: Libraries Unlimited, 1974. 137 p.

CHAPTER 18
SUMMARY AND CONCLUSIONS

This analysis of the 2,344 individuals who have been portrayed 3,336 times on 2,814 TIME covers has revealed some very interesting information on the newsmakers of the past 54 years.

There has been a very noticeable evolution in the style and contents of the covers. During the first 36 years of publication the covers usually just depicted one identifiable person and only a very small percentage could be considered as topical covers. In the last 18 years the covers have portrayed more persons and fewer covers depict anyone at all. Even though more and more covers have been portraying no identifiable individual, there are still more persons appearing on those covers which do depict identifiable personalities. If this trend were to continue at the present pace soon very few covers would have identifiable people on them. A future study could point out if this trend will lose momentum, be reversed or stay the same. TIME does assure us that even though many covers symbolize an event, a trend or an idea tht the individual will always reappear on the covers.

Americans make up over two-thirds of all individuals on the covers. However, this should be expected as TIME is an American newsmagazine written for the American public. The other one-third of the cover personalities represents 75 different countries from all parts of the globe. The most poorly-represented areas are Africa and Latin America. This is understandable as these areas, which are often called "third world," do not play very significant roles in world affairs. Europe is highly represented on the covers, which is indubitably due to Europe's important role in the past as well as the present, and also to our own cultural heritage. Great Britain is the most represented country after the United States, which again is probably because of our language and cultural heritage. The five countries (the United States, the Soviet Union, Great Britain, France and China) which are the only permanent members of the Security Council of the United Nations are among the six most represented countries on the covers. Individuals from these five countries account for 82.45 percent of all persons who have appeared on TIME.

Politicians appear more often than any other professional group. Almost one-half of all persons are in politics or related to someone in political affairs. TIME's cover figures are representative of all of man's major endeavors or professions. Even biblical personages are used occasionally on the covers. Jesus Christ appeared for the first time on the cover of December 17, 1928, and thirteen times thereafter; the Virgin Mary is the most often portrayed female.

It is quite surprising how consistent the number of times each of the thirty major professional groups was represented in each of the six periods into which the fifty-four years of the study were divided. The consistency is such that it gives the impression that it was planned that way, but more than likely it is just that people in the news do come from all fields of endeavor and TIME makes careful and judicious selections for its cover subjects.

Women have appeared on TIME since its twenty-second issue, but still only one out of every ten persons who "makes" a cover is a female. There is no doubt that the traditional role and position of the female have prevented their frequent portrayal on the covers. But, this is changing; the percentage of females has increased in the past twenty years, and it will be interesting to see if the percentage of females will increase even more in the next decade or two. American women form a higher percentage of all women on the covers than do all Americans in general when compared to the total number of foreigners. African and Latin American women are the least represented of all women from other geographic areas.

Individuals of all ages appear on TIME. The youngest ever to be portrayed was the infant son of Charles A. Lindbergh who was shown on a cover just before he would have had his second birthday. The oldest was the famous football coach, Amos Alonzo Stagg, who had already celebrated his ninety-sixth birthday when he was portrayed for the first and only time.

The average age for all persons is 51 years; for men it is 53 and for women just 38. The average age depends greatly on the profession; sports persons and entertainers (actors, singers, dancers, etc.) have a much lower average than those who are in such fields as psychology, religion or the creative arts (painting, architecture, writing, etc.). Politicians, on the other hand, fall very close to the overall average; they have an average age of 54. Or, perhaps it is that the overall average falls close to the average age of the politicians since they make up almost one-half of all persons on the covers.

Richard M. Nixon, the most frequently portrayed individual, appeared more than twice the number of times than either the second or third most frequently portrayed individuals, Lyndon B. Johnson and Gerald R. Ford. Also, Nixon appeared on 36 covers during his presidency; no other person ever appeared that many times. However, when one takes into account the number of covers issued under each president and the number of times each president appeared during his presidency, one finds that Gerald Ford was on a higher percentage of covers during his presidency than was Richard Nixon. During the years that Nixon served as Vice-President under President Eisenhower he "made" the covers 10 times; Eisenhower appeared on 10 covers during his presidency. No vice-president was ever portrayed as often as was Nixon during his vice-presidency; and Nixon is the only vice-president that appeared on as many covers as did the president under which he served. Patricia Nixon was on TIME more than any other

First Lady. There is no reason to doubt that Nixon will prove to be the biggest newsmaker of this era.

Forty-eight (56.5 percent) of the 85 most frequently portrayed individuals are Americans. This is a little lower than the overall percentage for Americans which is 68.8 percent. There were 32 from this group of 85 who received a score of 100 or more when the number of covers on which each appeared was multiplied by the number of years thoughout which each was portrayed on the covers of TIME. These individuals who are listed in Column C of Table 16-A and in Tabled 16-B can be considered to be among the most important newsmakers since TIME's inception in 1923.

There have been 65 different individuals selected as the Person of the Year. Yet, only 20 (31 percent) of these are among those who were portrayed four or more times. This leads one to believe that the Person of the Year may have been the "biggest newsmaker" of a given year, but still he may have been of only temporary importance, or performed a feat that may be of historical significance but no longer newsworthy. The individuals who are repeatedly in the news are much more likely to be remembered in history, than those who are in the news for a short period, regardless of how important they may have been at one time.

Even though all American presidents, except Herbert Hoover, were depicted on the covers during their presidencies, it is quite surprising how much more frequently the recent presidents are portrayed than were those who were presidents prior to Dwight D. Eisenhower. Since Calvin Coolidge, each president, without exception, has been on a higher percentage of the covers issued under his presidency than the preceding ones. Will Jimmy Carter appear on a higher percentage of covers than did Gerald Ford? Only TIME will tell.

TIME's policy of selecting the "newsmaker of the week" for its cover subject places some restriction on the use of non-living persons on the covers, but still those from the past do appear from time to time. Quite often they appear as background for other cover subjects, but occasionally they are the principal objects of the covers. No American president who dies during his term in office is ever portrayed on a cover at the time of his death. Since 1923 three presidents have died in office, viz., Harding, Roosevelt and Kennedy. When Roosevelt and Kennedy died the very next cover portrayed the new president; after Harding's death Coolidge did not appear on a cover until almost five years later.

Almost 70 percent of all persons on the covers have been Americans, and 97 percent of these Americans are white, yet only 82 percent of the American population is white. The two largest minority groups in the United States are blacks and Spanish-surnamed. Blacks have made 57 appearances on the covers. Spanish-surnamed Americans form a group that is almost one-half as large as that of American blacks, yet there have been only four Spanish-surnamed Americans on TIME. There must be a reason for this lack of Spanish-surnamed American newsmakers; TIME has proven that race or national origin is no barrier to "make" its covers. Perhaps future studies of TIME's covers will show that the number of newsmakers from the minority groups has increased.

Queens, kings, princesses, princes and other members of the world's royal families are frequently in the news and their portrayals on TIME have been consistent since the first year of publication. The longest reigning monarch, Emperor Hirohito, has appeared seven times; more than any other member of royalty. Second to him is Queen Elizabeth II with six cover portrayals (and also she is the second most frequently portrayed female); even though she has not reigned as long as some others, she has been on TIME over a longer span of years than any other person who has appeared four or more times. Her grandfather, George V, appeared five times in a period of just eleven years. No other monarch was on TIME so often in such a short period of time.

The covers of TIME are not just mere portrayals of the newsmaker of the week, but most of them are works of art per se which were created for the covers of TIME. But, occasionally there have been works of art on the covers which were not originally created or commissioned by TIME for its covers. Twenty-nine such works have appeared on TIME, some of these were cover subjects, and others were background for persons. More than one-half of these twenty-nine works of art were paintings; other art forms used include statues and sculptures, a tapestry, a stained glass window, figures from a Nativity scene, and architectural works which can be considered as national symbols. The most frequently used was the U.S. Capitol which was depicted on no less than sixteen covers.

All works of art used for Christmas covers were the subjects of those covers. Only ten of the other works were the principal cover subjects. The remaining depictions of art works were all used as background material for individuals.

Animals have appeared on one out of every six covers. They have been used as cover subjects, background material, symbols representing ideas, national symbols, and also as cover decoration and design. An excellent example of the symbolic use of animals was the cover which portrayed Dr. Alfred C. Kinsey (Aug. 24, 1953), the famous researcher of human sexual behavior; in the background were "the birds and the bees."

Inanimate objects have also been used quite frequently on the covers either as symbols, part of the design, or just incidentally. These include many modes of transportation, such as airplanes, ships, automobiles and motorcycles; food; flowers; musical instruments; and rockets and missiles. A study of the symbols used for the background of the covers would prove to be quite fascinating. Unfortunately, probably too few of TIME's readers either notice, appreciate or understand the great amount of symbolism that is used in the background of many of TIME's covers. Symbolism in the cover design is especially prevalent in the covers published since 1940.

Comparisons of the personalities from TIME's covers with those qho were included in some collections of biographical sketches of so-called "important people of the twentieth century," and also with those who have been honored on U.S. postage stamps pointed out that TIME's selections for its covers are done with a very careful and sagacious analysis of current events. There can be little doubt that those who are the most frequently portrayed on TIME's covers are the very people who will be included in the history books of the future.

During the years 1923 to 1976 there seem to have been four major events which dominated the news and determined the subjects for many of TIME's covers, viz., World War II, the Korean conflict, the war in Vietnam and the Watergate affair.

If one were to establish the dates of the Second World War from January 2, 1939, until August 20, 1945, then it could be stated that TIME published 347 issued during World War II. Of those 347 covers there were at least 156 (45 percent) that were related to persons or events involved in the War.

The involvement of the United States in the Korean conflict began on June 27, 1950, when President Truman ordered General Douglas MacArthur to aid South Korea, and it ended on July 23, 1953, when an armistice was signed. During this period there were 161 issues of TIME and 23 (14.3 percent) were directly related to this "conflict."

For the United States the was in Vietnam began on August 2, 1964, and lasted until the troop evacuation on March 29, 1973. During this eight and one-half years there were 452 issues of TIME and there were no less than 44 covers (9.93 percent) which dealt with persons and events directly related to this war; this includes the covers showing the protests in the United States against American intervention and involvement in Southeast Asia.

The other event which influenced TIME's covers was the Watergate affair that began with the arrest of five men on June 17, 1972, for having broken into the offices of the Democratic National Committee in the Watergate office complex in Washington, D.C. TIME's first cover on this "affair" portrayed Senator Sam Ervin as the "Watergate prober"; the date was April 16, 1973. From this date until Nixon's resignation on August 9, 1974, a period of 17 months, 69 issues of TIME were published. Of these 69 issues, 26 (38 percent) were related to persons and events connected to the Watergate affair and its many ramifications. No fewer than 15 (21.73 percent) of these covers portrayed Nixon's likeness.

Thus, it can be seen that there were two of these four events which thoroughly dominated the news while they were taking place: World War II and the Watergate affair. Even though World War II is of great historic importance, there is no single person who can be termed the "most important" of the War. This is not true for the Watergate affair, in which case Richard M. Nixon can be called the "most important" personality of this "political affair."

World War II affected both the national and international news, but no matter of national concern ever influenced the news as much as did that of the Watergate affair and our first president ever to resign his office. This is, of course, based on the news as reflected by TIME's covers. And, as was pointed out earlier Nixon has proved to be the "big newsmaker" of the past fifty-four years.

This study of the 2,814 covers published between March 3, 1923, and January 3, 1977, has shown that the covers of TIME are symbols of the times which represent domestic and international affairs; American life and society; science and technology; the fine arts; trends in the history of civilization; and all other aspects of man's role in the world in which he lives. If the future can be judged from the past, then TIME's readers can rest assured that the covers will continue to represent the world's great men and women, both the notable and the notorious, as well as all the important events, feats and exploits on earth and in the universe. The covers of the last fifty-four years have done so, and those of the future will undoubtedly keep on doing so until the end of TIME.

APPENDIX I

PERSONS WHO HAVE APPEARED ON THE COVERS OF TIME

The following is an alphabetical list of all identified persons who appeared on the covers of TIME from March 3, 1923 to January 3, 1977. Each name is followed by the years of birth and death and the dates of each issue on which the person appeared. In some cases it was impossible to ascertain the exact birth and death years because of conflicts in different reference sources or the paucity of biographical data. However, all possible was done to try to supply the correct years of birth and death.

A

ABBAS, Ferhat (1899-)
  Oct. 13, 1958
ABBOTT, Charles (1963-)
  Feb. 19, 1973
ABBOTT, Daniel (1961-)
  Feb. 19, 1973
ABBOTT, Dorothy (1959-)
  Feb. 19, 1973
ABBOTT, Elizabeth (1963-)
  Feb. 19, 1973
ABBOTT, Joan (Mrs. Joseph) (1939-)
  Feb. 19, 1973
ABBOTT, Joan (1957-)
  Feb. 19, 1973
ABBOTT, Joseph (1935-)
  Feb. 19, 1973
ABBOTT, Joseph (1960-)
  Feb. 19, 1973
ABBOTT, Matthew (1967-)
  Feb. 19, 1973
ABD-EL-KRIM (1885-1963)
  Aug. 17, 1925
ABDUL AZIZ IBN SAUD,
  King of Saudi Arabia (1880-1953)
  Mar. 5, 1945
ABDULLAH IBN HUSSEIN,
  King of Jordan (1882-1951)
  May 24, 1948
ABRAMS, Creighton W. (1914-1974)
  Oct. 14, 1961; Apr. 19, 1968; Feb. 15, 1971
ACHESON, Dean G. (1893-1971)
  Feb. 28, 1949; Jan. 8, 1951
ADAMS, Charles Francis (1866-1954)
  Nov. 4, 1944
ADAMS, Edward Dean (1846-1931)
  May 27, 1929
ADAMS, Sherman (1899-)
  Jan. 9, 1956; June 30, 1958
ADAMS, Theodore F. (1898-)
  Dec. 5, 1955
ADAMS, William H. (1861-1954)
  June 10, 1929
ADENAUER, Konrad (1876-1967)
  Dec. 5, 1949; Aug. 31, 1953; Jan. 4, 1954
ADLER, Mortimer (1902-)
  Mar. 17, 1952

AGNELLI, Giovanni (1922-)
  Jan. 17, 1969
AGNEW, Spiro (1918-)
  Aug. 16, 1968; Sept. 20, 1968; Nov. 14, 1969;
  Nov. 21, 1969; Oct. 26, 1970; Aug. 28, 1972;
  Aug. 20, 1973; Aug. 27, 1973; Oct. 1, 1973;
  Oct. 8, 1973
AGUSTSSON, Linda (1948-)
  Dec. 28, 1972
AIKEN, George (1892-)
  Jan. 15, 1973
AISHA LALLA, Princess of Morocco
  (1930-)
  Nov. 11, 1957
ALBERT I, King of Belgium (1875-1934)
  Aug. 6, 1928
ALBERT, Carl Bert (1909-)
  Jan. 15, 1965; Feb. 1, 1971; Jan. 15, 1973;
  Oct. 8, 1973; Jan. 27, 1975
ALDRICH, Winthrop William (1885-1974)
  Aug. 31, 1931
ALEMÁN, Miguel (1905-)
  Apr. 28, 1947
ALEXANDER, King of Yugoslavia
  (1888-1934)
  Feb. 11, 1929
ALEXANDER, Harold (1891-1969)
  Sept. 14, 1942; June 5, 1944
ALEXANDER, Henry C. (1902-1969)
  Nov. 2, 1959
ALFONSO XIII, King of Spain (1886-1941)
  Dec. 22, 1924; July 23, 1928; Apr. 6, 1931
ALI, Muhammad (1942-)
  Mar. 22, 1963; Mar. 8, 1971
ALINGTON, Cyril (1872-1955)
  June 29, 1931
ALLEN, Fred (1894-1956)
  Apr. 7, 1947
ALLEN, George E. (1896-1955)
  Aug. 12, 1946
ALLEN, Terry (1888-1969)
  Aug. 9, 1943
ALLEN, William M. (1900-)
  July 19, 1954
ALLEN, Woody, (1935-)
  July 3, 1972

ALLENDE, Salvador (1908-1973)
Oct. 19, 1970; Sept. 24, 1973
ALLRED, James V. (1889-1959)
June 8, 1936
ALMOND, Edward Mallory (1892-1979)
Oct. 23, 1950
ALMOND, James Lindsay (1898-)
Sept. 22, 1958
ALPHAND, Nicole (1917-1979)
Nov. 22, 1963
AMARAL, Afranio Do (1894-)
Jan. 28, 1929
AMERY, Leopold (1873-1955)
Jan. 3, 1927
ANDERS, William A. (1933-)
Jan. 3, 1969
ANDERSON, George (1906-)
Nov. 2, 1962
ANDERSON, Ian (1948-)
Feb. 12, 1973
ANDERSON, John (1927-)
Jan. 15, 1973; May 20, 1974
ANDERSON, Judith (1898-)
Dec. 21, 1942
ANDERSON, Kenneth A. N. (1891-1951)
May 3, 1943
ANDERSON, Marian (1902-)
Dec. 30, 1946
ANDERSON, Maxwell (1888-1959)
Dec. 10, 1934
ANDERSON, Michael (1939-)
July 2, 1965
ANDERSON, Robert Bernard (1910-)
Nov. 23, 1959
ANDERSON, Wendell Richard (1933-)
Aug. 13, 1973
ANDREWS, Elmer Frank (1890-1964)
Nov. 21, 1938
ANDREWS, Frank Maxwell (1884-1943)
Sept. 1, 1941
ANDREWS, Jack Northman (1923-)
Apr. 3, 1972
ANDREWS, Julie (1935-)
July 23, 1956; Dec. 23, 1966
ANDREWS, Lincoln Clark (1867-1950)
Aug. 3, 1925
ANDREWS, Roy Chapman (1884-1960)
Oct. 29, 1923
ANDRUS, Cecil D. (1931-)
Dec. 20, 1976
ANGELL, James Rowland (1869-1949)
June 15, 1936
ANNE-MARIE, Princess of Denmark
(1945-)
July 3, 1964
ARAFAT, Yasser (1930-)
Dec. 13, 1968; Nov. 11, 1974
ARAKI, Sadao (1877-1966)
Jan. 23, 1933
ARAMBURU, Pedro Eugenio (1903-1970)
June 3, 1957
ARANHA, Oswaldo (1894-1960)
Jan. 19, 1942
ARBENZ, Jacobo (1913-)
June 28, 1954
ARCARO, Eddie (1916-)
May 17, 1948

ARDEN, Elizabeth (1891-1966)
May 6, 1946
ARENDS, Leslie (1895-1974)
Jan. 15, 1973
AREVALO, Juan José (1904-)
June 28, 1954
ARISTOTLE (384-322 B.C.)
Nov. 24, 1961
ARKIN, Alan (1934-)
June 15, 1970
ARLEN, Michael (1895-1956)
May 2, 1927
ARLISS, George (1868-1946)
Mar. 26, 1934
ARMSTRONG, Louis (1900-1971)
Feb. 21, 1949
ARMSTRONG, Neil (1930-)
July 25, 1969
ARNESS, James (1923-)
Mar. 30, 1959
ARNOLD, Henry Harley (1886-1950)
June 22, 1942
ARONS, Arnold (1916-)
May 6, 1966
ARRUPE, Pedro (1907-)
Apr. 23, 1973
ARTHUR, Bea (1926-)
Sept. 25, 1972
ASQUITH, Herbert H. (1852-1928)
Oct. 8, 1923
ASSAD, Hafez (1928-)
Apr. 1, 1974
ASTOR, Nancy Langhorne (1879-1964)
Oct. 15, 1928
ASTOR, Vincent (1891-)
Feb. 6, 1928; Apr. 9, 1934
ATATURK, Kemal (1881-1938)
Mar. 24, 1923; Feb. 21, 1926
ATHLONE, Alexander (1874-1957)
Sept. 2, 1940
ATHLONE, Alice (1883-)
Sept. 2, 1940
ATHOS, ANTHONY (1934-)
May 6, 1966
ATTERBURY, William Wallace (1886-1935)
Feb. 20, 1933
ATTLEE, Clement R. (1883-1967)
Aug. 6, 1945; Feb. 6, 1950; Sept. 20, 1954
AUCHINLECK, Claude (1884-)
Dec. 1, 1941
AURIOL, Jules Vincent (1884-1966)
Apr. 2, 1951
AUSTIN, Warren (1877-)
Feb. 5, 1951
AYDELOTTE, Frank (1880-1956)
June 5, 1933
AYUB KHAN (1908-1974)
Sept. 17, 1965
AZAÑO, Manuel (1880-1940)
Aug. 24, 1936

B

BACALL, Lauren (1924-)
July 29, 1966
BACH, Johann Sebastian (1685-1750)
Dec. 27, 1968

BACH, Richard (1936-)
Nov. 13, 1972
BACON, Edmund Norwood (1910-)
Nov. 6, 1964
BADOGLIO, Pietro (1871-1956)
June 24, 1940
BAEKELAND, Leo H. (1863-1944)
Sept. 22, 1924
BAEZ, Joan (1941-)
Nov. 23, 1962
BAGWELL, Paul Douglas (1913-1973)
Oct. 24, 1960
BAILEY, Charles P. (1910-)
Mar. 25, 1957
BAILEY, F. Lee (1933-)
Feb. 16, 1976
BAKER, George Fisher (1840-1931) ·
Apr. 14, 1924
BAKER, Howard (1925-)
Jan. 15, 1973
BAKER, Newton Diehl (1871-1937)
Nov. 14, 1927; May 23, 1932
BAKER, Robert "Bobby" Eugene (1928-)
Mar. 6, 1964
BALANCHINE, George (1904-)
Jan. 25, 1954
BALBO, Italo (1896-1940)
June 26, 1933
BALDWIN, James (1924-)
May 17, 1963
BALDWIN, Stanley (1867-1947)
Aug. 10, 1925; Dec. 26, 1927; Apr. 1, 1929;
Sept. 7, 1931; June 17, 1935
BALEWA, Abubakar (1912-1966)
Dec. 5, 1960
BALFOUR, Arthur (1848-1930)
Apr. 13,1925
BALIEFF, Nikita (1877-1936)
Oct. 17, 1927
BALL, Joseph H. (1905-)
Mar. 3, 1947
BALL, Lucille (1911-)
May 26, 1952
BALLARD, Florence (1944-1976)
May 21, 1965
BALTHASAR, wise man of the Three Magi
Dec. 26, 1938; Dec. 23, 1940; Dec. 25, 1950;
Dec. 28, 1959; Dec. 30, 1974
BANCROFT, Anne (1931-)
Dec. 21, 1959
BAND (The), music group
Jan. 12, 1970
BANKHEAD, Tallulah (1903-1968)
Nov. 22, 1948
BANKHEAD, William Brockman (1874-1940)
Nov. 29, 1937
BANTING, Frederick Grant (1891-1941)
Aug. 27, 1923
BAO DAI, Emperor of Vietnam (1913-)
May 29, 1950
BARKLEY, ALBEN (1877-1956)
Aug. 23, 1937; July 28, 1952
BARNARD, Christiaan (1922-)
Dec. 15, 1967
BARNES, Julius Howland (1873-1959)
May 5, 1930

BARRATT, Arthur Sheridan (1891-1966)
May 27, 1940
BARRY, Philip (1896-1949)
Jan. 25, 1932
BARRYMORE, ETHEL (1879-1959)
Nov. 10, 1924
BARRYMORE, John (1882-1942)
Mar. 7, 1932
BARRYMORE, Lionel (1878-1954)
Mar. 7, 1932
BARTH, Karl (1886-1968)
Apr. 20, 1962
BARTHOU, Louis (1862-1934)
Sept. 24, 1934
BARUCH, Bernard Mannes (1870-1965)
Feb. 25, 1924; Mar. 12, 1928; June 28, 1943
BARYSHNIKOV, Mikhail (1948-)
May 19, 1975
BARZUN, Jacques (1907-)
June 11, 1956
BATES, John Grenville (1881-1944)
Feb. 21, 1938
BATISTA, Fulgencio (1901-1973)
Apr. 26, 1937; Apr. 21, 1952
BATTEN, Harry Albert (1897-)
Oct. 12, 1962
BAUDOUIN I, King of Belgium (1930-)
July 30, 1951
BAUDOUIN, Paul (1895-1964)
June 17, 1940
BAUER, Henry "Hank" Albert (1922-)
Sept. 11, 1964
BEACH BOYS, music group
May 21, 1965
BEADLE, George W. (1903-)
July 14, 1958; Jan. 2, 1961
BEAME, Abraham David (1906-)
Oct. 20, 1975
BEATLES (The), music group
Sept. 22, 1967
BEATTY, Clyde (1903-1965)
Mar. 29, 1937
BEATTY, Warren (1938-)
Nov. 3, 1967
BEAVERBROOK, William M. A. (1879-1964)
Nov. 28, 1938; Sept. 16, 1940
BECK, David (1894-)
Nov. 29, 1946; Apr. 8, 1957
BECK, James Montgomery (1861-1936)
May 5, 1923
BECK, Josef (1894-1944)
Mar. 6, 1939
BEDFORD, Gunning (1747-1812)
Aug. 6, 1973
BEECHAM, Thomas (1879-1961)
Apr. 5, 1943
BELAFONTE, Harry (1927-)
Mar. 2, 1959
BALAUNDE-TERRY, Fernando (1913-)
Mar. 12, 1965
BELLANCA, Giuseppe Mario (1886-1960)
July 4, 1927
BELMONTE, Juan (1892-1962)
Jan. 5, 1925
BENCH, Johnny (1947-)
July 10, 1972

BENES, Eduard (1884-1948)
Mar. 23, 1925; June 27, 1938; Oct. 22, 1945
BEN-GURION, David (1886-1973)
Aug. 16, 1948; Jan. 16, 1956; Mar. 11, 1957
BENKHEDDA, Benyoussef (1920-)
Mar. 16, 1962
BENNETT, Richard Bedford (1870-1947)
July 28, 1930
BENNETT, William A. C. (1900-1979)
Sept. 30, 1966
BENSON, Ezra T. (1899-)
Apr. 13, 1953; May 5, 1956
BENTON, Thomas Hart (1859-1975)
Dec. 24, 1934
BENTSEN, Lloyd (1921-)
Oct. 26, 1970
BERENGER, Victor Henry (1867-1952)
Feb. 1, 1926
BERENSON, Marisa (1947-)
Dec. 15, 1975
BERGEN, Edgar (1903-1978)
Nov. 20, 1944
BERGGRAV, Eivind Josef (1884-1959)
Dec. 26, 1944
BERGLAND, Bob (1928-)
Dec. 20, 1976
BERGMAN, Ingmar (1918-)
Mar. 14, 1960
BERGMAN, Ingrid (1917-)
Aug. 2, 1943; Jan. 8, 1945
BERIA, Laventry (1899-1954)
Mar. 22, 1948; July 20, 1953
BERLE, Milton (1908-)
May 16, 1949
BERLIN, Irving (1888-)
May 28, 1934
BERLINGUER, Enrico (1922-)
June 14, 1976
BERNHARD, Prince of the Netherlands
(1911-)
May 3, 1976
BERNSTEIN, Leonard (1918-)
Feb. 4, 1957
BERRIGAN, Daniel (1922-)
Jan. 25, 1971
BERRIGAN, Philip (1924-)
Jan. 25, 1971
BESSBOROUGH, see PONSONBY
BETANCOURT, Rómulo (1908-)
Feb. 8, 1960
BETZ, Pauline (1919-)
Sept. 2, 1946
BEVAN, Aneurin (1897-1960)
Mar. 21, 1949
BEVIN, Ernest (1884-1951)
Feb. 18, 1946
BHAVE, Vinoba (1895-)
May 11, 1953
BHUMIBOL ADULYADEJ, King of Thailand
(1927-)
Apr. 3, 1950; May 27, 1966
BING, Rudolf (1902-)
Jan. 15, 1951; Sept. 23, 1966
BLACK, Eugene R. (1898-)
June 25, 1956
BLACK, Hugo Lafayette (1886-1971)
Aug. 26, 1935; Oct. 9, 1964

BLACK, Shirley Temple (1928-)
Apr. 27, 1936; Jan. 8, 1945
BLACKMUN, Harry A. (1909-)
July 22, 1974
BLAIR, John (1732-1800)
Aug. 6, 1973
BLAKE, Eugene Carson (1906-)
May 26, 1961
BLANCHARD, Felix "Doc" (1924-)
Nov. 12, 1945
BLOCK, Joseph L. (1902-)
May 31, 1963
BLOOM, Claire (1931-)
Nov. 17, 1952
BLOUGH, Roger Miles (1904-)
June 20, 1959
BLOUNT, William (1749-1800)
Aug. 6, 1973
BLUE, Vida (1949-)
Aug. 23, 1971
BLUHDORN, Charles (1926-)
Dec. 3, 1965; Mar. 7, 1969
BLUM, Leon (1872-1950)
Mar. 9, 1936
BLUMENTHAL, W. Michael (1926-)
Dec. 20, 1976
BLYTHE, Samuel George (1868-1947)
Aug. 13, 1923
BO, MAI VAN (1917-)
May 10, 1968
BOAS, Franz (1858-1942)
May 11, 1936
BOCHENSKI, Judy (1955-)
Apr. 26, 1971
BOCK, Fedor von (1880-1945)
Dec. 8, 1941; Sept. 21, 1942
BOGART, Humphrey (1899-1957)
June 7, 1954
BOGGAN, Tim (1920-)
Apr. 26, 1971
BOHNENBLUST, H. Frederick (1906-)
May 6, 1966
BOK, Curtis (1897-)
July 17, 1933
BOND, Ward (1904-)
Mar. 30, 1959
BONO, Cher (1947-)
Mar. 17, 1975
BOONE, Richard (1918-)
Mar. 30, 1959
BOOTH, Shirley (1909-)
Aug. 10, 1953
BORAH, William Edgar (1865-1940)
May 5, 1924; Jan. 26, 1931; Mar. 30, 1936
BORBON y BATTENBERG, Juan (1913-)
June 22, 1962
BOREN, David L. (1941-)
Nov. 18, 1974
BORI, Lucrezia (1887-1960)
June 30, 1930
BORIS III, King of Bulgaria (1894-1943)
Jan. 20, 1941
BORMAN, Frank (1928-)
Mar. 14, 1969
BOSE, Subhas C. (1897-1945)
Mar. 7, 1938

BOWHILL, Frederick (1880-)
Oct. 20, 1941
BOWLES, Chester Bliss (1901-)
Mar. 4, 1946
BOWMAN, Isaiah (1878-1950)
Mar. 23, 1936
BOWRON, Fletcher (1888-)
July 4, 1949
BOYD, William (1895-1972)
Nov. 27, 1950
BOYLE, William M. (1902-)
Oct. 8, 1951
BRADEN, Spruille (1894-1978)
Nov. 5, 1945
BRADLEY, Edward Riley (1859-)
May 7, 1934
BRADLEY, Omar Nelson (1893-)
May 1, 1944; Dec. 4, 1944; April 1, 1946;
July 24, 1950
BRADSHAW, Terry (1948-)
Oct. 1, 1972
BRAGG, William Lawrence (1890-1971)
Oct. 3, 1938
BRAITHWAITE, George (1935-)
Apr. 26, 1971
BRANDEIS, Louis D. (1856-1941)
Oct. 19, 1925; July 7, 1930; Nov. 15, 1937
BRANDO, Marlon (1924-)
Oct. 11, 1954; Jan. 22, 1973
BRANDT, Willy (1913-)
May 25, 1959; Oct. 10, 1969; Jan. 4, 1971
BRANNAN, Charles Franklin (1904-)
June 19, 1950
BRATIANO, Jon (1864-1927)
July 11, 1927
BRAUCHITSCH, Heinrich (1881-1948)
Sept. 25, 1939
BREASLEY, David (1745-1790)
Aug. 6, 1973
BREASTED, James Henry (1865-1935)
Dec. 14, 1931
BRENNAN, George E. (1865-1928)
Aug. 9, 1926
BRENNAN, William J. (1906-)
July 22, 1974
BRENT, Charles Henry (1862-1929)
Aug. 29, 1927
BRERETON, Lewis Hyde (1890-1967)
May 4, 1942
BREWSTER, Kingman (1919-)
June 23, 1967
BREZHNEV, Leonid I. (1906-)
Feb. 21, 1964; Oct. 23, 1964; June 13, 1969;
Aug. 15, 1969; May 4, 1970; Mar. 29, 1971;
May 29, 1972; June 5, 1972; Jan. 29, 1973;
June 25, 1973; Apr. 1, 1974; July 1, 1974;
Aug. 4, 1975
BRIAND, Aristide (1862-1932)
Nov. 9, 1925; Dec. 19, 1927; Sept. 28, 1931
BRIARD, Barbara (1910-)
June 2, 1975
BRIARD, William (1905-)
June 2, 1975
BRICKER, John W. (1893-)
Apr. 26, 1943
BRIDGEMAN, Bill (1917-)
Apr. 27, 1953

BRIDGES, Harry (1900-)
July 19, 1937
BRIDGES, Robert (1844-1930)
Dec. 2, 1929
BRINKLEY, David (1920-)
Nov. 21, 1969
BRISBANE, Arthur (1864-1936)
Aug. 16, 1926
BRITTEN, Benjamin (1914-)
Feb. 16, 1948
BROCK, William (1931-)
Oct. 26, 1970; Nov. 16, 1970
BROOKE, Alan F. (1883-1963)
Aug. 5, 1940
BROOKE, Edward (1919-)
Nov. 18, 1966; Feb. 17, 1967
BROOKS, Van Wyck (1886-1963)
Oct. 2, 1944
BROOM, Jacob (1752-1810)
Aug. 6, 1973
BROWDER, Earl (1891-1973)
May 30, 1938
BROWER, Charles Hendrickson (1902-)
Oct. 12, 1962
BROWN, Clide (1942-)
May 26, 1967
BROWN, Edmund G. "Pat" (1905-)
Sept. 15, 1958; Nov. 24, 1958
BROWN, Edmund G. "Jerry" (1928-)
Oct. 21, 1974; Nov. 18, 1974
BROWN, Harold (1927-)
Dec. 20, 1976
BROWN, James "Jimmy" N. (1936-)
Nov. 26, 1965
BROWN, Lewis H. (1894-)
Apr. 3, 1939
BROWN, Walter Folger (1869-1961)
June 13, 1932
BROWNELL, Herbert (1904-)
Feb. 16, 1953; May 13, 1957
BROWNING, James R. (1918-)
Jan. 27, 1961
BROWNMILLER, Susan (1936-)
Jan. 5, 1976
BRUBECK, Dave (1920-)
Nov. 8, 1954
BRUNING, Heinrich (1885-1970)
June 15, 1931
BUCHAN, John (1875-1940)
Oct. 21, 1935
BUCHER, Lloyd M. (1928-)
Feb. 2, 1968
BUCHMAN, Frank N. D. (1878-1961)
Apr. 20, 1936
BUCKLEY, James (1923-)
Oct. 26, 1970; Nov. 16, 1970
BUCKLEY, William F. (1925-)
Nov. 3, 1967
BUCKNER, Simon Bolivar (1886-1945)
Apr. 16, 1945
BUDDHA (563-483 B.C.)
Aug. 30, 1954; Dec. 11, 1964
BUDENNY, Semion (1883-1973)
Oct. 13, 1941
BUDGE, Donald (1915-)
Sept. 2, 1935

BULGANIN, Nikolai (1895-1975)
July 25, 1955; Aug. 1, 1955
BULKLEY, Robert Johns (1880-1965)
Nov. 24, 1930
BUMPERS, Dale (1925-)
Nov. 18, 1974
BUNDY, McGeorge (1919-)
June 25, 1965
BUNTING, Mary I. (1910-)
Nov. 3, 1961
BURCH, Dean (1927-)
Nov. 21, 1969
BURGER, Warren (1907-)
May 30, 1969; July 22, 1974
BURKE, Arleigh Albert (1902-)
May 21, 1956
BURNETT, Leo (1898-)
Oct. 12, 1962
BURNS, Arthur F. (1904-)
June 1, 1970; Aug. 16, 1971
BURR, Raymond (1917-)
Oct. 26, 1959
BURTON, Richard (1925-)
Apr. 26, 1963
BURTON, Theodore Elijah (1851-1929)
June 29, 1925
BUSCH, August Anheuser (1899-)
July 11, 1955
BUSH, George (1924-)
Oct. 26, 1970; Nov. 17, 1975
BUSH, Vannevar (1890-1974)
Apr. 3, 1944
BUTLER, Nicholas Murray (1862-1947)
June 27, 1927; Feb. 15, 1932
BUTLER, Pierce (1744-1822)
Aug. 6, 1973
BUTLER, Richard A. (1903-)
Apr. 5, 1954
BUTLER, Smedley Darlington (1881-1940)
June 20, 1927
BUTLER, William Morgan (1861-)
Oct. 10, 1927
BYERLY, Kathleen (1944-)
Jan. 5, 1976
BYNG, Julian H.G. (1862-1935)
July 16, 1928
BYRD, Harry Flood (1887-1966)
Oct. 15, 1928; May 13, 1935; Aug. 17, 1962
BYRD, Richard Evelyn (1888-1957)
Aug. 20, 1928
BYRNES, James Francis (1879-1972)
Jan. 11, 1943; Sept. 17, 1945; Jan. 6, 1947
BYRNS, Joseph W. (1869-1936)
Apr. 22, 1935

C

CAETANI, GELASIO (1877-1934)
Apr. 28, 1924
CAFE FILHO, Joao (1899-)
Dec. 6, 1954
CAGLE, Christian Keener (1905-)
Sept. 23, 1929
CAHILL, Holger (1887-1960)
Sept. 5, 1938
CAILLAUX, Joseph (1863-1944)
Sept. 7, 1925

CALDWELL, Sarah (1924-)
Nov. 10, 1975
CALIFANO, Joseph A. (1931-)
Dec. 20, 1976
CALLAS, Maria (1923-1977)
Oct. 29, 1956
CALLES, Plutarco (1877-1945)
Dec. 8, 1924
CALLEY, William Laws (1943-)
Dec. 5, 1969; Apr. 12, 1971
CAMACHO, Manuel Avila (1897-1955)
Dec. 9, 1940; Apr. 19, 1943
CAMPANELLA, Roy (1921-)
Aug. 8, 1955
CAMPBELL, Tom Donald (1882-)
Jan. 9, 1928
CANBY, Henry Seidel (1878-1961)
May 19, 1924
CANIFF, Milton (1907-)
Jan. 13, 1947
CANNON, Clarence Andrew (1879- 1964)
Feb. 2, 1959
CANNON, Joseph Gurney (1836-1926)
Mar. 3, 1923; Jan. 15, 1973
CAPABLANCA, José R. (1888-1942)
Dec. 7, 1925
CAPLIN, Mortimer M. (1917-)
Feb. 1, 1963
CAPONE, Alphonse (1899-1947)
Mar. 24, 1930
CAPP, Al (1909-1979)
Nov. 6, 1950
CAPPER, Arthur (1865-1951)
Jan. 18, 1926
CAPRA, Frank (1897-1939)
Aug. 8, 1938
CÁRDENAS, Lázaro (1895-1970)
Dec. 3, 1934; Aug. 29, 1938
CARDOZO, Benjamin N. (1870-1939)
Nov. 26, 1934
CAREY, Hugh (1919-)
Nov. 18, 1974
CAREY, Philip (1925-)
Oct. 26, 1959
CARL XVI GUSTAF, King of Sweden
(1946-)
May 3, 1976
CARLSBERG, Arthur (1933-)
Dec. 3, 1965
CARLSEN, Anton Julius (1875-1956)
Feb. 10, 1941
CARLSON, Paul Earle (1928-1964)
Dec. 4, 1964
CARNE, Judy (1939-)
Oct. 11, 1968
CARNERA, Primo (1906-1967)
Oct. 5, 1931
CAROL II, King of Rumania (1893-1953)
Nov. 13, 1939
CARREL, Alexis (1873-1944)
Sept. 16, 1935; June 13, 1938
CARSON, Johnny (1925-)
May 19, 1967
CARTER, Amy (1967-)
July 26, 1976
CARTER, Jimmy (1924-)
May 31, 1971; Mar. 8, 1976; May 10, 1976;

June 21, 1976; July 26, 1976; Oct. 4, 1976;
Nov. 8, 1976; Nov. 15, 1976; Dec. 20, 1976;
Jan. 3, 1977
CARTER, Rosalynn (1927-)
July 26, 1976
CARY, Joyce (1888-1957)
Oct. 20, 1952
CASE, Clifford (1904-)
Dec. 27, 1954
CASPARY, Anita (1916-)
Feb. 23, 1970
CASTANEDA, Carlos (1931-)
Mar. 5, 1973
CASTILLO, Ramon S. (1873-1944)
May 5, 1941
CASTRO, Fidel (1926-)
Jan. 26, 1959; Oct. 3, 1960; July 21, 1961;
Oct. 8, 1965; June 13, 1969
CATHER, Willa S. (1873-1947)
Aug. 3, 1931
CATT, Carrie Chapman (1859-1947)
June 14, 1926
CAVETT, Dick (1936-)
June 7, 1971
CEAUSESCU, Nicolae (1918-)
Mar. 18, 1966; June 13, 1969; Aug. 15, 1969
CERF, Bennett (1898-1971)
Dec. 16, 1966
CHABOT, LORNE (1900-)
Feb. 11, 1935
CHAFFEE, Roger (1936-1967)
Feb. 3, 1967
CHAGALL, Marc (1887-)
July 30, 1965
CHALKLEY, Otway Hebron (1886-)
July 4, 1938
CHAMBERLAIN, Austen (1863-1937)
Nov. 30, 1925
CHAMBERLAIN, Charles Ernest (1917-)
Oct. 27, 1958
CHAMBERLAIN, Neville (1869-1940)
Apr. 25, 1932; June 19, 1933; Oct. 17, 1938
CHANDLER, Albert B. (1998-)
Aug. 1, 1938
CHANDLER, Dorothy Buffun (1901-)
Dec. 18, 1964
CHANDLER, Norman (1900-1973)
July 15, 1957
CHANDOR, Valentine (1878-)
Oct. 8, 1934
CHANNING, Carol (1923-)
Jan. 9, 1950
CHAPLIN, Charlie (1889-1977)
July 6, 1925; Feb. 9, 1931
CHAPPUIS, Robert Richard (1923-)
Nov. 3, 1947
CHARLES, Prince of Wales (1948-)
June 27, 1969
CHAVEZ, Cesar (1927-)
July 4, 1969
CHEEK, Alison (1928-)
Jan. 5, 1976
CHEEVER, John (1913-)
Mar. 27, 1964
CHEN, Li-fu (1899-)
May 26, 1947

CHEN, Yi (1901-1972)
Feb. 26, 1965
CHENG, Chen (1900-1965)
June 16, 1941
CHENNAULT, Claire (1890-1958)
Dec. 6, 1943
CHESSMAN, Caryl (1922-1964)
Mar. 21, 1960
CHESTER, Colby Mitchell (1877-1965)
Dec. 13, 1937
CHIANG, Kai-shek (1886-1975)
Apr. 4, 1927; Oct. 26, 1931; Dec. 11, 1933;
Feb. 24, 1936; Nov. 9, 1936; Jan. 3, 1938;
June 1, 1942; Sept. 3, 1945; Dec. 6, 1948;
Apr. 18, 1955
CHIANG, Mei-ling (1897-)
Oct. 26, 1931; Jan. 3, 1938; Mar. 1, 1943
CHIDLAW, Benjamin Wiley (1900-)
Dec. 20, 1954
CHILD, Julia (1912-)
Nov. 25, 1966
CHILES, Lawton (1930-)
Oct. 26, 1970
CHOU, En-lai (1898-1975)
June 18, 1951; May 10, 1954; Sept. 13, 1963;
Nov. 13, 1964; Nov. 8, 1971; Mar. 6, 1972;
Dec. 17, 1973; Feb. 3, 1975
CHRIST, see JESUS CHRIST
CHRISTIAN X, King of Denmark (1870-
1947)
May 17, 1937; Jan. 2, 1939
CHRYSLER, Walter Percy (1875-1940)
Apr. 20, 1925; Jan. 7, 1929; Jan. 8, 1934
CHURCHILL, Winston (1874-1965)
Apr. 14, 1923; May 11, 1925; Sept. 4, 1939;
Sept. 30, 1940; Jan. 6, 1941; Jan. 5, 1942;
Jan. 2, 1950; Nov. 5, 1951
CIANO, Edda (1910-)
July 24, 1939
CLAIRE, Ina Fagan (1892-)
Sept. 30, 1929
CLAPP, Margaret (1911-)
Oct. 10, 1949
CLARK, Jim (1936-1968)
July 9, 1965
CLARK, Mark (1896-)
Oct. 4, 1943; June 25, 1946; July 7, 1952
CLARK, Petula (1934-)
May 21, 1965
CLARKE, John Hessin (1857-1945)
Feb. 11, 1924
CLAUDEL, Paul L. C. (1868-1955)
Mar. 21, 1927
CLAY, Lucius (1897-1978)
June 25, 1945; July 12, 1948; Oct. 2, 1950
CLAYTON, William L. (1880-1966)
Aug. 17, 1936
CLEMENCEAU, Georges (1841-1929)
Jan. 4, 1926
CLEMENT, Martin Withington (1881-1966)
Mar. 16, 1936
CLEVELAND, Grover (1837-1908)
May 28, 1945; Feb. 23, 1976
CLIBURN, Van (1934-)
May 19, 1958
CLIFFORD, Clark (1906-)
Mar. 15, 1948

CLOONEY, Rosemary (1928-)
Feb. 23, 1953
CLYMER, George (1739-1813)
Aug. 6, 1973
COCHRANE, Mickey (1903-)
Oct. 7, 1935
COFFEY, Walter Bernard (1868-1944)
May 25, 1931
COFFIN, Henry Sloane (1877-1954)
Nov. 15, 1926
COHAN, George Michael (1878-1942)
Oct. 9, 1933
COHEN, Benjamin Victor (1894-)
Sept. 12, 1938
COHEN, William (1941-)
July 29, 1974
COHN, Roy (1928-)
Mar. 22, 1954
COLAVITO, Rocky (1933-)
Aug. 24, 1959
COLBERT, Lester Lum (1906-)
Jan. 29, 1951; May 12, 1958
COLBY, Anita (1914-)
Jan. 8, 1945
COLBY, William Egan (1920-)
Sept. 30, 1974
COLE, Edward N. (1909-1977)
Oct. 5, 1959
COLES, Robert (1930-)
Feb. 14, 1972
COLLINS, John Frederick (1920-)
Mar. 23, 1962
COLLINS, LeRoy (1909-)
Dec. 19, 1955
COLOMBO, Joe (1923-1978)
July 12, 1971
COMANECI, Nadia (1962-)
Aug. 2, 1976
COMMONER, Barry (1918-)
Feb. 2, 1970
COMPTON, Arthur Holly (1892-1962)
Jan. 13, 1936
CONABLE, Barber (1923-)
Jan. 15, 1973
CONANT, James Bryant (1893-1978)
Feb. 5, 1934; Sept. 28, 1936; Sept. 23, 1946;
Sept. 14, 1959
CONE, Fairfax Mastick (1903-)
Oct. 12, 1962
CONFUCIUS (ca. 551-479 B.C.)
May 26, 1947
CONINGHAM, Arthur (1895-1948)
Aug. 14, 1944
CONKLIN, Edwin G. (1863-1952)
July 3, 1939
CONNALLY, John Bowden (1917-)
Jan. 17, 1964; Aug. 30, 1971; Oct. 18, 1971;
May 17, 1976
CONNALLY, Thomas Terry (1877-1963)
Mar. 13, 1944
CONNERS, Grace Isabell Hammond
(1900-)
May 25, 1931
CONNORS, Jimmy (1953-)
Apr. 28, 1975
CONRAD, Joseph (1857-1924)
Apr. 7, 1923

CONSTANTINE, King of Greece (1940-)
Apr. 28, 1967
CONWAY, Jill Ker (1935-)
Jan. 5, 1976
COOK, Barbara (1927-)
July 21, 1958
COOLIDGE, Calvin (1872-1933)
Jan. 16, 1928
COOLIDGE, Grace Anna Goodhue (1879-
1957)
Sept. 17, 1928
COOPER, Gary (1901-1961)
Mar. 3, 1941
COOPER, Gordon (1927-)
May 24, 1963
COOPER, John S. (1901-)
July 5, 1954
COPELAND, Charles Townsend (1860-1952)
Jan. 17, 1927
COPELAND, Lammot DuPont (1905-)
May 31, 1963; Nov. 27, 1964
CORCORAN, Thomas Gardiner (1900-)
Sept. 12, 1938
CORD, Errett Lobban (1894-1974)
Jan. 18, 1932; Apr. 23, 1934
CORDINER, Ralph J. (1900-)
Jan. 12, 1959
CORMIER, Lucia Marie (1912-)
Sept. 5, 1960
CORNELL, Katherine (1893-1974)
Dec. 26, 1932; Dec. 21, 1942
CORTISSOZ, Royal (1869-1948)
Mar. 10, 1930
COSTA e SILVA, Arthur da (1902-1969)
Apr. 21, 1967
COSTA GOMES, Francisco da (1914-)
Aug. 11, 1975
COSTELLO, Frank (1891-1973)
Nov. 28, 1949
COUCH, Virgil (1907-)
Oct. 20, 1961
COUGHLIN, Charles Edward (1891-1979)
Jan. 15, 1934
COUSTEAU, Jacques Yves (1911-)
Mar. 28, 1960
COUVE de MURVILLE, Maurice (1907-)
Feb. 7, 1964
COUZENS, James (1872-1936)
July 16, 1923
COWAN, Glenn (1951-)
Apr. 26, 1971
COWARD, Noel (1899-1973)
Feb. 6, 1933
COWLES, John (1899-)
July 1, 1935
COX, Archibald (1912-)
Oct. 29, 1973
COX, Eddie (1946-)
June 14, 1971
COX, Tricia Nixon (1946-)
June 14, 1971
COZZENS, James G. (1903-1978)
Sept. 2, 1957
CRAIG, Eddie (1896-)
Aug. 14, 1950
CRAIG, George (1909-)
Mar. 7, 1955

CRAIG, James, Viscount of Craigavon (1871-1940)
May 26, 1924
CRAM, Ralph Adams (1863-1942)
Dec. 13, 1926
CRAMER, William C. (1922-)
Oct. 26, 1970
CRAMM, Gottfried von (1909-)
Sept. 13, 1937
CRANE, Charles Richard (1858-1939)
Mar. 9, 1931
CRAWFORD, Jack (1908-)
Sept. 4, 1933
CRERAR, Henry Duncan (1888-1965)
Sept. 18, 1944
CRESAP, Mark (1910-)
May 31, 1963
CRIPPS, Stafford (1889-1952)
Apr. 13, 1942; Nov. 10, 1947
CRONKITE, Walter (1916-)
Oct. 14, 1966; Nov. 21, 1969
CROSBY, Bing (1904-1977)
Apr. 7, 1941
CRUMP, Edward H. (1876-1954)
May 27, 1946
CUNNINGHAM, Andrew (1883-1963)
Feb. 17, 1941; May 24, 1943
CUNNINGHAM, Briggs Swift (1907-)
Apr. 26, 1954
CUNNINGHAM, John Philip (1897-)
Oct. 12, 1962
CUMMINGS, Edith (1900-)
Aug. 24, 1924
CUMMINS, Albert Baird (1850-1926)
Dec. 10, 1923
CURIE, Eve (1904-)
Feb. 12, 1940
CURRAN, Joe (1906-)
June 17, 1946
CURRY, John Francis (1873-1957)
Mar. 23, 1931
CURTER, Lewis Wesley (1905-)
Mar. 23, 1962
CURTICE, Harlow H. (1893-1962)
June 14, 1954; Jan. 2, 1956; May 12, 1958
CURTIN, John (1885-1945)
Apr. 24, 1944
CURTIS, Charles (1860-1936)
Dec. 20, 1926; June 18, 1928; Dec. 5, 1932
CURTISS, Glenn Hammond (1878-1930)
Oct. 13, 1924
CUSHING, Alexander C. (1913-)
Feb. 9, 1959
CUSHING, Richard (1895-1970)
Aug. 21, 1964
CUTTEN, Arthur W. (1871-1936)
Dec. 10, 1928

D

DALADIER, Edouard (1884-1970)
May 29, 1933; June 5, 1939
DALAI LAMA (1936-)
Apr. 20, 1959
DALEY, Richard Joseph (1903-1976)
Mar. 23, 1962; Mar. 15, 1963; Sept. 6, 1968

DALI, Salvador (1904-)
Dec. 14, 1936
DAMASKINOS, Archbishop of Greece (1891-)
Oct. 1, 1945
DANKO, Rick (1943-)
Jan. 12, 1970
DARLAN, Alain (1881-1942)
May 26, 1941
DAUGHERTY, Duffy (1915-)
Oct. 8, 1956
DAVIDSON, Jo (1883-1952)
Sept. 9, 1946
DAVIES, Joseph Edward (1876-1958)
Mar. 15, 1937
DAVIES, Marjorie Post Hutton (1887-1973)
Mar. 15, 1937
DAVILA, Carlos Guillermo (1887-1955)
June 20, 1932
DAVIS, Bette (1908-)
Mar. 28, 1938
DAVIS, Dwight Filley (1879-1945)
Dec. 15, 1924
DAVIS, Elmer Holmes (1890-1958)
Mar. 15, 1943
DAVIS, Glenn (1925-)
Nov. 12, 1945
DAVIS, J. Mason (1936-)
June 17, 1974
DAVIS, James J. (1873-1947)
Jan. 10, 1927; Dec. 1, 1930
DAVIS, Jay (1963-)
June 17, 1974
DAVIS, June (1942-)
June 17, 1974
DAVIS, Karen (1958-)
June 17, 1974
DAVIS, Norman H. (1878-1944)
Dec. 12, 1932
DAVISON, F. Trubee (1896-1974)
Aug. 24, 1925
DAWES, Charles Gates (1865-1951)
Dec. 14, 1925; June 11, 1928
DAWES, Rufus Cutler (1867-1940)
May 21, 1933
DAWSON, Bertrand (1864-1945)
Sept. 1, 1930
DAYAN, Moshe (1915-)
June 16, 1967
DAYAN, Yael (1939-)
Apr. 10, 1972
DEAN, Gordon (1906-)
Jan. 14, 1952
DEAN, Jerome Hermann "Dizzy" (1911-1974)
Apr. 15, 1935
DEAN, John Wesley (1939-)
Apr. 30, 1973; May 28, 1973; July 2, 1973; July 9, 1973
DEAN, William Frische (1899-)
Dec. 7, 1953
DeBAKEY, Michael (1908-)
May 28, 1965
DECIO, Arthur Julius (1930-)
Dec. 3, 1965
DeGASPERI, Alcide (1881-1954)
Apr. 19, 1948; May 25, 1953

DeHAVILLAND, Olivia (1916-   )
Dec. 20, 1948
DELANO, William Adams (1874-1960)
June 2, 1930
DeLEE, Joseph (1869-1942)
May 25, 1936
DeMILLE, Cecil B. (1881-1959)
Aug. 27, 1934
DEMPSEY, Jack (1895-   )
Sept. 10, 1923
DEMPSEY, Miles Christopher (1896-   )
Mar. 19, 1945
DENNIS, Eugene (1905-   )
Apr. 25, 1949
DENNIS, Sandy (1937-   )
Sept. 1, 1967
DEPEW, Chauncy Mitchell (1834-1928)
Dec. 1, 1924
DeSAPIO, Carmine (1909-   )
Aug. 22, 1955
DeVALERA, Eamon (1882-1975)
Apr. 11, 1932; Mar. 25, 1940
DEWEY, John (1859-1952)
June 4, 1928
DEWEY, Thomas Edward (1902-1971)
Feb. 1, 1937; Feb. 26, 1940; Nov. 1, 1943;
Oct. 23, 1944; July 5, 1948; Nov. 1, 1948
DIAMOND, Martin (1920-   )
May 6, 1966
DIBELIUS, Otto (1880-1967)
Apr. 6, 1953
DICKINSON, John (1732-1808)
Aug. 6, 1973
DIEBOLD, John (1926-   )
Dec. 3, 1965
DIEFENBAKER, John G. (1895-1979)
Aug. 5, 1957
DIEM, Ngo Dinh (1901-   )
Apr. 4, 1955; Aug. 4, 1961
DIETRICH, Marlene (1904-   )
Nov. 30, 1936
DILLON, C. Douglas (1909-   )
Aug. 18, 1961
DILLON, Richard C. (1877-1966)
June 10, 1929
DiMAGGIO, Joe (1915-   )
July 13, 1936; Oct. 4, 1948
DIONNE, Annette (1934-   )
May 31, 1937
DIONNE, Cecile (1934-   )
May 31, 1937
DIONNE, Emille (1934-1954)
May 31, 1937
DIONNE, Marie (1934-1970)
May 31, 1937
DIONNE, Yvonne (1934-   )
May 31, 1937
DIOR, Christian (1905-   )
Mar. 4, 1957
DIRKSEN, Everett (1896-1969)
Sept. 14, 1962; June 19, 1964; July 10, 1964
DiSALLE, Michael V. (1908-   )
Mar. 19, 1951
DISNEY, Walt (1901-1966)
Dec. 27, 1937; Dec. 27, 1954
DODDS, Harold Willis (1889-   )
June 18, 1934

DODGE, Joseph Morrell (1890-1964)
Jan. 24, 1955
DOENITZ, Karl (1891-   )
Feb. 2, 1942; May 10, 1943
DOLE, Robert (1923-   )
Aug. 30, 1976
DOLLAR, Robert (1844-1932)
Mar. 19, 1928
DOLLFUSS, Engelbert (1892-1934)
Sept. 25, 1933
DONNER, Frederic Garrett (1903-   )
May 18, 1962
DOOLITTLE, James Harold (1896-   )
Nov. 23, 1942
DOS PASSOS, John R. (1896-1970)
Aug. 10, 1936
DOUGHERTY, Denis Joseph (1865-1951)
Feb. 15, 1937
DOUGHTON, Robert Lee (1863-1954)
Apr. 30, 1934
DOUGLAS, Donald Wills (1892-   )
May 23, 1938; Nov. 22, 1943
DOUGLAS, Lewis (1894-1974)
Dec. 1, 1947
DOUGLAS, Paul H. (1892-1976)
Jan. 16, 1950; Jan. 22, 1951; Apr. 16, 1956
DOUGLAS, William Orville (1898-1980)
Oct. 11, 1937; July 22, 1974
DOUGLAS-HOME, Alec (1903-   )
Oct. 25, 1963
DOUMERGUE, Gaston (1863-1937)
July 21, 1924; Aug. 2, 1926; Mar. 12, 1934
DOWNEY, Morton (1901-   )
June 22, 1931
DOWNEY, Sheridan (1884-1961)
Oct. 24, 1938
DRAPER, Charles Stark (1901-   )
Jan. 2, 1961
DRESSLER, Marie (1873-1934)
Aug. 7, 1933
DRYDEN, Franklin B. (1915-   )
Jan. 27, 1961
DUBCEK, Alexander (1921-   )
Apr. 5, 1968
DUBINSKY, David (1892-   )
Aug. 29, 1949
DuBRIDGE, Lee Alvin (1901-   )
May 16, 1955
DUFF, James Henderson (1883-1970)
June 21, 1948
DUFFIELD, Edward Dickinson (1871-1938)
Sept. 26, 1932
DUKAKIS, Michael (1933-   )
Nov. 18, 1974
DUKE, Nanaline (1871-1962)
Apr. 27, 1931
DULLES, Allen W. (1893-1969)
Aug. 3, 1953
DULLES, John Foster (1888-1959)
Aug. 13, 1951; Oct. 12, 1953; Jan. 3, 1955;
Apr. 16, 1956
DUNAWAY, Faye (1941-   )
Dec. 8, 1967
DUNLOP, John T. (1914-   )
Dec. 20, 1976
DuPONT, Ethel (1916-   )
June 28, 1937

DuPONT, Pierre S. (1870-1928)
Jan. 31, 1927
DURANTE, Jimmy (1893-1980)
Jan. 24, 1944
DUROCHER, Leo (1907-)
Apr. 14, 1947
DUSE, Eleanora (1859-1924)
July 30, 1923

E

EAGLETON, Thomas (1930-)
July 24, 1972; Aug. 7, 1972
EAKER, Ira Clarence (1896-)
Aug. 30, 1943
EARLE, George Howard (1890-1974)
July 5, 1937
EARLY, Stephen Tyree (1889-1951)
Dec. 17, 1934
EASTLAND, James Oliver (1905-)
Mar. 26, 1956
EASTMAN, Ben (1911-)
July 11, 1932
EASTMAN, George (1854-1932)
Mar. 31, 1924; Apr. 16, 1928
EATON, Cyrus Stephen (1884-1979)
Feb. 24, 1930
EBERLE, Edward W. (1864-1929)
Feb. 4, 1924
ECCLES, Marriner Stoddard (1890-1977)
Feb. 10, 1936
ECKNER, Hugo (1868-1954)
Sept. 16, 1929
EDDINGTON, Arthur Stanley (1882-1944)
Apr. 16, 1934
EDEN, Anthony (1897-1977)
Apr. 8, 1935; Feb. 8, 1943; Feb. 11, 1952;
May 23, 1955; Aug. 1, 1955; Nov. 19, 1956
EDISON, Charles (1890-1969)
Feb. 20, 1939
EDISON, Thomas Alva (1847-1931)
May 25, 1925
EDWARD, Duke of Windsor (1894-1972)
Aug. 8, 1927; April 1, 1929
EDWARDS, William Hanford (1876-)
Oct. 4, 1926
EHRLICHMAN, JOHN (1925-)
June 8, 1970; May 28, 1973
EICHELBERGER, Robert Lawrence (1886-1961)
Sept. 10, 1945
EINSTEIN, Albert (1879-1955)
Feb. 18, 1929; Apr. 4, 1938; July 1, 1946
EINSTEIN, Elsa (1874-1936)
Dec. 22, 1930
EISEN, Louis (1914-)
Mar. 11, 1946
EISENHOWER, Dwight David (1890-1969)
Nov. 16, 1942; Sept. 13, 1943; June 19, 1944;
Jan. 1, 1945; June 23, 1947; Feb. 12, 1951;
June 16, 1952; Nov. 3, 1952; Nov. 10, 1952;
July 4, 1955; Aug. 1, 1955; Apr. 16, 1956;
June 18, 1956; Nov. 12, 1956; Jan. 27, 1958;
Sept. 7, 1959; Jan. 4, 1960; May 23, 1960;
Aug. 15, 1960; July 21, 1961; Apr. 4, 1969
EISENHOWER, Mamie Dowd (1896-1979)
Jan. 19, 1953

EISENHOWER, Milton Stover (1899-)
Sept. 8, 1958
ELIOT, T. S. (1888-1965)
Mar. 6, 1950
ELIZABETH II, Queen of Great Britain (1926-)
Apr. 29, 1929; Mar. 31, 1947; Feb. 18, 1952;
Jan. 5, 1953; June 29, 1959; May 3, 1976
ELIZABETH BOWES-LYON, consort of George VI (1900-)
Aug. 11, 1930; Oct. 9, 1939
ELLINGTON, Duke (1899-1974)
Aug. 20, 1956
ELLSBERG, Daniel (1930-)
July 5, 1971
ELSTEIN, Kenneth (1948-)
July 17, 1972
EMANUEL, Victor (1898-1960)
Oct. 7, 1946
EMERSON, Frank Collins (1882-1931)
June 10, 1929
ENDERS, John Franklin (1897-)
Jan. 2, 1961; Nov. 17, 1961
ERHARD, Ludwig (1897-1977)
Oct. 28, 1957; Nov. 1, 1963
ERVIN, Sam (1896-)
Jan. 15, 1973; Apr. 16, 1973; July 30, 1973
ESCOBEDO, Danny, (1938-)
Apr. 29, 1966
ESHKOL, Levi (1895-1969)
June 9, 1967
ESTES, Billie Sol (1925-)
May 25, 1962
EVANS, Daniel J. (1926-)
Aug. 9, 1968
EVANS, Hiram Wesley (1881-)
June 23, 1924
EVE, first woman in the Bible
Oct. 25, 1954
EVTUSHENKO, Evgeny (1934-)
Apr. 13, 1962
EWING, James (1866-1943)
Jan. 12, 1931

F

FAIRCHILD, John Burr (1927-)
Sept. 14, 1970
FAIRCHILD, Sherman Mills (1896-1971)
July 25, 1960
FAIRLESS, Benjamin F. (1891-)
Nov. 12, 1951
FAISAL, King of Saudi Arabia (1905-1975)
Nov. 19, 1973; Jan. 6, 1975; Apr. 7, 1975
FALK, Peter (1927-)
Nov. 26, 1973
FALKENHORST, Nikolaus von (1885-1969)
May 13, 1940
FARLEY, James A. (1888-1976)
Oct. 31, 1932; May 21, 1934
FAROUK I, King of Egypt (1920-1965)
Aug. 9, 1937; Sept. 10, 1951
FARRAND, Livingston (1867-1939)
June 17, 1929
FARRAR, Geraldine (1882-1967)
Dec. 5, 1927

FARRELL, James A. (1863-1943)
June 6, 1927
FARRINGTON, Joseph Rider (1897-1954)
Dec. 22, 1947
FARRINGTON, Wallace Rider (1871-1933)
July 25, 1927
FARROW, Mia (1946-   )
Feb. 7, 1969; Mar. 18, 1974
FAUBUS, Orval (1910-   )
Sept. 23, 1957
FAULKNER, William (1897-1962)
Jan. 23, 1939; July 17, 1964
FAURE, Edgar (1908-   )
Aug. 1, 1955
FAWCETT—MAJORS, Farrah (1946-   )
Nov. 22, 1976
FECHNER, Robert (1876-1939)
Feb. 6, 1939
FELLER, Bob (1919-   )
Aug. 19, 1937
FELT, Harry Donald (1902-   )
Jan. 6, 1961
FENG, Yu-hsiang (1880-1948)
July 2, 1928
FENHOLT, Jeff (1950-   )
Oct. 25, 1971
FERKAUF, Eugene (1921-   )
Nov. 23, 1962
FIELDING, Temple H. (1914-   )
June 16, 1969
FINCH, Robert Hutchison (1926-   )
May 2, 1969
FINE, John Sydney (1893-1978)
June 20, 1952
FINKELSTEIN, Louis (1895-   )
Oct. 15, 1951
FINLEY, Charles O. (1918-   )
Aug. 18, 1975
FISHBEIN, Morris (1889-1976)
June 21, 1937
FISCHER, Bobby (1943-   )
July 31, 1972
FISHER, Geoffrey Francis (1887-1972)
Sept. 6, 1954
FITZGERALD, John (1863-1950)
July 11, 1960
FITZHUGH, Gilbert (1910-   )
May 31, 1963
FITZSIMMONS, Thomas (1741-1811)
Aug. 6, 1973
FLACK, Roberta (1940-   )
Feb. 12, 1973
FLAGSTAD, Kirsten (1895-1962)
Dec. 23, 1935
FLANDIN, Pierre Etienne (1889-1958)
Feb. 4, 1935
FLEET, Reuben Hollis (1887-1975)
Nov. 17, 1941
FLEMING, Alexander (1881-1955)
May 15, 1944
FLETCHER, Henry P. (1873-1959)
Nov. 5, 1934
FLYNN, Edward Joseph (1891-1953)
Oct. 12, 1942
FOCH, Ferdinand (1851-1929)
Mar. 16, 1925

FOKKER, Anthony H. G. (1890-1939)
Dec. 31, 1923
FONCK, Rene (1894-1953)
Aug. 23, 1926
FONDA, Henry (1905-   )
Feb. 16, 1970
FONDA, Jane (1937-   )
Feb. 16, 1970
FONDA, Peter (1939-   )
Feb. 16, 1970
FONSSAGRIVES, Lisa (1911-   )
Sept. 19, 1949
FONTAINE, Joan (1917-   )
Jan. 8, 1945
FONTANNE, Lynn (1887-   )
Nov. 8, 1937
FONTEYN, Margot (1919-   )
Nov. 14, 1949
FORD, Benson (1920-   )
May 18, 1953
FORD, Betty (1918-   )
Dec. 17, 1973; Oct. 7, 1974; July 28, 1975;
Jan. 5, 1976
FORD, Gayle (1951-   )
July 28, 1975
FORD, Gerald (1913-   )
Jan. 15, 1973; Oct. 22, 1973; Dec. 17, 1973;
Aug. 19, 1974; Aug. 26, 1974; Sept. 23, 1974;
Oct. 13, 1974; Jan. 20, 1975; Apr. 21, 1975;
May 26, 1975; July 28, 1975; Aug. 4, 1975;
Oct. 6, 1975; Nov. 17, 1975; May 17, 1976;
June 21, 1976; Aug. 9, 1976; Aug. 30, 1976;
Oct. 4, 1976; Oct. 18, 1976; Nov. 8, 1976
FORD, Henry (1863-1947)
July 27, 1925; Jan. 14, 1935; Mar. 17, 1941;
Mar. 23, 1942; Feb. 4, 1946
FORD, Henry (1917-   )
May 18, 1953; Feb. 4, 1946; May 12, 1958;
July 20, 1970
FORD, Jack (1952-   )
July 28, 1975
FORD, Mike (1950-   )
July 28, 1975
FORD, Steve (1956-   )
July 28, 1975
FORD, Susan (1957-   )
July 28, 1975
FORD, William (1925-   )
May 18, 1953
FORRESTAL, James V. (1892-1949)
Oct. 29, 1945
FORTAS, Abe (1910-   )
July 5, 1968
FOSDICK, Harry Emerson (1878-1969)
Sept. 21, 1925; Oct. 6, 1930
FOWLER, Henry H. (1908-   )
Sept. 10, 1965
FOXX, Jimmy (1908-1967)
July 29, 1929
FOXX, Redd (1922-   )
Sept. 25, 1972
FRANCIS, Alec B. (1885-1934)
Dec. 25, 1933
FRANCO, Francisco (1892-1975)
Aug. 24, 1936, Sept. 6, 1937; Jan. 2, 1939;
Mar. 27, 1939; Oct. 18, 1943; Mar. 18, 1946;
Jan. 21, 1966; Nov. 3, 1975

FRANK, Jerome New (1889-1957)
Mar. 11, 1940
FRANKLIN, Aretha (1942-)
June 28, 1968
FRANKLIN, Benjamin (1706-1790)
Aug. 6, 1973
FRANKLIN, Philip Albright Small (1871-1939)
May 17, 1926
FRANKS, Oliver (1905-)
Sept. 26, 1949
FRAZIER, Joe (1944-)
Mar. 8, 1971
FREDERIKA, Queen of Greece (1917-)
Oct. 26, 1953
FREEMAN, Douglas Southall (1886-1953)
Oct. 18, 1948
FREEMAN, James Edward (1866-1943)
Oct. 24, 1927; May 9, 1932
FREEMAN, Orville (1918-)
Apr. 5, 1963
FREUD, Sigmund (1856-1939)
Oct. 27, 1924; June 26, 1939; Apr. 23, 1956
FRIEDMAN, Milton (1912-)
Dec. 19, 1969
FROMME, Lynette (1948-)
Sept. 15, 1975
FRONDIZI, Arturo (1909-)
Mar. 30, 1962
FROST, Robert Lee (1874-1963)
Oct. 9, 1950
FRY, Christopher (1907-)
Nov. 20, 1950
FRY, Franklin Clark (1900-)
Apr. 7, 1958
FUAD I, King of Egypt (1868-1936)
Apr. 28, 1923
FULBRIGHT, William (1905-)
Jan. 22, 1965
FULLER, R. Buckminster (1895-)
Jan. 10, 1964
FUNSTON, Keith (1910-)
Nov. 21, 1955

G

GABLE, Clark (1901-1960)
Aug. 31, 1936
GADDAFI, Muammar (1942-)
Apr. 2, 1973
GAGARIN, Yuri (1934-1968)
Apr. 21, 1961
GALBRAITH, John Kenneth (1909-)
Jan. 12, 1962; Feb. 16, 1968
GALLO, Ernest (1909-)
Nov. 27, 1972
GALLO, Julio (1910-)
Nov. 27, 1972
GALLUP, George (1901-)
May 3, 1948
GAMELIN, Maurice G. (1872-1958)
Aug. 14, 1939
GANDHI, Indira (1917-)
Jan. 28, 1966; Dec. 6, 1971
GANDHI, Mahatma (1869-1948)
Mar. 31, 1930; Jan. 5, 1931; Aug. 24, 1942;
June 30, 1947; May 11, 1953

GANGER, Robert Mondell (1903-)
Oct. 12, 1962
GARBETT, Cyril F. (1875-1955)
Apr. 17, 1944
GARDEN, Mary (1874-1967)
Dec. 15, 1930
GARDNER, Ava (1922-)
Sept. 3 1951; Aug. 29, 1955
GARDNER, John W. (1912-)
Jan. 20, 1967
GARNER, James (1928-)
Mar. 30, 1959
GARNER, John Nance (1868-1967)
Dec. 7, 1931; June 3, 1935; Mar. 20, 1939
GARSON, Greer (1908-)
Dec. 20, 1943
GARY, Elbert Henry (1846-1927)
July 5, 1926
GASPAR, wise man of the Three Magi
Dec. 26, 1938; Dec. 23, 1940; Dec. 28, 1959;
Dec. 30, 1974
GATTI-CASAZZA, Giulio (1869-1940)
Nov. 5, 1923; Nov. 1, 1926
GAULLE, Charles de (1890-1970)
Aug. 4, 1941; May 29, 1944; Nov. 17, 1947;
May 26, 1958; Jan. 5, 1959; May 23, 1960;
July 21, 1961; Dec. 7, 1962; Feb. 8, 1963;
Feb. 7, 1964; July 1, 1966; May 31, 1968;
Nov. 29, 1968
GEDDES, Barbara Bel (1922-)
Apr. 9, 1951
GEHRIG, Lou (1903-1941)
Oct. 5, 1936
GENEEN, Harold S. (1910-)
Sept. 8, 1967
GEORGE, Duke of Kent (1902-)
Aug. 8, 1927
GEORGE V, King of Great Britain (1865-1936)
Apr. 7, 1924; May 30, 1927; Oct. 27, 1930;
Oct. 10, 1932; May 6, 1935
GEORGE VI, King of Great Britain (1895-1952)
Jan. 12, 1925, Mar. 8, 1937; May 15, 1939;
Mar. 6, 1944
GEORGE II, King of Greece (1890-1947)
Nov. 4, 1940; Feb. 24, 1947
GEORGE, Harold Lee (1895-)
May 17, 1943
GEORGE, Walter (1878-1957)
July 19, 1943; Apr. 25, 1955
GERNREICH, Rudi (1922-)
Dec. 1, 1967
GERSHWIN, George (1898-1937)
July 20, 1925
GETTY, J. Paul (1892-1976)
Feb. 24, 1958
GHEORGHIU-DEJ, Gheorghe (1901-1965)
Oct. 3, 1960
GHORMLEY, Robert Lee (1883-1958)
Aug. 17, 1942
GIANNINI, Amadeo Peter (1870-1949)
Apr. 2, 1928; Apr. 15, 1946
GIAP, Vo Nguyen (1911-)
June 17, 1966; Feb. 9, 1968; May 15, 1972
GIBBS, William Francis (1886-1967)
Sept. 28, 1942

GIBSON, Althea (1927-)
Aug. 26, 1957
GIBSON, Charles Dana (1867-1931)
Mar. 28, 1927
GIBSON, Hugh (1883-1954)
Nov. 26, 1923; July 18, 1927; Feb. 8, 1932
GILBERT, H. Edward (1906-)
July 26, 1963
GILBERT, S. Parker (1892-1938)
Sept. 15, 1924
GILDERSLEEVE, Virginia C. (1877-1965)
Oct. 8, 1934
GILLETT, Frederick Huntington (1851-1935)
Nov. 17, 1924
GILMAN, Nicholas (1755-1814)
Aug. 6, 1973
GIMBEL, Sophie (1898-)
Sept. 15, 1947
GIRAUD, Henri (1879-1949)
Mar. 29, 1943
GLASER, Donald Arthur (1926-)
Jan. 2, 1961
GLASS, Carter (1858-1946)
June 9, 1924; Feb. 6, 1933
GLEASON, Jackie (1916-)
Dec. 29, 1961
GLENN, John Herschel (1922-)
Mar. 2, 1962; Nov. 18, 1974
GLOUCESTER, Duke of, Henry (1900-1974)
Aug. 8, 1927
GLUECK, Nelson (1900-1971)
Dec. 13, 1963
GODFREY, Arthur (1903-)
Feb. 27, 1950
GOEBBELS, Joseph Paul (1897-1945)
July 10, 1933
GOLDBERG, Arthur J. (1908-)
Sept. 22, 1961
GOLDWATER, Barry (1909-)
June 23, 1961; June 14, 1963; June 12, 1964;
July 10, 1964; July 24, 1964; Sept. 25, 1964
GOLIKOV, Filip Ivanovich (1900-)
Feb. 22, 1943
GOMEZ, Vernon (1910-)
July 9, 1934
GOMPERS, Samuel (1850-1924)
Oct. 1, 1923
GOMULKA, Wladyslaw (1905-)
Dec. 10, 1956; Oct. 3, 1960
GONÇALVES, Vasco dos Santos (1921-)
Aug. 11, 1975
GOOD, James William (1866-1929)
Sept. 24, 1928; Sept. 2, 1929
GOOD, Robert Alan (1923-)
Mar. 19, 1973
GOODELL, Charles (1926-)
Oct. 26, 1970
GOODMAN, Johnny (1910-)
June 6, 1938
GORDON, John F. (1900-1978)
May 31, 1963
GORDON, Ruth (1896-)
Dec. 21, 1942
GORE, Albert (1908-)
Oct. 26, 1970
GOREN, Charles Henry (1901-)
Sept. 29, 1958

GÖRING, HERMANN (1893-1946)
Aug. 21, 1933; Apr. 1, 1940; Dec. 10, 1945
GORSHKOV, Sergei (1911-)
Feb. 23, 1968
GORT, John S. (1886-1946)
Oct. 26, 1942
GOULD, Elliott (1933-)
Sept. 7, 1970
GOULD, Samuel B. (1911-)
Jan. 12, 1968
GRABLE, Betty (1916-1973)
Aug. 23, 1948
GRAHAM, Billy (1918-)
Oct. 25, 1954
GRAHAM, Philip L. (1916-)
Apr. 16, 1956
GRANDI, Dino (1895-)
Nov. 16, 1931
GRANGE, "Red" Harold (1902-)
Oct. 5, 1925
GRANT, Harry J. (1881-1963)
Feb. 1, 1954
GRANT, Heber Jedediah (1856-1945)
Apr. 7, 1930
GRASS, Gunter (1927-)
Apr. 13, 1970
GRASSO, Ella (1919-)
Nov. 18, 1974; Jan. 5, 1976
GRAY, Bowman (1907-)
Apr. 11, 1960
GRAY, L. Patrick (1917-)
Mar. 26, 1973
GREEN, William (1873-1952)
Oct. 19, 1931; Oct. 4, 1937; Oct. 13, 1947
GREENE, Graham (1904-)
Oct. 29, 1951
GREENE, Joe (1946-)
Dec. 8, 1975
GREENE, Wallace Martin (1908-)
Feb. 5, 1965
GREENEWALT, Crawford H. (1902-)
Apr. 16, 1951
GREENWOOD, L. C. (1946-)
Dec. 8, 1975
GREW, Joseph Clark (1880-1965)
Nov. 12, 1934
GRIBBIN, George Homer (1907-)
Oct. 12, 1962
GRIESE, Bob (1946-)
Jan. 17, 1972; Oct. 16, 1972
GRIFFITHS, Martha (1912-)
Jan. 15, 1973
GRISSOM, Virgil (1927-1967)
Feb. 3, 1967
GRISWOLD, Alfred Whitney (1906-1963)
June 11, 1951
GROMYKO, Andrei (1909-)
Aug. 18, 1947
GROSS, Calvin Edward (1919-)
Nov. 15, 1963
GROSS, Courtlandt (1905-)
May 31, 1963; Feb. 11, 1966
GROSS, Robert E. (1897-1961)
Jan. 14, 1946
GROSVENOR, Graham Bethune (1884-1943)
Sept. 9, 1929

GRUENING, Ernest (1887-1974)
June 16, 1947
GRUENTHER, Alfred (1899-)
Feb. 6, 1956
GRUMMAN, Leroy Randle (1895-)
Sept. 11, 1944
GRZEBYK, Anthony (1906-)
Nov. 16, 1936
GUDERIAN, Heinz (1886-1954)
Aug. 7, 1944
GUEST, Lucy Douglas Cochrane (1920-)
July 20, 1962
GUEVARA, Che (1928-1967)
Aug. 8, 1960
GUGGENHEIM, Henry Frank (1890-1971)
Oct. 21, 1929
GUINNESS, Alec (1914-)
Apr. 21, 1958
GUNTHER, John (1901-1970)
Apr. 14, 1958
GUSTAF V, King of Sweden (1858-1950)
Jan. 2, 1939; Oct. 30, 1939; Apr. 29, 1940
GUSTAF VI, King of Sweden (1882-1973)
May 31, 1943
GUSTAFSON, Carol (1951-)
Mar. 22, 1976

H

HAAKON VII, King of Norway (1872-1957)
May 3, 1926; Dec. 8, 1930; Jan. 2, 1939
HAGERTY, James Campbell (1910-)
Jan. 27, 1958
HAGGARD, Merle (1937-)
May 6, 1974
HAIDER, Michael Lawrence (1904-)
Dec. 29, 1967
HAILE SELASSIE, Emperor of Ethiopia
(1891-1975)
Nov. 3, 1930; Jan. 6, 1936
HAILSHAM, 1st Viscount, Douglas McGarel
Hogg (1872-1950)
Apr. 1, 1929
HAISE, Fred W. (1934-)
Apr. 27, 1970
HALABY, Najeeb Elias (1916-)
Jan. 19, 1970
HALDEMAN, Harry Robbins (1926-)
June 8, 1970; Apr. 30, 1973; May 28, 1973
HALDER, Franz (1884-1972)
June 29, 1942
HALIFAX, Edward F. L. W. (1881-1959)
Apr. 12, 1926; Jan. 15, 1940
HALL, Leonard (1900-1979)
Mar. 12, 1956
HALLECK, Charles Abraham (1901-)
June 8, 1959
HALSEY, William F. (1882-1959)
Nov. 30, 1942; July 23, 1945
HAMILL, Dorothy (1955-)
Feb. 2, 1976
HAMILTON, Alexander (1757-1804)
Nov. 23, 1959; Sept. 10, 1965; Aug. 6, 1973
HAMILTON, John D. M. (1892-1973)
Sept. 21, 1936
HAMMARSKJOLD, Dag (1905-1961)
June 27, 1955; Nov. 26, 1956; Aug. 22, 1960

HAMMERSTEIN, Oscar (1895-1960)
Oct. 20, 1947
HAMMOND, John Hays (1855-1936)
May 10, 1926
HAMPDEN, Walter (1879-1955)
Mar. 4, 1929
HANRATTY, Terry (1946-)
Oct. 28, 1966
HARDING, Warren G. (1865-1923)
Mar. 10, 1923
HARDISON, Osborne Bennett (1929-)
May 6, 1966
HARKINS, Paul D. (1905-)
May 11, 1962
HARLOW, Jean (1911-1937)
Aug. 19, 1935
HARMON, Thomas Dudley (1919-)
Nov. 6, 1939
HARPER, Marion (1916-)
Oct. 12, 1962
HARPER, Valerie (1941-)
Oct. 28, 1974
HARRIMAN, W. Averell (1891-)
Nov. 14, 1955; Aug. 2, 1963; May 10, 1968
HARRIS, Arthur Travers (1892-1946)
June 7, 1943
HARRIS, Jed (1900-1979)
Sept. 3, 1928
HARRIS, Julie (1925-)
Nov. 28, 1955
HARRISON, George (1943-)
Sept. 22, 1967
HARRISON, Pat.(1881-1941)
Feb. 27, 1933; June 1, 1936
HARRISON, Rex (1908-)
July 23, 1956
HARRISON, Richard Berry (1864-1935)
Mar. 4, 1935
HARRISON, Rufford (1931-)
Apr. 26, 1971
HARRISON, Wallace K. (1895-)
Sept. 22, 1952
HART, Gary (1938-)
Nov. 18, 1974
HART, Lorenz (1895-1943)
Sept. 26, 1938
HART, Thomas (1877-1971)
Nov. 24, 1941
HARTACK, Willie (1932-)
Feb. 10, 1958
HARTFORD, George Ludlum (1864-1957)
Nov. 13, 1950
HARTFORD, John Augustine (1872-1951)
Nov. 13, 1950
HARVARD, John (1607-1638)
Mar. 1, 1954; Apr. 18, 1969
HARVEY, George B. M. (1864-1928)
Oct. 25, 1926
HASTINGS, Patrick (1880-1952)
Oct. 20, 1924
HATFIELD, Bob (1940-)
May 21, 1965
HATFIELD, Mark (1922-)
Nov. 18, 1966
HATOYAMA, Ichiro (1883-1959)
Mar. 14, 1955

HAYES, Bill (1926-   )
Jan. 12, 1976
HAYES, Helen (1900-   )
Dec. 30, 1935
HAYES, Patrick Joseph (1867-1938)
Sept. 30, 1935
HAYES, Susan Seaforth (1944-   )
Jan. 12, 1976
HAYNES, Roy Asa (1881-1940)
July 23, 1923
HAYS, William Harrison (1879-1954)
Sept. 13, 1926
HAYWORTH, Rita (1918-   )
Nov. 10, 1941
HEALD, Henry Townley (1905-   )
June 10, 1957
HEARST, Patricia (1954-   )
Apr. 29, 1974; Sept. 29, 1975; Feb. 16, 1976
HEARST, William Randolph (1863-1951)
Aug. 15, 1927; May 1, 1933; Mar. 13, 1939
HEARST, William Randolph (1908-   )
May 20, 1974
HEATH, Edward R. (1916-   )
July 13, 1962; June 29, 1970
HEFNER, Hugh (1927-   )
Mar. 3, 1967
HEIL, Julius P. (1876-1949)
Jan. 16, 1939
HELFRICH, Conrad (1887-1962)
Mar. 9, 1942
HELLER, John Roderick (1905-   )
July 27, 1959
HELLER, Walter W. (1916-   )
Mar. 3, 1961; June 8, 1962
HELMS, Richard McGarrah (1924-   )
Feb. 24, 1967
HEMINGWAY, Ernest (1899-1961)
Oct. 18, 1937; Oct. 4, 1954
HEMINGWAY, Margaux (1955-   )
June 16, 1975
HENDERSON, Leon (1895-   )
May 12, 1941
HENIE, Sonja (1913-1969)
July 17, 1939
HENRY, Charlotte (1916-   )
Dec. 31, 1933
HENRY, Duke of Gloucester (1900-1974)
Aug. 8, 1927
HENRY-HAYE, Gaston (1889-   )
Mar. 10, 1941
HEPBURN, Audrey (1929-   )
Sept. 7, 1953
HEPBURN, Katherine (1909-   )
Sept. 1, 1952
HEPBURN, Mitchell F. (1896-1953)
Sept. 20, 1937
HERMAN (1949-   )
May 21, 1965
HERRICK, Myron Timothy (1854-1929)
Jan. 30, 1928
HERRING, Clyde Laverne (1879-1945)
Sept. 9, 1935
HERRIOT, Edouard (1872-1957)
May 16, 1932
HERTER, Christian A. (1895-1966)
Aug. 17, 1953; Apr. 27, 1959

HERTZ, Alfred (1872-1942)
Oct. 31, 1927
HERTZOG, James B. (1866-1942)
Apr. 27, 1925
HESBURGH, Theodore (1918-   )
Feb. 9, 1962
HESS, Rudolf (1894-   )
Dec. 10, 1945
HEYDRICK, Reinhard (1904-1942)
Feb. 23, 1942
HILLMAN, Sidney (1887-1946)
Dec. 2, 1940; July 24, 1944
HILLS, Carla (1934-   )
Jan. 5, 1976
HILTON, Conrad (1887-1979)
Dec. 12, 1949; July 19, 1963
HIMMLER, Heinrich (1900-1945)
Apr. 24, 1939; Oct. 11, 1943; Feb. 12, 1945
HINDENBURG, Paul von (1847-1934)
July 27, 1931; Mar. 22, 1926; July 16, 1934;
July 14, 1941
HIROHITO, Emperor of Japan (1901-   )
Nov. 19, 1928; June 6, 1932; Feb. 24, 1936;
Dec. 28, 1936; Oct. 30, 1944; May 21, 1945;
Oct. 4, 1971
HIROTA, Koki (1878-1948)
May 21, 1934
HITCHCOCK, Louise Eustis (1865-1934)
Aug. 18, 1930
HITLER, Adolf (1889-1945)
Dec. 21, 1931; Mar. 13, 1933; Apr. 13, 1936;
Jan. 2, 1939; Apr. 14, 1941; May 7, 1945
HO, Chi Minh (1890-1969)
Nov. 22, 1954; July 16, 1965; Jan. 14, 1966;
Sept. 12, 1969; May 12, 1975
HOAN, Daniel Webster (1881-1961)
Apr. 6, 1936
HOARE, Samuel (1880-1959)
Sept. 23, 1935; June 29, 1936
HOBBY, Oveta Culp (1905-   )
Jan. 17, 1944; May 4, 1953
HODGES, Courtney Hicks (1887-1966)
Oct. 16, 1944
HOEGH, Leo (1908-   )
Oct. 22, 1956
HOFFA, James Riddle (1913-1975?)
Sept. 9, 1957; Aug. 31, 1959
HOFFMAN, Dustin (1937-   )
Feb. 7, 1969; Mar. 29, 1976
HOFFMAN, Paul Gray (1891-1974)
Sept. 6, 1943; Apr. 11, 1949
HOGAN, Ben (1912-   )
Jan. 10, 1949
HOGAN, Frank J. (1877-1945)
Mar. 11, 1935
HOLCOMB, Thomas (1879-1965)
Nov. 11, 1940
HOLDEN, William (1918-   )
Feb. 27, 1956
HOLLOWAY, James Lemuel (1898-   )
Aug. 4, 1958
HOLLOWAY, William J. (1888-1970)
June 10, 1929
HOLM, Eleanor (1913-   )
Aug. 21, 1939
HOLMAN, Eugene (1895-1962)
Mar. 24, 1947

HOLMES, Dyer Brainerd (1921-   )
Aug. 10, 1962
HOLMES, Ernie (1948-   )
Dec. 8, 1975
HOLMES, Oliver Wendell (1841-1935)
Mar. 15, 1926
HOME, Alec Douglas (1903-   )
Oct. 25, 1963
HOMER, (fl. ca. 1000 B.C.)
Nov. 24, 1961
HOOVER, Herbert Clark (1874-1964)
Nov. 16, 1925; Mar. 26, 1928; Oct. 14, 1935;
Dec. 18, 1939
HOOVER, Herbert Clark (1904-   )
July 14, 1930
HOOVER, J. Edgar (1895-1972)
Aug. 5, 1935; Aug. 8, 1949; Apr. 16, 1956;
Dec. 22, 1975
HOOVER, Lou Henry (1875-1944)
May 13, 1929
HOPE, Bob (1903-   )
Sept. 20, 1943; Dec. 22, 1967
HOPE, Victor A.J. (1887-1951)
Oct. 12, 1936; Mar. 16, 1942
HOPKINS, Harry Lloyd (1890-1946)
Feb. 19, 1934; July 18, 1938; Jan. 22, 1945
HOPKINS, Miriam (1902-1972)
May 27, 1935
HOPPER, Edward (1882-1967)
Dec. 24, 1956
HOPPER, Hedda (1890-1966)
July 28, 1947
HORNSBY, Rogers (1896-1963)
July 9, 1928
HOUDE, Camillien (1889-1958)
Aug. 5, 1946
HOUGHTON, Alanson Bigelow (1863-1941)
Apr. 5, 1926
HOUSE, Edward Mandell (1858-1938)
June 25, 1923
HOUSSER, Harry B. (1885-   )
Apr. 5, 1937
HOWARD, Jack (1935-   )
Apr. 26, 1971
HOWARD, Roy Wilson (1883-1964)
Apr. 13, 1931
HOWARD, Sidney Coe (1891-1939)
June 7, 1937
HOWE, Clarence Decatur (1886-1961)
Feb. 4, 1952
HOWE, Louis McHenry (1871-1936)
Dec. 17, 1934
HUBBELL, Carl (1903-   )
Oct. 5, 1936
HUBBLE, Edwin P. (1889-1953)
Feb. 9, 1948
HUDSON, Garth (1943-   )
Jan. 12, 1970
HUFF, Sam (1934-   )
Nov. 30, 1959
HUGHES, Charles Evans (1862-1948)
Dec. 29, 1924; Feb. 17, 1930; Mar. 1, 1937
HUGHES, Charles Frederick (1866-1934)
May 9, 1927; Feb. 20, 1928
HUGHES, Howard (1906-1976)
July 19, 1948; Jan. 24, 1972; Apr. 19, 1976;
Dec. 13, 1976

HUGHES, Rowland R. (1896-1957)
Jan. 23, 1956
HULL, Bobby (1939-   )
Mar. 1, 1968
HULL, Cordell (1871-1955)
Apr. 17, 1933; Dec. 7, 1936; Jan. 8, 1940
HUMBER, John Davis (1895-   )
May 25, 1931
HUMPHREY, George (1890-1970)
Jan. 26, 1953
HUMPHREY, Hubert H. (1911-1978)
Jan. 17, 1949; Nov. 24, 1958; Feb. 1, 1960;
Sept. 4, 1964; Apr. 1, 1966; Apr. 14, 1967;
May 5, 1967; Jan. 5, 1968; May 3, 1968;
July 26, 1968; Sept. 6, 1968; Mar. 8, 1976
HUNT, E. Howard (1921-   )
May 28, 1973
HUNTLEY, Chester (1911-1974)
Nov. 21, 1969
HURJA, Emil Edward (1892-1953)
Mar. 2, 1936
HURLEY, Patrick Jay (1883-1963)
Sept. 14, 1931
HUSSEIN, King of Jordan (1936-   )
Apr. 2, 1956; May 6, 1957; July 14, 1967
HUTCHINS, Robert Maynard (1899-   )
June 25, 1935; Nov. 21, 1949
HUTTON, Betty (1921-   )
Apr. 24, 1950
HUTTON, James (1932-   )
Dec. 7, 1970
HYDE, Arthur Mastick (1877-1947)
Aug. 5, 1929

I

IACOCCA, Lee (1925-   )
Apr. 17, 1964
ICKES, Harold L. (1874-1952)
July 24, 1933; Sept. 15, 1941
ILLINGWORTH, Cyril G. (1884-1959)
Aug. 11, 1947
INGALLS, David Sinton (1899-   )
Mar. 2, 1931
INGE, William Ralph (1860-1954)
Nov. 24, 1924
INGERSOLL, Jared (1722-1781)
Aug. 6, 1973
INONU, Ismet (1884-1973)
May 19, 1941
INSULL, Samuel (1859-1938)
Nov. 29, 1926; Nov. 4, 1929; May 14, 1934
INUKAI, Ki (1855-1932)
Dec. 28, 1931
IRVING, Clifford (1930-   )
Feb. 21, 1972
IRVING, Washington (1783-1859)
Oct. 2, 1944
IRWIN, Baron (Edward F. L. Wood) (1881-1959)
Apr. 21, 1926; Jan. 15, 1940
IRWIN, James B. (1930-   )
Aug. 9, 1971
ISAACS, Rufus D. (1860-1935)
Oct. 24, 1932
ISELIN, Columbus O'Donnell (1904-   )
July 6, 1959

ITAGAKI, Seishiro (1885-1948)
Aug. 3, 1942

J

JACKSON, Henry M. (1912-)
July 1, 1974; Feb. 17, 1975; Mar. 8, 1976
JACKSON, Jesse (1941-)
Apr. 6, 1970
JACKSON, Kate (1949-)
Nov. 22, 1976
JACKSON, Reggie (1946-)
June 3, 1974
JACKSON, William (1759-1828)
Aug. 6, 1973
JACOBS, Helen Hull (1908-)
Sept. 14, 1936
JACOBSEN, Alfred (1890-1967)
Dec. 1, 1952
JAMIESON, John Kenneth (1911-)
Feb. 18, 1974
JANSEN, William (1887-1968)
Oct. 19, 1953
JANSSEN, David (1930-1980)
Oct. 26, 1959
JARDINE, Alan (1942-)
May 21, 1965
JAVITS, Jacob (1904-)
June 24, 1966
JAWORSKI, Leon (1906-)
Mar. 11, 1974
JEFFERS, Robinson (1887-1962)
Apr. 4, 1932
JEFFERS, William Martin (1876-1953)
July 30, 1945
JEFFERSON, Thomas (1743-1826)
Special 1776 issue, 1976
JENKINS, Ray Howard (1897-)
May 17, 1954
JERITZA, Maria (1887-)
Nov. 12, 1928
JESUS CHRIST (ca. 4 B.C. - 29 A.D.)
Dec. 27, 1928; May 12, 1930; Dec. 26, 1938;
Dec. 23, 1940; Dec. 24, 1945; Dec. 29, 1947;
Dec. 25, 1950; Dec. 24, 1951; Dec. 26, 1955;
Dec. 28, 1959; Feb. 9, 1962; Sept. 27, 1963;
Dec. 25, 1964; June 21, 1971
JINNAH, Mohamed Ali (1876-1948)
Apr. 22, 1946
JOAN OF ARC (1412-1431)
Aug. 4, 1941
JOHN XXIII, Pope (1881-1963)
Nov. 10, 1958; Oct. 5, 1962; Jan. 4, 1963;
June 7, 1963
JOHN, Augustus Edwin (1878-1961)
Sept. 10, 1928; May 31, 1948
JOHN, Elton (1947-)
July 7, 1975
JOHNSON, Arte (1929-)
Oct. 11, 1968
JOHNSON, Edward (1881-1959)
Dec. 21, 1936
JOHNSON, Frank Minis (1918-)
May 12, 1967
JOHNSON, Harold Keith (1913-)
Feb. 5, 1965; Dec. 10, 1965

JOHNSON, Hiram Warren (1866-1945)
Sept. 29, 1924
JOHNSON, Hugh Samuel (1882-1942)
July 3, 1933; Jan. 1, 1934
JOHNSON, Lady Bird (1912-)
Aug. 28, 1964
JOHNSON, Louis Arthur (1891-1966)
Aug. 22, 1938; June 6, 1949
JOHNSON, Luci B. (1947-)
Aug. 5, 1966
JOHNSON, Lyndon Baines (1908-1973)
June 22, 1953; Mar. 17, 1958; Nov. 24, 1958;
Apr. 25, 1960; July 18, 1960; Aug. 15, 1960;
Jan. 27, 1961; Nov. 29, 1963; May 1, 1964;
Sept. 4, 1964; Sept. 25, 1964; Oct. 23, 1964;
Nov. 4, 1964; Jan. 1, 1965; Aug. 6, 1965;
Oct. 29, 1965; Jan. 14, 1966; Nov. 4, 1966;
Apr. 14, 1967; June 30, 1967; Jan. 5, 1968;
Apr. 12, 1968; Nov. 8, 1968
JOHNSON, Nelson T. (1887-1954)
Dec. 11, 1939
JOHNSON, Rafer (1935-)
Aug. 29, 1960
JOHNSON, Virginia (1925-)
May 25, 1970
JOHNSON, William Samuel (1727-1819)
Aug. 6, 1973
JONES, Ben (1881-1961)
May 30, 1949
JONES, Howard Harding (1885-1941)
Nov. 14, 1932
JONES, Jennifer (1919-)
Jan. 8, 1945
JONES, Jesse H. (1874-1956)
Jan. 22, 1934; Jan. 13, 1941
JONES, Robert Tyre (1902-1971)
Aug. 31, 1925; Sept. 22, 1930
JONES, Thomas Victor (1920-)
Oct. 27, 1961
JORDAN, Barbara (1936-)
Jan. 5, 1976; Dec. 20, 1976
JORDAN, David Starr (1851-1931)
June 8, 1931
JORDAN, Hamilton (1944-)
Dec. 20, 1976
JOSEPH, husband of the Virgin Mary
Dec. 26, 1938; Dec. 24, 1945; Dec. 25, 1950;
Dec. 28, 1959
JOYCE, James (1882-1941)
Jan. 29, 1934; May 8, 1939
JUAN CARLOS, King of Spain (1938-)
Nov. 3, 1975; May 3, 1976
JUAN de BORBÓN y BATTENBERG
(1913-)
June 22, 1962
JUDD, Lawrence McCully (1887-1968)
July 8, 1929
JULIANA, Queen of the Netherlands
(1909-)
Sept. 6, 1948; May 3, 1976
JUNG, Carl Gustav (1875-1961)
Feb. 14, 1955

K

KADAR, Janos (1912-1979)
Oct. 3, 1960

KISSINGER, Henry (1923-   )
 Feb. 14, 1969; June 8, 1970; July 26, 1971;
 Feb. 7, 1972; Oct. 30, 1972; Jan. 1, 1973;
 Jan. 29, 1973; Feb. 5, 1973; Sept. 3, 1973;
 Apr. 1, 1974; June 10, 1974; Mar. 10, 1975;
 Apr. 7, 1975; Aug. 25, 1975; Nov. 17, 1975
KLEBERG, Robert J. (1896-   )
 Dec. 15, 1947
KLEIN, Julius (1887-1958)
 May 16, 1927
KNIGHT, Carolyn (1927-   )
 May 30, 1955
KNIGHT, Goodwin (1896-1970)
 May 30, 1955
KNIGHT, Marilyn (1929-   )
 May 30, 1955
KNOWLAND, William Fife (1908-1974)
 Jan. 14, 1957
KNOX, Frank (1874-1944)
 Sept. 7, 1942
KNUDSEN, William S. (1879-1948)
 Jan. 18, 1937; Oct. 7, 1940
KOGA, Mineichi (1885-1943)
 Nov. 8, 1943
KONOYE, Prince of Japan (1891-1945)
 July 26, 1937; July 27, 1940
KOSYGIN, Aleksei (1904-   )
 Oct. 23, 1964; Nov. 13, 1964; June 30, 1967;
 Nov. 10, 1967; Apr. 1, 1974
KOUSSEVITZKY, Sergei A. (1874-1951)
 Oct. 13, 1930; Oct. 10, 1938
KOZLOV, Frol Romanovich (1909-1965)
 July 13, 1959
KRAFT, Christopher Columbus (1924-   )
 Aug. 27, 1965
KRAMER, John Albert "Jake" (1921-   )
 Sept. 1, 1947
KREISLER, Fritz (1875-1962)
 Feb. 2, 1925
KREUGER, Ivar (1880-1932)
 Oct. 28, 1929
KRISHNA MENON, Vengalil Krishnan
 (1896-1974)
 Feb. 2, 1962
KRUEGER, Walter (1881-1967)
 Jan. 29, 1945
KRUPP, Alfried (1907-1967)
 Aug. 19, 1957
KUBITSCHEK, Juscelino (1902-1976)
 Feb. 13, 1956
KUESTER, Gustav T. (1888-   )
 Apr. 29, 1946
KY, Nguyen Cao (1930-   )
 Feb. 18, 1966

L

LaFOLLETTE, Philip Fox (1897-1965)
 Oct. 22, 1928
LaFOLLETTE, Robert Marion (1855-1925)
 Dec. 3, 1923
LaFOLLETTE, Robert Marion (1895-1953)
 Dec. 12, 1927; Nov. 19, 1934
LaGUARDIA, Fiorello H. (1882-1947)
 Oct. 23, 1933; Aug. 2, 1937
LAHR, Bert (1895-1967)
 Oct. 1, 1951

LAIRD, Melvin (1922-   )
 Aug. 15, 1969; Aug. 29, 1969
LALLA AISHA, Princess of Morocco
 (1930-   )
 Nov. 11, 1957
LAMONT, Thomas William (1870-1948)
 Nov. 14, 1929
LAND, Edwin Herbert (1909-   )
 June 26, 1972
LAND, Emory Scott (1879-1971)
 Mar. 31, 1941
LANDON, Alfred (1887-   )
 May 18, 1936
LANDRY, Greg (1946-   )
 Oct. 1, 1972
LANG, Alois (1892-1971)
 May 12, 1930
LANG, Anton (1875-1938)
 Dec. 17, 1923
LANG, Cosmo Gordon (1864-1945)
 Apr. 1, 1929; May 24, 1937
LANG, Jessica (1949-   )
 Oct. 25, 1976
LANGDON, John (1741-1819)
 Aug. 6, 1973
LANGLE, Eugenie (1896-   )
 Aug. 3, 1970
LANGLIE, Arthur B. (1900-1966)
 Sept. 3, 1956
LANGMUIR, Irving (1881-1957)
 Aug. 28, 1950
LANSDOWNE, Zachary (1888-   )
 Sept. 14, 1925
LANZA, Mario (1921-   )
 Aug. 6, 1951
LAPHAM, Roger D. (1883-1966)
 July 15, 1946
LARAGH, John Henry (1925-   )
 Jan. 13, 1975
LARSON, Leonard Winfield (1898-   )
 July 7, 1961
LATTNER, John (1931-   )
 Nov. 9, 1953
LAUGHTON, Charles (1899-1962)
 Mar. 31, 1952
LAUSCHE, Frank John (1895-   )
 Feb. 20, 1956
LAVAL, Pierre (1883-1945)
 Sept. 28, 1931; Jan. 4, 1932; Apr. 27, 1942
LAWES, Lewis Edward (1883-1947)
 Nov. 18, 1929
LAWFORD, Patricia Kennedy (1924-   )
 July 11, 1960
LAWRENCE, Andrea Mead (1933-   )
 Jan. 21, 1952
LAWRENCE, Ernest Orlando (1901-1958)
 Nov. 1, 1937
LAWRENCE, Gertrude (1901-1952)
 Feb. 3, 1941
LAWRENCE, T. E. (1888-1935)
 Nov. 28, 1932
LAWRENCE, William (1850-1941)
 Jan. 28, 1924
LAYNE, Robert Lawrence "Bobby" (1927-   )
 Nov. 29, 1954
LAZARUS, Ralph (1914-   )
 May 31, 1963

LONGWORTH, Alice Roosevelt (1884-1980)
Feb. 7, 1927
LONGWORTH, Nicholas (1869-1931)
Mar. 9, 1925; Dec. 16, 1929
LOPEZ, Trini (1937-   )
May 21, 1965
LOPEZ-MATEOS, Adolfo (1910-1969)
Dec. 8, 1958
LOREN, Sophia (1934-   )
Apr. 6, 1962
LOUDON, John Hugo (1906-   )
May 9, 1960
LOUIS XIV, King of France (1638-1715)
Feb. 8, 1963
LOUIS, Joe (1914-   )
Sept. 29, 1941
LOVE, Mike (1941-   )
May 21, 1965
LOVELL, James A. (1928-   )
Jan. 3, 1969; Apr. 27, 1970
LOVETT, Robert A. (1895-   )
Feb. 9, 1942; Mar. 29, 1948
LOWDEN, Florence Pullman (1869-1937)
Nov. 28, 1927
LOWDEN, Frank Orren (1861-1943)
Aug. 13, 1923; Nov. 28, 1927
LOWELL, Abbott Lawrence (1856-1943)
June 21, 1926
LOWELL, Amy (1874-1925)
Mar. 2, 1925
LOWELL, Robert (1917-1977)
June 2, 1967
LUCE, Henry Robinson (1898-1967)
Mar. 10, 1967
LUCKMAN, Charles (1909-   )
June 10, 1946
LUDENDORFF, Erich F. W. (1865-1937)
Nov. 19, 1923
LULL, Richard Swann (1867-1957)
June 1, 1925
LUNT, Alfred (1893-1977)
Nov. 8, 1937
LUSK, Robert Emmett (1902-   )
Oct. 12, 1962
LUTHER, Martin (1483-1546)
Mar. 24, 1967
LYAUTEY, Hubert (1854-1934)
May 11, 1931
LYONS, Joseph Aloysius (1879-1939)
July 8, 1935

M

McADOO, William Gibbs (1863-1941)
Jan. 7, 1924; Aug. 29, 1932
McAFEE, Mildred (1900-   )
Mar. 12, 1945
MacARTHUR, Douglas (1880-1964)
Mar. 12, 1935; Dec. 29, 1941; Mar. 30, 1942;
Oct. 30, 1944; Aug. 27, 1945; May 9, 1949;
July 10, 1950; Apr. 30, 1951
MacARTHUR, Douglas (1909-   )
June 27, 1960
MACAULEY, Alvan (1872-1952)
July 22, 1929; Nov. 4, 1935
McBRIDE, Francis Scott (1872-1955)
June 3, 1929

McCARDELL, Claire (1905-   )
May 2, 1955
McCARTHY, Eugene (1916-   )
Mar. 22, 1968; July 26, 1968
McCARTHY, Glenn (1908-   )
Feb. 13, 1950
McCARTHY, Joseph Raymond (1908-1957)
Oct. 22, 1951; Mar. 8, 1954
McCARTHY, Michael W. (1903-   )
May 31, 1963
McCARTNEY, Paul (1942-   )
Sept. 22, 1967; May 31, 1976
McCLELLAN, John Little (1896-1977)
May 27, 1957
McCLORY, Robert (1908-   )
July 29, 1974
McCLOY, John Jay (1895-   )
June 20, 1949
McCONNELL, John Paul (1908-   )
Feb. 5, 1965
McCORD, James W. (1927-   )
Apr. 30, 1973; May 28, 1973
McCORMACK, John (1891-   )
Feb. 2, 1959; Jan. 19, 1962; May 5, 1967
McCORMICK, Robert Rutherford (1880-
1955)
May 7, 1928; Nov. 2, 1936; June 9, 1947
McCORMICK, Ruth Hanna (1880-1944)
Apr. 23, 1928
MacCRACKEN, Henry Noble (1880-1970)
Oct. 1, 1934
McDIVITT, James Alton (1929-   )
June 11, 1965
McDONALD, David John (1902-1979)
July 9, 1956
McDONALD, David Lamar (1907-   )
Feb. 5, 1965
MacDONALD, Ramsay (1866-1937)
Aug. 18, 1924; Oct. 7, 1929; Sept. 7, 1931
McDONNELL, James S. (1899-   )
Mar. 31, 1967
McELROY, Neil Hosler (1905-1973)
Oct. 5, 1953; Jan. 13, 1958
McGAREL, Douglas (1872-1950)
Apr. 1, 1929
McGILLICUDDY, Cornelius (1862-1956)
Apr. 11, 1927
McGINLEY, Phyllis (1905-1978)
June 18, 1965
McGOVERN, Eleanor (1920-   )
Oct. 9, 1972
McGOVERN, George (1922-   )
May 8, 1972; July 24, 1972; Aug. 14, 1972;
Oct. 2, 1972
McGRADY, Edward Francis (1872-1960)
Nov. 23, 1936
MacGRAW, Ali (1939-   )
Jan. 11, 1971
McGRAW, John Joseph (1873-1934)
June 27, 1927
McGUIRE, Dorothy (1919-   )
Jan. 8, 1945
MACHADO, Gerardo (1871-1939)
Jan. 19, 1931; May 15, 1933
McHENRY, James (1753-1816)
Aug. 6, 1973

McINTYRE, Marvin Hunter (1878-1943)
Dec. 17, 1934
MACK, Connie (1862-1956)
Apr. 11, 1927
McKAY, Douglas (1893-1959)
Aug. 23, 1954; Apr. 16, 1956
McKEE, Joseph Vincent (1889-1956)
Oct. 23, 1933
McKELVIE, Samuel Roy (1881-1956)
June 1, 1931
McKENNA, Reginald (1863-1943)
Mar. 3, 1924
McKONE, John (1933-)
Feb. 3, 1961
McLAIN, Denny (1944-)
Sept. 13, 1968
MacLAINE, Shirley (1934-)
June 22, 1959
MACMILLAN, Harold (1894-)
Jan. 21, 1957; Oct. 19, 1959; May 23, 1960
McNAIR, Lesley James (1883-1944)
Dec. 28, 1942
McNAMARA, Robert S. (1916-)
Apr. 7, 1961; Feb. 15, 1963; July 8, 1966
McNAMEE, Graham (1888-1942)
Oct. 3, 1927
McNAUGHTON, Andrew G. L. (1887-1966)
Aug. 10, 1942
McNINCH, Frank Ramsay (1873-1950)
May 16, 1938
McNUTT, Paul Vories (1891-1955)
July 10, 1939; Oct. 5, 1942
MADISON, James (1751-1836)
Aug. 6, 1973
MAGILL, Roswell (1895-1963)
Jan. 31, 1938
MAGLOIRE, Paul Eugene (1907-)
Feb. 22, 1954
MAGRUDER, Jeb Stuart (1935-)
Apr. 30, 1973
MAGSAYSAY, Ramon (1907-1957)
Nov. 26, 1951
MAHESH, Maharishi (1911-)
Oct. 13, 1975
MAILER, Norman (1923-)
July 16, 1973
MALAN, Daniel F. (1874-1959)
May 5, 1952
MALENKOV, Georgi M. (1902-)
Mar. 20, 1950; Oct. 6, 1952; Mar. 23, 1953
MALIK, Jacob (1906-1980)
Aug. 21, 1950
MALINOVSKY, Rodion (1898-1967)
May 30, 1960
MALRAUX, Andre (1901-1976)
Nov. 7, 1938; July 18, 1955
MANN, Thomas (1875-1955)
June 11, 1934
MANN, Thomas C. (1913-)
Jan. 31, 1964
MANNERHEIM, Carl Gustaf Emil von (1867-1951)
Feb. 5, 1940
MANNERS, Diana (1892-)
Feb. 15, 1926
MANNING, Harry (1897-1974)
June 23, 1952

MANSFIELD, Mike (1903-)
Mar. 20, 1964; Jan. 15, 1973
MANSTEIN, Fritz (1887-1973)
Jan. 10, 1944
MANTLE, Mickey (1932-)
June 15, 1953
MANUEL, Richard (1946-)
Jan. 12, 1969
MAO, Tse-Tung (1893-1976)
Feb. 7, 1949; Dec. 11, 1950; Dec. 1, 1958;
Aug. 8, 1960; July 21, 1961; Nov. 30, 1962;
Sept. 13, 1963; Jan. 13, 1967; June 13, 1969;
Mar. 6, 1972; Apr. 1, 1974; Sept. 20, 1976
MARCONI, Guglielmo (1874-1937)
Dec. 6, 1926
MARCOS, Ferdinand Edralin (1917-)
Oct. 21, 1966
MARGARET, Princess of Great Britain
(1930-)
June 13, 1949; Nov. 7, 1955
MARGRETHE, Queen of Denmark
(1940-)
May 3, 1976
MARGULIS, Gordon (1931-)
Dec. 13, 1976
MARICHAL, Juan (1939-)
June 10, 1966
MARIE, Queen of Romania (1875-1938)
Aug. 4, 1924
MARQUAND, John P. (1893-1960)
Mar. 7, 1949
MARSHALL, George Catlett (1880-1959)
July 29, 1940; Oct. 19, 1942; Jan. 3, 1944;
Mar. 25, 1946; Mar. 10, 1947; Jan. 5, 1948
MARSHALL, Thurgood (1908-)
Sept. 19, 1955; July 22, 1974
MARTHA, Princess of Sweden (1901-1954)
Mar. 25, 1929
MARTIN, Dick (1922-)
Oct. 11, 1968
MARTIN, Edward (1879-1967)
Oct. 28, 1946
MARTIN, Glenn L. (1886-1955)
May 29, 1939
MARTIN, Joe (1884-1968)
Apr. 11, 1938; Sept. 9, 1940; Nov. 18, 1946;
Aug. 9, 1954
MARTIN, William McChesney (1907-)
Aug. 15, 1938; Sept. 10, 1956
MARX, Chico (1891-1961)
Aug. 15, 1932
MARX, Groucho (1895-1977)
Aug. 15, 1932; Dec. 31, 1951
MARX, Harpo (1893-1964)
Aug. 15, 1932
MARX, Karl Heinrich (1818-1883)
Feb. 23, 1948; Sept. 13, 1963
MARX, Louis (1896-)
Dec. 12, 1955
MARX, Zeppo (1901-1979)
Aug. 15, 1932
MARY, mother of Jesus
Dec. 26, 1938; Dec. 23, 1940; Dec. 24, 1945;
Dec. 29, 1947; Dec. 25, 1950; Dec. 24, 1951;
Apr. 11, 1955; Dec. 26, 1955; Dec. 28, 1959;
Feb. 9, 1962

MARY COLUMBA (1892-   )
Apr. 11, 1955
MARY LILIANE de RETHY, Queen of
Belgium (1911-   )
July 18, 1949
MARY of TECK, consort of George V
(1867-1953)
May 30, 1927; Mar. 17, 1930; Oct. 27, 1930
MASARYK, Jan (1886-1948)
Mar. 27, 1944
MASARYK, Thomas Garrigue (1850-1937)
Mar. 5, 1928
MASCAGNI, Pietro (1863-1945)
Sept. 6, 1926
MASTERS, William Howell (1916-   )
May 25, 1970
MATHIAS, Bob (1931-   )
July 21, 1952
MATHIAS, Charles (1923-   )
Jan. 15, 1973
MATISSE, Henri (1869-1954)
Oct. 20, 1930
MATLOVICH, Leonard (1943-   )
Sept. 8, 1975
MATSUOKA, Yosuke (1880-1946)
July 7, 1941
MATSUSHITA, Konosuke (1894-   )
Feb. 23, 1962
MAUCH, Billy (1924-   )
May 3, 1937
MAUCH, Bobby (1924-   )
May 3, 1937
MAULDIN, Bill (1921-   )
July 21, 1961
MAYO, Charles H. (1865-1939)
June 22, 1925
MAYS, Willie (1931-   )
July 26, 1954
MAZUROV, Kirill (1917-   )
Mar. 29, 1971
MBOYA, Tom (1930-1969)
Mar. 7, 1960
MEANY, George (1894-1980)
Mar. 21, 1955; Sept. 6, 1971
MEDINA, Harold (1888-   )
Oct. 24, 1949
MEDLEY, Bill (1940-   )
May 21, 1965
MEHTA, Zubin (1936-   )
Jan. 19, 1968
MEIKLEJOHN, Alexander (1872-1964)
Oct. 1, 1928
MEIR, Golda (1898-1978)
Sept. 19, 1969; Apr. 1, 1974
MELBA, Nellie (1861-1931)
Apr. 11, 1927
MELCHIOR, wise man of the Three Magi
Dec. 26, 1938; Dec. 23, 1940; Dec. 28, 1959;
Dec. 30, 1974
MELCHIOR, Lauritz (1890-1973)
Jan. 22, 1940
MELLER, Raquel (1888-   )
Apr. 26, 1926
MELLON, Andrew William (1855-1937)
July 2, 1923; May 28, 1928
MELLON, Richard King (1899-1970)
Oct. 3, 1949

MENDERES, Adnan (1899-1961)
Feb. 3, 1958
MENDES-FRANCE, Pierre (1907-   )
July 12, 1954
MENNINGER, William C. (1899-1966)
Oct. 25, 1948
MENON, Krishna (1896-1974)
Feb. 2, 1962
MENOTTI, Gian-Carlo (1911-   )
May 1, 1950
MENUHIN, Yehudi (1916-   )
Feb. 22, 1932
MENZHINSKY, Viacheslav (1874-1934)
Feb. 23, 1931
MENZIES, Robert Gordon (1894-1978)
Apr. 4, 1960
MERCK, George W. (1894-1957)
Aug. 18, 1952
MERMAN, Ethel (1909-   )
Oct. 28, 1940
MERRICK, David (1911-   )
Mar. 25, 1966
MESSERSMITH, George (1883-1960)
Dec. 2, 1946
MESTA, Perle (1890-1975)
Mar. 14, 1949
METZENBAUM, Howard (1917-   )
Oct. 26, 1970
MEYER, Eugene (1875-1959)
May 30, 1932
MEYNER, Robert Baumle (1908-   )
Nov. 24, 1958
MICHAEL, King of Romania (1921-   )
Aug. 1, 1927
MICKELSON, Merlyn Francis (1927-   )
Dec. 3, 1965
MIFFLIN, Thomas (1744-1800)
Aug. 6, 1973
MIHAILOVICH, Draja (1893-1946)
May 25, 1942
MIKOLAJCZYK, Stanislaw (1901-1966)
Feb. 11, 1946
MIKOYAN, Anastas (1896-1978)
Sept. 16, 1957
MILBURN, Devereux (1881-1942)
Sept. 5, 1927
MILCH, Erhard (1892-1972)
Aug. 26, 1940
MILLER, George William (1926-   )
Mar. 7, 1969
MILLETT, Kate (1934-   )
Aug. 31, 1970
MILLIKAN, Robert Andrews (1868-1953)
Apr. 25, 1927
MILLS, Ogden Livingston (1884-1937)
Oct. 11, 1926; July 13, 1931
MILLS, Wilbur Daigh (1910-   )
Feb. 2, 1959; Jan. 11, 1963; Jan. 5, 1968;
Jan. 15, 1973
MINDSZENTY, Jozsef (1892-1975)
Feb. 14, 1949
MINER, Dwight (1905-   )
May 6, 1966
MINER, Leroy (1882-   )
July 27, 1936
MINH, Van Doung (1916-   )
Nov. 8, 1963

MINNELLI, Liza (1946-   )
Feb. 28, 1972
MIRO-CARDONA, José (1903-   )
Apr. 28, 1961
MITCHELL, John (1913-   )
June 8, 1970; Apr. 30, 1973; May 21, 1973;
July 23, 1973
MITCHELL, Joni (1950-   )
Dec. 16, 1974
MITCHELL, Martha (1918-1976)
Nov. 30, 1970
MITCHELL, William DeWitt (1874-1955)
Jan. 27, 1930
MOHAMMED V, King of Morocco
(1910-   )
Apr. 22, 1957
MOHAMMED REZA PAHLAVI, Shah of
Iran (1919-   )
Dec. 17, 1945; Sept. 12, 1960; Nov. 4, 1974
MOLA, Emilio (1887-1937)
Aug. 24, 1936
MOLEY, Raymond (1886-1975)
May 8, 1933
MOLOTOV, Viacheslav (1890-   )
July 15, 1940; Oct. 25, 1943; Aug. 19, 1946;
Apr. 20, 1953
MOND, Alfred Moritz (1868-1930)
Oct. 29, 1928
MONDALE, Joan (1931-   )
July 26, 1976
MONDALE, Walter (1933-   )
Jan. 15, 1973; July 26, 1976; Dec. 20, 1976
MONK, Thelonius (1918-   )
Feb. 28, 1964
MONNET, Jean (1888-1979)
Oct. 6, 1961
MONROE, James (1758-1831)
Sept. 21, 1962
MONROE, Marilyn (1926-1962)
May 14, 1956; July 16, 1973
MONTESSORI, Maria (1870-1952)
Feb. 3, 1930
MONTGOMERY, Bernard Law (1887-1976)
Feb. 1, 1943; July 10, 1944
MOODY, Daniel J. (1893-1966)
June 10, 1929
MOOK, Hubertus (1895-1965)
Aug. 18, 1941
MOORE, Francis D. (1914-   )
May 3, 1963
MOORE, Henry (1898-   )
Sept. 21, 1959
MOORE, Joe (1934-   )
Oct. 24, 1955
MOORE, Mary Tyler (1937-   )
Oct. 28, 1974
MORAN, James Martin (1919-   )
Mar. 24, 1961
MOREAU, Jeanne (1928-   )
Mar. 5, 1965
MORGAN, John Pierpont (1867-1943)
Sept. 24, 1923; Feb. 25, 1929, Jan. 20, 1936
MORGENTHAU, Henry (1891-1967)
Sept. 17, 1934
MORITA, Akio (1921-   )
May 10, 1971

MOROZOV, Platon (1906-   )
Feb. 24, 1961
MORRIS, Gouverneur (1752-1816)
Aug. 6, 1973
MORRISON, DeLesseps (1912-   )
Nov. 24, 1947
MORRISON, Harry W. (1885-1971)
May 3, 1954
MORRISON, Herbert Stanley (1888-1965)
July 29, 1946
MORROW, Dwight Whitney (1873-1931)
Oct. 12, 1925; Sept. 29, 1930
MORSE, Wayne Lyman (1900-1974)
Jan. 17, 1955
MORTIMER, Charles Greenough (1900-   )
Dec. 7, 1959
MOSBACHER, Bus (1922-   )
Aug. 18, 1967
MOSES, Anna Mary Robertson "Grandma"
(1860-1961)
Dec. 28, 1953
MOSES, Robert (1888-   )
June 5, 1964
MOSLEY, Oswald Ernald (1896-   )
Mar. 16, 1931
MOSSADEQ, Mohamed (1880-1967)
June 4, 1951; Jan. 7, 1952
MOUNTBATTEN, Louis (1900-1979)
June 8, 1942
MOYERS, Bill Don (1934-   )
Oct. 29, 1965
MOYNIHAN, Daniel Patrick (1927-   )
July 28, 1967; Jan. 26, 1976
MUMFORD, Lewis (1895-   )
Apr. 18, 1938
MUNCH, Charles (1891-1968)
Dec. 19, 1949
MUNDELEIN, George William (1872-1939)
May 31, 1926
MUNI, Paul (1895-1967)
Aug. 16, 1937
MUÑOZ-MARÍN, Luis (1898-   )
May 2, 1949; June 23, 1958
MUNSEL, Patrice (1925-   )
Dec. 3, 1951
MURCHISON, Clinton W. (1895-1969)
May 24, 1954
MURCHISON, Clinton W. (1924-   )
June 16, 1961
MURCHISON, John Dabney (1922-1979)
June 16, 1961
MURPHY, Frank (1890-1949)
Aug. 28, 1939
MURPHY, George (1902-   )
Oct. 16, 1964; Oct. 26, 1970
MURPHY, Robert Daniel (1894-1978)
Aug. 25, 1958
MURRAY, John Courtney (1904-1967)
Dec. 12, 1960
MURRAY, Philip (1886-1952)
Jan. 27, 1941; Jan. 21, 1946; Aug. 4, 1952
MURRAY, William Henry (1869-1956)
Feb. 29, 1932
MURROW, Edward R. (1908-1965)
Sept. 30, 1957
MUSIAL, Stan (1920-   )
Sept. 5, 1949

MUSICK, Edwin C. (1894-1938)
Dec. 2, 1935
MUSKIE, Edmund (1914-)
Sept. 6, 1968; Sept. 13, 1971
MUSSOLINI, Benito (1883-1945)
Aug. 6, 1923; July 12, 1926; Oct. 28, 1935;
July 20, 1936; Jan. 2, 1939; Apr. 8, 1940;
June 24, 1940; June 9, 1941; June 21, 1943
MUSSOLINI, Bruno (1918-)
Oct. 28, 1935
MUSSOLINI, Vittorio (1917-)
Oct. 28, 1935

N

NABOKOV, Helene (1876-1937)
May 23, 1969
NABOKOV, Vladimir (1899-1977)
May 23, 1969
NADER, Ralph (1934-)
Dec. 12, 1969
NAGANO, Osami (1888-1947)
Feb. 15, 1943
NAGUIB, Mohammed (1901-)
Sept. 8, 1952
NAMATH, Joe (1943-)
Oct. 16, 1972
NAPOLEON BONAPARTE (1769-1821)
July 14, 1941; Dec. 22, 1952
NASSER, Gamal Abdel (1918-1970)
Sept. 26, 1955; Aug. 27, 1956; July 28, 1958;
Mar. 29, 1963; May 16, 1969; Oct. 12, 1970
NAVARRE, Henri Eugene (1898-)
Sept. 28, 1953
NEHRU, Jawaharlal (1889-1964)
Aug. 24, 1942; Oct. 17, 1949; May 7, 1951;
July 30, 1956; Dec. 14, 1959; Nov. 30, 1962
NELSON, Donald Marr (1888-1959)
Feb. 24, 1941
NESMEYANOV, Aleksandr (1900-)
June 2, 1958
NESTERENKO, Alexei (1904-)
Feb. 24, 1961
NEUBERGER, Richard Lewis (1912-1960)
Jan. 17, 1955
NEUTRA, Richard J. (1892-1970)
Aug. 15, 1949
NEVILLE, Wendell Cushing (1870-1930)
Dec. 23, 1929
NEW, Harry Stewart (1858-1937)
Feb. 16, 1925
NEWALL, Cyril (1886-1963)
Oct. 23, 1939
NEWHOUSE, Samuel I. (1895-1979)
July 27, 1962
NEYLAN, John Francis (1885-1960)
Apr. 29, 1935
NHU, Tran Le Xuan (1925-)
Aug. 9, 1963
NIARCHOS, Starvos (1909-)
Aug. 6, 1956
NICHOLS, Mike (1931-)
June 15, 1970
NICHOLSON, Jack (1937-)
Aug. 12, 1974
NICKLAUS, Jack (1940-)
June 29, 1962

NIEBUHR, Reinhold (1892-1971)
Mar. 8, 1948
NIEMOLLER, Martin (1892-)
Jan. 2, 1939; Dec. 23, 1940
NIKOLAYEV, Andrian G. (1931-)
Aug. 24, 1962
NILSSON, Harry (1942-)
Feb. 12, 1973
NIMITZ, Chester William (1885-1966)
May 18, 1942; Feb. 26, 1945
NIXON, Patricia (1912-)
Feb. 29, 1960; Mar. 6, 1972; June 5, 1972;
Oct. 2, 1972; Oct. 9, 1972; Oct. 7, 1974
NIXON, Richard (1913-)
Aug. 25, 1952; Nov. 10, 1952; Jan. 18, 1954;
Oct. 10, 1955; Apr. 16, 1956; Nov. 5, 1956;
Nov. 12, 1956; Dec. 9, 1957; Aug. 3, 1959;
Aug. 1, 1960; Aug. 15, 1960; Oct. 31, 1960;
July 21, 1961; Apr. 14, 1967; Mar. 8, 1968;
July 26, 1968; Aug. 16, 1968; Nov. 15, 1968;
Jan. 24, 1969; Feb. 28, 1969; Aug. 15, 1969;
Oct. 24, 1969; Nov. 21, 1969; Apr. 20, 1970;
June 8, 1970; Oct. 5, 1970; Oct. 26, 1970;
July 26, 1971; Aug. 30, 1971; Jan. 3, 1972;
Mar. 6, 1972; May 1, 1972; June 5, 1972;
Aug. 28, 1972; Oct. 2, 1972; Nov. 20, 1972;
Jan. 1, 1973; Jan. 29, 1973; Apr. 30, 1973;
May 14, 1973; June 4, 1973; June 18, 1973;
July 9, 1973; July 30, 1973; Aug. 20, 1973;
Aug. 27, 1973; Oct. 8, 1973; Oct. 29, 1973;
Nov. 5, 1973; Apr. 15, 1974; May 13, 1974;
June 24, 1974; July 1, 1974; July 22, 1974;
Sept. 16, 1974
NKRUMAH, Kwame (1909-1972)
Feb. 9, 1953
NOBLE, Percy (1880-1955)
Apr. 28, 1941
NOMURA, Kichisaburo (1877-1964)
Sept. 22, 1941
NOONE, Peter (1949-)
May 21, 1965
NORDHOFF, Heinz (1899-1968)
Feb. 15, 1954
NORMAN, Montagu Collett (1871-1950)
Aug. 19, 1929
NORRIS, Geoge William (1861-1944)
Jan. 11, 1937
NORRIS, Kathleen (1880-1966)
Jan. 28, 1935
NORSTAD, Lauris (1907-)
Dec. 16, 1957
NORTH, Warren (1914-)
Mar. 9, 1959
NOVAK, Kim (1933-)
July 29, 1957
NOVIKOV, Aleksandr (1902-)
July 31, 1944
NOVOTNY, Antonin (1905-1975)
Oct. 3, 1960
NU, U (1907-)
Aug. 30, 1954
NUGENT, Patrick (1943-)
Aug. 5, 1966
NUREYEV, Rudolf (1939-)
Apr. 16, 1965
NURI-AL-SAID (1888-1958)
June 17, 1957

NUTHALL, Betty (1912-)
July 6, 1931
NYERERE, Julius K. (1922-)
Mar. 13, 1964

O

OBERHOLTZER, Kenneth Edison (1903-)
Feb. 20, 1950
O'BRIAN, Hugh (1927-)
Mar. 30, 1959
O'BRIEN, John Patrick (1873-1951)
Oct. 23, 1933
O'BRIEN, Lawrence F. (1917-)
Sept. 1, 1961
O'BRIEN, Parry (1932-)
Dec. 3, 1956
OCHS, Adolph S. (1858-1935)
Sept. 1, 1924
O'CONNELL, William Henry (1859-1944)
Dec. 24, 1928
O'CONNOR, Carroll (1925-)
Sept. 25, 1972
ODETS, Clifford (1906-1963)
Dec. 5, 1938
O'DWYER, William (1890-1964)
June 7, 1948
OGILVY, David MacKenzie (1911-)
Oct. 12, 1962
OGLE, William E. (1917-)
May 4, 1962
OJUKWU, Odumegwu (1933-)
Aug. 23, 1968
OLAF V, King of Norway (1903-)
Mar. 25, 1929
OLIVIER, Laurence (1907-)
Apr. 8, 1946
OLMSTEAD, Bruce (1936-)
Feb. 3, 1961
O'MALLEY, Walter (1903-1979)
Apr. 28, 1958
ONASSIS, Aristotle (1900-1975)
Oct. 25, 1968
ONASSIS, Jacqueline (1929-)
July 11, 1960; Jan. 20, 1961; Oct. 25, 1968
O'NEILL, Eugene (1888-1953)
Mar. 17, 1924; Feb. 13, 1928; Nov. 2, 1931; Oct. 21, 1946
O'NEILL, Thomas "Tip" (1913-)
Jan. 15, 1973; Feb. 4, 1974
OPPENHEIM, Edward Phillips (1866-1946)
Sept. 12, 1927
OPPENHEIMER, Robert (1904-1967)
Nov. 8, 1948; June 14, 1954
ORTIZ-RUBIO, Pascual (1877-1963)
Dec. 30, 1929
OSBORN, Henry Fairfield (1857-1935)
Dec. 31, 1928
OSMAN ALI KHAN, Nizam of Hyderabad (1886-1967)
Feb. 22, 1937
OSWALD, Lee Harvey (1939-1963)
Oct. 2, 1964
OSWALD, Marina (1942-)
Feb. 14, 1964
OTT, Mel (1909-)
July 2, 1945

OTTINGER, Richard (1929-)
Oct. 26, 1970
OWINGS, Alexander (1903-)
Aug. 2, 1968
OXNAM, Bromley (1891-1963)
Sept. 13, 1948

P

PAAR, Jack (1917-)
Aug. 18, 1958
PACE, Frank (1913-)
Jan. 20, 1958
PACKWOOD, Bob (1933-)
Jan. 15, 1973
PADEREWSKI, Ignace Jan (1860-1941)
Jan. 23, 1928; Feb. 27, 1939
PADILLA, Ezequiel (1890-1971)
Apr. 6, 1942
PAGE, Irvine H. (1901-)
Oct. 31, 1955
PAINLEVE, Paul (1863-1933)
Nov. 9, 1925
PALEY, William S. (1902-)
Sept. 19, 1938
PALMER, Arnold (1929-)
May 2, 1960
PAPAGOS, Alexander (1883-1955)
Dec. 16, 1940
PAPEN, Franz von (1879-1969)
July 4, 1932
PARENT, Bernie Marcel (1945-)
Feb. 24, 1975
PARNELL, Harvey (1880-1936)
June 10, 1929
PARRAN, Thomas (1892-1968)
Oct. 26, 1936
PARSEGHIAN, Ara Raoul (1923-)
Nov. 20, 1964
PASTERNAK, Boris (1890-1960)
Dec. 15, 1958
PATCH, Alexander M. (1889-1945)
Aug. 28, 1944
PATEL, Vallabhbhai (1873-1950)
Jan. 27, 1947
PATERSON, William (1745-1806)
Aug. 6, 1973
PATRICK, Mason Mathews (1863-1942)
July 9, 1923
PATTERSON, Alicia (1907-)
Sept. 13, 1954
PATTERSON, John (1921-) June 2, 1961
PATTERSON, Joseph Medill (1879-1946)
May 7, 1928; Nov. 2, 1936
PATTERSON, William A. (1899-)
Apr. 21, 1947; May 31, 1963
PATTON, George Smith (1885-1945)
Apr. 12, 1943; July 26, 1943; Apr. 9, 1945
PATTON, Melvin Emery (1925-)
Aug. 2, 1948
PAUKER, Ana (1893-1960)
Sept. 20, 1948
PAUL VI, Pope (1897-1978)
June 28, 1963; Sept. 24, 1965; Nov. 22, 1968
PAUL, Prince of Yugoslavia (1893-1976)
Dec. 12, 1938

PAUL, Saint (died ca. 67 A.D.)
Apr. 18, 1960
PAULING, Linus Paul (1901-   )
Jan. 2, 1961
PAYNE, John Barton (1855-1935)
May 12, 1923
PEARSON, Drew (1897-1969)
Dec. 13, 1948
PEARSON, Lester B. (1897-1972)
Apr. 19, 1963
PECK, Gregory (1917-   )
Jan. 15, 1948
PECORA, Ferdinand (1882-1971)
June 12, 1933
PEEK, George N. (1873-1943)
Nov. 6, 1933
PELLEY, John Jeremiah (1878-1946)
Feb. 8, 1937
PEPPER, Claude (1900-   )
May 2, 1938
PERCY, Charles Harting (1919-   )
Sept. 18, 1964; Nov. 18, 1966
PEREIRA, William Leonard (1909-   )
Sept. 6, 1963
PEREZ-JIMENEZ, Marcos (1914-   )
Feb. 28, 1955
PERKINS, Frances, (1882-1965)
Aug. 14, 1933
PERKINS, Marlin (1905-   )
July 7, 1947
PERÓN, Eva (1919-1952)
July 14, 1947; May 21, 1951
PERÓN, Juan Domingo (1895-1974)
Nov. 27, 1944; May 21, 1951; Mar. 30, 1962
PERRY, Frederick John (1910-   )
Sept. 3, 1934
PERRY, James DeWolff (1871-1947)
. Oct. 15, 1934
PERSHING, John (1860-1948)
Aug. 11, 1924; Nov. 15, 1943
PETAIN, Henri Philippe (1856-1951)
June 17, 1940
PETERSON, Rudolph A. (1905-   )
May 31, 1963; Dec. 30, 1966
PETRILLO, James Caesar (1892-   )
Jan. 26, 1948
PEW, Joseph N. (1886-1963)
May 6, 1940
PFEIFFER, Jane Cahill (1932-   )
Dec. 20, 1976
PHILIP, Prince, consort of Elizabeth II
(1921-   )
Oct. 21, 1957
PHILLIPS, William (1878-1968)
Dec. 9, 1935
PHUMIPHON, King of Thailand (1927-   )
Apr. 3, 1950; May 27, 1966
PICASSO, Pablo (1881-1973)
Feb. 13, 1939; June 26, 1950
PICKERING, William H. (1910-   )
Mar. 8, 1963; July 23, 1965
PIKE, James A. (1913-1969)
Nov. 11, 1966
PILSUDSKI, Josef (1867-1935)
June 7, 1926
PINAY, Antoine (1891-   )
Dec. 22, 1952

PINCHOT, Gifford (1865-1946)
Nov. 23, 1925
PINCKNEY, Charles C. (1746-1825)
Aug. 6, 1973
PIUS XI, Pope (1857-1939)
June 16, 1924, Dec. 29, 1930; Apr. 3, 1933
PIUS XII, Pope (1876-1958)
Oct. 19, 1936; Aug. 16, 1943; Dec. 14, 1953
PLAYFAIR, Patrick Henry Lyon (1889-   )
May 27, 1940
PLUNKETT, Jim (1947-   )
Oct. 1, 1972
PODGORNY, Nikolai (1903-   )
June 5, 1972
POINCARE, Raymond (1860-1934)
Mar. 24, 1924
POINDEXTER, Joseph Boyd (1869-1951)
July 23, 1934
POLAINSKY, Dimitry (1917-   )
May 29, 1971
POMPIDOU, Georges (1911-1974)
May 9, 1969; Apr. 1, 1974
PONS, Lily (1904-1976)
Oct. 17, 1932; Dec. 30, 1940
PONSELLE, Rosa (1897-   )
Nov. 9, 1931
PONSONBY, Roberte de (1890-   )
July 25, 1932
PONSONBY, Vere Brabazon (1880-1956)
July 25, 1932
POORTEN, Hein ter (1887-   )
Jan. 26, 1942
POPOVICH, Pavel R. (1930-   )
Aug. 24, 1962
PORTAL, Charles (1893-1971)
July 28, 1941
PORTER, Cole (1893-1964)
Jan. 31, 1949
PORTER, Seton (1882-1953)
Dec. 4, 1933
PORTER, Sylvia Field (1913-   )
Nov. 28, 1960
POST, Marjorie Merriweather (1887-1973)
Mar. 15, 1937
POUJADE, Pierre (1921-   )
Mar. 19, 1956
POUND, Dudley (1877-1943)
Apr. 22, 1940
POWELL, Lewis (1907-   )
Nov. 1, 1971; July 22, 1974
POWERS, Bertram Anthony (1923-   )
Mar. 1, 1963
POWERS, Gary Francis (1930-1977)
May 16, 1960
POWNALL, Henry R. (1887-1961)
Jan. 12, 1942
POZAS, Sebastian (1876-1946)
Feb. 14, 1938
PRAJADHIPOK, King of Thailand (1893-1941)
Apr. 20, 1931
PRATT, Herbert L. (1871-1945)
June 11, 1923
PRESTES, Julio (1882-1946)
June 23, 1930
PRESTON, Robert (1918-   )
July 21, 1958

PRICE, Gwilym A. (1896-)
Mar. 2, 1953
PRICE, Leontyne (1927-)
Mar. 10, 1961
PRIDE, Alfred Melville (1897-)
Feb. 7, 1955
PRINCE, Harold Smith (1928-)
Dec. 3, 1965
PROCACCINO, Mario (1912-)
Oct. 3, 1969
PROCTER, William Cooper (1862-1934)
June 16, 1930
PROKOFIEV, Sergei (1891-1953)
Nov. 19, 1945
PU-YI, Henry, Emperor of China (1906-1967)
Mar. 5, 1934; Feb. 24, 1936
PUGMIRE, Ernest I. (1888-1953)
Dec. 26, 1949
PURCELL, Edward Mills (1912-)
Jan. 2, 1961
PUSEY, Nathan M. (1907-)
Mar. 1, 1954
PYLE, Ernie (1900-1945)
July 17, 1944

Q

QUADROS, Janio (1917-)
June 30, 1961
QUESADA, Pete (1905-)
Feb. 22, 1960
QUEZON, Manuel L. (1878-1944)
Nov. 25, 1935
QUINN, William Francis (1919-)
Aug. 10, 1959

R

RABI, Isidor Isaac (1898-)
Jan. 2, 1961
RABIN, Yitzak (1922-)
Dec. 2, 1974; Apr. 7, 1975; Aug. 25, 1975
RADFORD, Arthur William (1896-1973)
Sept. 11, 1950; Feb. 25, 1957
RAEDER, Erich (1876-1960)
Apr. 20, 1942
RAHMAN, Abdul (1903-)
Apr. 12, 1963
RAINEY, Henry Thomas (1860-1934)
Dec. 19, 1932
RAMA VII, King of Thailand (1893-1941)
Apr. 20, 1931
RAMA IX, King of Thailand (1927-)
Apr. 3, 1950; May 27, 1966
RAMO, Simon (1913-)
Apr. 29, 1957
RAMSEY, Arthur Michael (1904-)
Aug. 16, 1963
RANK, J. Arthur (1888-1972)
May 19, 1947
RATHBONE, Monroe Jackson (1900-1976)
May 31, 1963
RAUSCHENBERG, Robert (1925-)
Nov. 29, 1976
RAYBURN, Sam (1882-1961)
Sept. 27, 1943; Feb. 2, 1959; Feb. 10, 1961

REAGAN, Ronald (1911-)
Oct. 7, 1966; Nov. 18, 1966; Apr. 14, 1967;
Oct. 20, 1967; Nov. 24, 1975; May 13, 1976;
June 21, 1976
REDDIN, Tom (1916-)
July 19, 1968
REDEFER, Frederick Lovatt (1905-)
Oct. 31, 1938
REDFORD, Robert (1937-)
Mar. 18, 1974; Mar. 29, 1976
REDGRAVE, Lynn (1943-)
Mar. 17, 1967
REDGRAVE, Vanessa (1937-)
Mar. 17, 1967
REED, Clyde Martin (1871-1949)
June 10, 1929
REED, David Aiken (1880-1953)
July 21, 1930
REED, James A. (1861-1944)
Mar. 7, 1927 REED, Ralph Thomas (1890-1968)
Apr. 9, 1956
REEVES, Joseph Mason (1872-1948)
June 4, 1934
REHNQUIST, William (1924-)
Nov. 1, 1971
REID, Helen (1882-)
Oct. 8, 1934
REINHARDT, Max (1873-1943)
Aug. 22, 1927
REISCHAUER, Edwin Oldfather (1911-)
Jan. 12, 1962
RENTSCHLER, Frederick Brant (1887-1956)
May 28, 1951
RESEK, Erroll (1942-)
Apr. 26, 1971
RESEK, Mrs. Erroll (1945-)
Apr. 26, 1971
RESTON, James Barrett (1909-)
Feb. 15, 1960
REUTER, Ernst (1889-1953)
Sept. 18, 1950; May 25, 1959
REUTHER, Walter (1907-1970)
Dec. 3, 1945; June 20, 1955
REYNAUD, Paul (1878-1966)
June 17, 1940
REYNOLDS, Frank (1924-)
Nov. 21, 1969
REZA SHAH PAHLEVI, Shah of Iran
(1877-1944)
July 2, 1934; Sept. 8, 1941; Apr. 25, 1938
RHEE, Syngman (1875-1965)
Oct. 16, 1950; Mar. 9, 1953
RHOADS, Cornelius P. (1898-1959)
June 27, 1949
RHODES, John (1917-)
Jan. 22, 1973; May 20, 1974
RHYNE, Charles S. (1913-)
May 5, 1958
RIBBENTROP, Joachim von (1893-1946)
Dec. 10, 1945
RIBICOFF, Abraham (1911-)
Jan. 15, 1973
RICE, Craig (1908-)
Jan. 28, 1946
RICHARDSON, Elliot (1920-)
Oct. 8, 1973

RICHARDSON, James Otto (1878-1974)
July 1, 1940
RICHBERG, Donald R. (1881-1960)
Sept. 10, 1934
RICKENBACKER, Edward Vernon (1890-1973)
Apr. 17, 1950
RICKEY, Branch (1881-1965)
Apr. 14, 1947
RICKOVER, Hyman (1900-)
Jan. 11, 1954
RIDDLE, Oscar (1877-1968)
Jan. 9, 1939
RIDGWAY, Matthew Bunker (1895-)
Apr. 2, 1945; Mar. 5, 1951; July 16, 1951
RIEBER, Torkild (1882-1968)
May 4, 1936
RIEFENSTAHL, Leni (1908-)
Feb. 17, 1936
RIESMAN, David (1909-)
Sept. 27, 1954
RIGGS, Bobby (1918-)
Sept. 10, 1973
RIGHTEOUS BROTHERS, music group
May 21, 1965
RIGHTER, Carroll (1900-)
Mar. 21, 1969
RIJN, Titus van (1642-1668)
June 4, 1965
RINGLING, John T. (1866-1936)
Apr. 6, 1925
RISNER, Robbie (1925-)
Apr. 23, 1965
RITCHIE, Albert Cabell (1876-1936)
May 24, 1926
RIVERA, Diego (1866-1957)
Apr. 4, 1949
RIVERA, Miguel Primo de (1870-1930)
June 8, 1925
ROBERTS, Kenneth (1885-1957)
Nov. 25, 1940
ROBERTS, Robin Evan (1927-)
May 28, 1956
ROBERTS, Roy Allison (1887-1967)
Apr. 12, 1948
ROBERTSON, Dale (1922-)
Mar. 30, 1959
ROBERTSON, Oscar (1938-)
Feb. 17, 1961
ROBERTSON, Jaime (1944-)
Jan. 12, 1970
ROBINSON, Dwight P. (1900-)
June 1, 1959
ROBINSON, Jackie Roosevelt (1919-1972)
Sept. 22, 1947
ROBINSON, Joseph Taylor (1872-1937)
June 25, 1928; July 15, 1935
ROBINSON, Sugar Ray (1920-)
June 25, 1951
ROBINSON, Wilbert (1864-1934)
Aug. 25, 1930
ROCA, Blas (1909-)
Apr. 27, 1962
ROCHE, James Michael (1907-)
May 20, 1966
ROCKEFELLER, ABBY (1874-1948)
Jan. 27, 1936

ROCKEFELLER, David (1915-)
Sept. 7, 1962
ROCKEFELLER, James S. (1902-)
July 7, 1924
ROCKEFELLER, John Davison (1839-1937)
May 21, 1928
ROCKEFELLER, John Davison (1874-1960)
Jan. 19, 1925; Sept. 24, 1956
ROCKEFELLER, Nelson A. (1907-1979)
May 22, 1939; Oct. 6, 1958; Aug. 1, 1960;
June 15, 1962; May 22, 1964; Nov. 18, 1966;
Apr. 14, 1967; Oct. 20, 1967; Mar. 8, 1968;
July 26, 1968; Sept. 2, 1974; May 17, 1976
ROCKEFELLER, Winthrop (1912-1973)
Dec. 2, 1966
ROCKNE, Knute Kenneth (1888-1931)
Nov. 7, 1927
RODGERS, Richard (1902-1979)
Sept. 26, 1938
RODINO, Peter (1909-)
Aug. 5, 1974
RODZINSKI, Artur (1892-1958)
Feb. 17, 1947
ROGERS, Mrs. (Will Rogers' aunt) (1846-)
July 19, 1926
ROGERS, Ginger (1911-)
Apr. 10, 1939; Jan. 24, 1972
ROGERS, Will (1879-1935)
July 19, 1926
ROGERS, William P. (1913-)
Dec. 20, 1968; Aug. 10, 1970; Mar. 6, 1972
ROKOSSOVSKY, Konstantin (1896-1968)
Aug. 23, 1943
ROMMEL, Erwin (1891-1944)
July 13, 1942
ROMNEY, George (1907-)
Apr. 6, 1959; Nov. 16, 1962; Nov. 18, 1966;
Apr. 14, 1967
ROONEY, Mickey (1920-)
Mar. 18, 1940
ROOSEVELT, Eleanor (1884-1962)
Nov. 20, 1933; Oct. 8, 1934; Apr. 17, 1939;
Apr. 7, 1952
ROOSEVELT, Franklin Delano (1882-1945)
May 26, 1923; Feb. 1, 1932; Jan. 2, 1933;
Jan. 7, 1935; June 10, 1940; Jan. 5, 1942;
Nov. 29, 1943; Jan. 22, 1945
ROOSEVELT, Franklin (1914-)
June 28, 1937
ROOSEVELT, James (1908-)
Feb. 28, 1938
ROOSEVELT, Sara Delano (1855-1960)
Mar. 6, 1933
ROOSEVELT, Theodore (1858-1919)
Sept. 7, 1942; Mar. 3, 1958
ROOT, Elihu (1845-1937)
Oct. 18, 1926
ROSE, Billy (1899-1966)
June 2, 1947
ROSS, Diana (1944-)
May 21, 1965
ROSSBY, Carl-Gustaf (1899-1957)
Dec. 17, 1956
ROTHSCHILD, Guy de (1909-)
Dec. 20, 1963
ROWAN, Dan (1922-)
Oct. 11, 1968

ROXAS, Manuel A. (1892-1948)
July 8, 1946
RUBINSTEIN, Artur (1887-)
Feb. 25, 1966
RUIZ-CORTINES, Adolfo (1892-1973)
Sept. 14, 1953
RUMSFELD, Donald (1932-)
Nov. 17, 1975
RUNCIMAN, Walter (1870-1949)
Nov. 30, 1931
RUNDSTEDT, Karl von (1875-1953)
Aug. 31, 1942; Aug. 21, 1944
RUPPERT, Jacob (1867-1939)
Sept. 19, 1932
RUSK, Dean (1909-)
Dec. 26, 1960; Dec. 6, 1963; Feb. 4, 1966
RUSSELL, Donald J.M. (1900-)
Aug. 11, 1961
RUSSELL, Richard Brevard (1898-1971)
May 19, 1952, Aug. 12, 1957
RUSSELL, Rosalind (1912-)
Mar. 30, 1953
RUTH, Babe (1895-1948)
Apr. 26, 1976
RYKOV, Alexis I. (1881-1938)
July 14, 1924

S

SAARINEN, Eero (1910-1961)
July 2, 1956
SABIN, Pauline Morton (1887-)
July 18, 1932
SADAT, Anwar (1918-)
May 17, 1971; Apr. 1, 1974; June 24, 1974;
Apr. 7, 1975; June 9, 1975; Aug. 25, 1975
SAHL, Mort (1927-)
Aug. 15, 1960
ST. CLAIR, James (1921-)
Mar. 25, 1974
ST. GAUDENS, Homer (1880-1958)
May 12, 1924;
ST. LAURENT, Louis (1882-1973)
Sept. 12, 1949
SAITO, Hiroshi (1886-1939)
May 20, 1935
SALAN, Raoul (1899-)
Jan. 26, 1962
SALAZAR, Antonio (1889-1970)
July 22, 1946
SALINGER, J. D. (1919-)
Sept. 15, 1961
SALINGER, Pierre (1925-)
Oct. 16, 1964
SALK, Jonas E. (1914-)
Mar. 29, 1954
SALTONSTALL, Leverett (1892-1979)
Apr. 10, 1944
SANDBURG, Carl (1878-1967)
Dec. 4, 1939
SANFORD, Stephen "Laddie" (1898-)
Mar. 31, 1923
SANTAYANA, George (1863-1952)
Feb. 3, 1936
SARACOGLU, Sukru (1888-1953)
July 12, 1943

SARAVIA de CARVALHO, Otelo (1936-)
Aug. 11, 1975
SARNOFF, David (1891-1971)
July 15, 1929; July 23, 1951
SATO, Eisaku (1902-1975)
Feb. 10, 1967
SAUD, King of Saudi Arabia (1902-1969)
Jan. 28, 1957
SAUNDERS, Stuart Thomas (1910-)
Jan. 26, 1968
SAVAGE, Howard Paul (1884-1944)
Sept. 26, 1927
SAVANG VATTHANA, King of Laos
(1907-)
Mar. 17, 1961
SAVITT, Dick (1927-)
Aug. 27, 1951
SAWYER, Charles (1887-1978)
Jan. 20, 1950
SAXBE, William (1917-)
Jan. 15, 1973
SCHACHT, Hjalmar (1877-1970)
Dec. 10, 1945
SCHELL, Maria (1926-)
Dec. 30, 1957
SCHIAPARELLI, Elsa (1890-1973)
Aug. 13, 1934
SCHIFF, Mortimer Leo (1877-1931)
Feb. 14, 1927
SCHINE, David (1928-)
Mar. 22, 1954
SCHLEICHER, Kurt von (1882-1934)
Aug. 22, 1932
SCHLESINGER, Arthur (1917-)
Dec. 17, 1965
SCHLESINGER, James Rodney (1929-)
Feb. 11, 1974, Dec. 20, 1976
SCHMELING, Max (1905-)
June 24, 1929
SCHMIDT, Maarten (1930-)
Mar. 11, 1966
SCHMITT, Kurt (1886-1950)
Aug. 6, 1934
SCHOCKLEY, William (1911-)
Jan. 2, 1961
SCHORSKE, Carl (1915-)
May 6, 1966
SCHRIEVER, Ben (1911-)
Apr. 1, 1957
SCHULTZ, George Pratt (1921-)
Aug. 16, 1971; Feb. 26, 1978
SCHULTZE, Charles L. (1924-)
Dec. 20, 1976
SCHUMACHER, Kurt (1895-1952)
June 9, 1952
SCHUMAN, Charles Baker (1907-)
Sept. 3, 1965
SCHUMAN, Robert (1886-1963)
Mar. 1, 1948
SCHUSCHNIGG, Kurt von (1897-1977)
Mar. 21, 1938
SCHWAB, Charles Michael (1862-1939)
Nov. 22, 1926
SCHWEIKER, Richard (1926-)
May 20, 1974
SCHWEITZER, Albert (1875-1965)
July 11, 1949

SCHWEITZER, Pierre-Paul (1913-   )
Mar. 29, 1968
SCHWELLENBACH, Lewis B. (1894-1948)
Oct. 15, 1945
SCOTT, Barbara Ann (1929-   )
Feb. 2, 1948
SCOTT, David R. (1932-   )
Aug. 9, 1971
SCOTT, Hugh (1900-   )
May 20, 1974
SCRANTON, William (1917-   )
Oct. 19, 1962
SCRIPPS, Ellen Browning (1836-1932)
Feb. 22, 1926
SCULLY, Vincent (1921-   )
May 3, 1966
SEABORG, Glenn T. (1912-   )
Nov. 10, 1961
SEABURY, Samuel (1873-1953)
Aug. 17, 1931
SEGRE, Emilio Gino (1905-   )
Jan. 2, 1961
SERGEI, Ivan (1867-1944)
Dec. 27, 1943
SEYMOUR, James Patrick (1947-   )
Oct. 28, 1966
SHAKESPEARE, William (1564-1616)
July 4, 1960
SHANKS, Carrol M. (1898-1976)
Mar. 18, 1957
SHANNON, James P. (1921-   )
Feb. 23, 1970
SHAPLEY, Harlow (1885-1972)
July 29, 1935
SHAPOSHNIKOV, Boris (1882-1945)
Feb. 16, 1942
SHARP, Grant (1906-   )
Aug. 14, 1964
SHARP, Susie Marshall (1907-   )
Jan. 5, 1976
SHASTRI, Lal Bahadur (1904-1966)
Aug. 13, 1965; Sept. 17, 1965
SHAW, George Bernard (1856-1950)
Dec. 24, 1923; July 23, 1956
SHEEN, Fulton (1895-1979)
Apr. 14, 1952
SHEHU, Mehmet (1913-   )
Oct. 3, 1960
SHELEPIN, Aleksandr (1919-   )
Jan. 14, 1966; Mar. 29, 1971
SHEPARD, Alan B. (1923-   )
May 12, 1961
SHEPHERD, Lemuel (1896-   )
Nov. 24, 1952
SHERMAN, Forrest (1896-1951)
Mar. 13, 1950
SHERMAN, Roger (1721-1793)
Aug. 6, 1973
SHERRILL, Henry Knox (1890-   )
Mar. 26, 1951
SHIDEHARA, Kijuro (1872-1951)
Oct. 12, 1931
SHIELDS, Cornelius (1895-   )
July 27, 1953
SHIMADA, Shigetaro (1883-1976)
July 3, 1944

SHINDIG DANCERS
May 21, 1965
SHIVERS, Allan (1907-   )
Sept. 29, 1952
SHODA, Michiko (1935-   )
Mar. 23, 1959
SHOSTAKOVICH, Dmitri (1906-1975)
July 20, 1942
SHOUP, Paul (1874-1946)
Aug. 12, 1929
SHOUSE, Jouett (1879-1968)
Nov. 10, 1930
SHRIVER, Eunice Kennedy (1922-   )
July 11, 1960
SHRIVER, Sargent (1915-   )
July 5, 1963; May 13, 1966; Aug. 7, 1972
SHULA, Don (1930-   )
Dec. 11, 1972
SIBELIUS, Jean (1865-1957)
Dec. 6, 1937
SIGERIST, Henry E. (1891-1957)
Jan. 30, 1939
SIHANOUK, Prince of Cambodia (1922-   )
Apr. 3, 1964
SIKORSKY, Igor (1889-1972)
Nov. 16, 1953
SILLS, Beverly (1929-   )
Nov. 22, 1971
SIMMONS, Jean (1929-   )
June 28, 1948
SIMON, John Allsebrook (1873-1954)
Mar. 21, 1932; Apr. 8, 1935
SIMON, Norton (1907-   )
June 4, 1965
SIMON, William E. (1927-   )
Jan. 21, 1974
SIMOVITCH, Dusan (1882-1962)
Apr. 21, 1941
SIMPSON, James (1874-   )
Jan. 21, 1929
SIMPSON, Wallis Warfield (1896-   )
Jan. 4, 1937
SIMPSON, William (1889-   )
Feb. 19, 1945
SIMS, William S. (1858-1936)
Oct. 26, 1925
SINATRA, Frank (1917-   )
Aug. 29, 1955
SINCLAIR, Harry Ford (1876-1956)
Apr. 9, 1928
SINCLAIR, Upton (1878-1968)
Oct. 22, 1934
SINGLETON, Trinette (1945-   )
Mar. 15, 1968
SIPLE, Paul-Allman (1908-   )
Dec. 31, 1956
SIRICA, John J. (1904-   )
Jan. 7, 1974
SIRIKIT, Queen of Thailand (1932-   )
May 27, 1966
SISLER, George Harold (1893-1973)
Mar. 30, 1925
SKINNER, B. F. (1904-   )
Sept. 20, 1971
SLIM, Mongi (1908-   )
Sept. 19, 1961

SLOAN, Alfred Pritchard (1875-1966)
Dec. 27, 1926; Sept. 24, 1945
SMIGLY-RYDZ, Edward (1886-1941)
Sept. 11, 1939
SMITH, Adam (1723-1790)
July 14, 1975
SMITH, Alexis (1922-)
May 3, 1971
SMITH, Alfred E. (1873-1944)
July 13, 1925; Apr. 30, 1928; June 27, 1932
SMITH, Cyrus Rowlett (1899-)
Nov. 17, 1958
SMITH, Frederick Edwin (1872-1930)
Aug. 20, 1923
SMITH, George Albert (1870-1951)
July 21, 1947
SMITH, Guy (1945-)
Sept. 29, 1967
SMITH, Harold Dewey (1898-)
June 14, 1943
SMITH, Harsen A. (1908-)
May 18, 1959
SMITH, Holland M. (1882-1967)
Feb. 21, 1944
SMITH, Howard Worth (1883-1976)
Feb. 2, 1959
SMITH, Ian Douglas (1919-)
Nov. 5, 1965; Oct. 11, 1976
SMITH, Jaclyn (1948-)
Nov. 22, 1976
SMITH, Jean Kennedy (1928-)
July 11, 1960
SMITH, John William (1935-)
July 21, 1967
SMITH, Margaret Chase (1897-)
Sept. 5, 1960
SMITH, Oliver, Prince (1893-1977)
Sept. 25, 1950
SMITH, Peggy (1949-)
Sept. 29, 1967
SMITH, Tony (1912-)
Oct. 13, 1967
SMOOT, Reed (1862-1941)
Apr. 8, 1929
SMUTS, Jan C. (1870-1950)
May 22, 1944
SNEAD, Sam (1912-)
June 21, 1954
SNOWDEN, Philip (1864-1937)
Apr. 24, 1930
SOLTI, Georg (1912-)
May 7, 1973
SOLTESZ, Olga (1954-)
Apr. 26, 1971
SOLZHENITSYN, Alexander (1918-)
Sept. 27, 1968; Feb. 25, 1974
SOMOZA, Anastasio (1896-1956)
Nov. 15, 1948
SOMERVELL, Brehon (1892-1955)
June 15, 1942
SOONG, Tse-ven (1894-1971)
Dec. 18, 1944
SOUSTELLE, Jacques (1912-)
Aug. 17, 1959
SPAAK, Paul Henri (1899-1972)
May 10, 1948

SPAIGHT, Richard Dobbs (1758-1802)
Aug. 6, 1973
SPANGLER, Harrison E. (1880-1965)
Feb. 14, 1944
SPARKMAN, Ivo Hall (1901-)
Jan. 27, 1961
SPARKMAN, John J. (1899-)
Aug. 11, 1952
SPASSKY, Boris (1937-)
July 31, 1972
SPAATZ, Carl (1891-1974)
Mar. 22, 1943, June 12, 1944
SPELLMAN, Francis Joseph (1889-1967)
Feb. 25, 1946
SPITZ, Mark (1950-)
Sept. 11, 1972
SPRINGSTEEN, Bruce (1947-)
Oct. 27, 1975
SPROUL, Robert G. (1891-1975)
Oct. 6, 1947
SPROULE, William (1858-1935)
July 28, 1924
SPRUANCE, Raymond Ames (1886-1969)
June 26, 1944
STAGG, Amos Alonzo (1862-1965)
Oct. 20, 1958
STAKHANOV, Alexei (1905-)
Dec. 16, 1935
STALIN, Joseph (1879-1953)
June 9, 1930; Feb. 24, 1936; Dec. 20, 1937;
Jan. 1, 1940; June 30, 1941; Oct. 27, 1941;
Jan. 5, 1942; Jan. 4, 1943; Feb.5, 1945;
July 17, 1950; Sept. 17, 1951; Oct. 6, 1952;
Mar. 16, 1953; June 28, 1954; Apr. 30, 1956;
Sept. 13, 1963; Nov. 10, 1967
STALIN, Vasily (1921-)
Aug. 20, 1951
STANKY, Eddie (1917-)
Apr. 28, 1952
STANLEY, Edward George Villiers
(1865-1948)
May 26, 1930
STANS, Maurice (1898-)
Apr. 30, 1973
STANTON, Frank Nicholas (1908-)
Dec. 4, 1950
STAPP, John Paul (1910-)
Sept. 12, 1955
STARR, Ringo (1940-)
Sept. 22, 1967
STASSEN, Harold (1907-)
Aug. 26, 1947
STAUBACH, Roger Thomas (1942-)
Oct. 18, 1963; Jan. 17, 1972
STEARNS, Alfred E. (1871-1949)
Feb. 8, 1926
STEENHOVEN, Graham B. (1912-)
Apr. 26, 1971
STEIN, Gertrude (1874-1946)
Sept. 11, 1933
STEIN, Howard (1927-)
Aug. 24, 1970
STENGEL, Casey (1891-1975)
Oct. 3, 1955
STEPOVICH, Michael (1919-)
June 9, 1958

STERLING, Ross S. (1875-1949)
Sept. 21, 1931
STETTINIUS, Edward R. (1900-)
Dec. 11, 1944
STEVENS, Craig (1920-)
Oct. 26, 1959
STEVENS, Henry Leonidas (1894-)
Sept. 12, 1932
STEVENSON, Adlai E. (1900-1965)
Jan. 28, 1952; Oct. 27, 1952; Apr. 26, 1956
July 16, 1956; Nov. 24, 1958; Aug. 15, 1960;
Dec. 14, 1962
STEVENSON, Adlai E. (1931-)
Nov. 16, 1970
STEWART, Potter (1915-)
July 22, 1974
STILWELL, Joseph W. (1883-1946)
Nov. 13, 1944
STIMSON, Henry Louis (1867-1950)
Mar. 11, 1929; Aug. 25, 1941
STINNES, Hugo (1870-1924)
Mar. 17, 1923
STOKES, Carl (1927-)
Nov. 17, 1967
STOKOWSKI, Leopold (1882-1977)
Apr. 28, 1930; Nov. 18, 1941
STONE, Edward Durell (1902-)
Mar. 31, 1958
STONE, Harlan Fiske (1872-1946)
May 6, 1929
STONE, Warren Sanford (1860-1925)
Mar. 10, 1924
STOUT, Wesley W. (1890-1971)
Jan. 10, 1938
STRAUS, Jack Isidor (1900-)
Jan. 8, 1965
STRAUS, Percy Selden (1876-1944)
Oct. 16, 1933
STRAUSS, Franz Joseph (1915-)
Dec. 19, 1960
STRAUSS, Lewis L. (1896-1974)
Sept. 21, 1953; Apr. 16, 1956; June 15, 1959
STRAUSS, Richard (1864-1949)
Jan. 24, 1927; July 25, 1938
STRAVINSKY, Igor (1882-1971)
July 26, 1948
STREET, Gabby (1882-1951)
Mar. 28, 1932
STREISAND, Barbra (1942-)
Apr. 10, 1964
STREIT, Clarence K. (1896-)
Mar. 27, 1950
STROUSE, Norman Hulbert (1907-)
Oct. 12, 1962
SUHARTO (1921-)
July 15, 1966
SUKARNO (1901-1970)
Dec. 23, 1946; Mar. 10, 1958
SULLIVAN, Ed (1902-1974)
Oct. 17, 1955
SULLIVAN, Mark (1874-1952)
Nov. 18, 1935
SULZBURGER, Arthur H. (1891-1968)
May 8, 1950
SUPREMES (The), music group
May 21, 1965

SUTTON, Carol (1933-)
Jan. 5, 1976
SUZUKI, Pat (1930-)
Dec. 22, 1958
SWEERIS, Connie (1951-)
Apr. 26, 1971
SWIGERT, John L. (1932-)
Apr. 27, 1970
SWOPE, Herbert Bayard (1882-1958)
Jan. 28, 1924
SYMINGTON, W. Stuart (1901-)
Jan. 19, 1948; Nov. 24, 1958; Nov. 9, 1959
SZELL, George (1897-1970)
Feb. 22, 1963

T

TAFT, Charles Phelps (1897-)
Aug. 3, 1936
TAFT, Robert Alphonso (1889-1953)
Jan. 29, 1940; Jan. 20, 1947; Oct. 30, 1950;
June 2, 1952
TAFT, Robert Alphonso (1917-)
Oct. 26, 1970
TAFT, William Howard (1857-1930)
June 30, 1924; Oct. 8, 1928
TALLEY, Marion Nevada (1907-)
Mar. 1, 1926
TALMADGE, Eugene (1885-1946)
Sept. 7, 1936
TALMADGE, Herman Eugene (1913-)
Oct. 15, 1956
TANNEHILL, John (1952-)
Apr. 26, 1971
TANNER, Charles (1932-)
Dec. 7, 1970
TARDIEU, André (1876-1945)
May 23, 1927; Jan. 20, 1930
TARKINGTON, Booth (1869-1946)
Dec. 21, 1925
TASSIGNY, Jean (1889-1952)
Aug. 1, 1949; Sept. 24, 1951
TAYLOR, Elizabeth (1932-)
Aug. 22, 1949
TAYLOR, Francis Henry (1903-)
Dec. 29, 1952
TAYLOR, James, (1948-)
Mar. 1, 1971
TAYLOR, John Thomas (1885-1965)
Jan. 21, 1935
TAYLOR, Joseph Deems (1885-1966)
Feb. 16, 1931
TAYLOR, Maxwell (1901-)
July 28, 1961
TAYLOR, Myron Charles (1874-1959)
Apr. 22, 1929
TEAD, Clara (1891-)
Oct. 8, 1934
TEAGLE, Walter Clark (1878-1962)
Dec. 9, 1929
TEBALDI, Renata (1922-)
Nov. 3, 1958
TEBBETTS, George Robert (1913-)
July 8, 1957
TEDDER, Arthur (1890-1967)
Nov. 9, 1942

TELLER, Edward (1908-   )
Nov. 8, 1957; Jan. 2, 1961
TEMPLE, Gertrude (1895-   )
Apr. 27, 1936
TEMPLE, Shirley (1928-   )
Apr. 27, 1936; Jan. 8, 1945
TEMPLER, Gerald (1898-   )
Dec. 15, 1952
TENG, Hsiao-ping (1904-   )
Jan. 19, 1976
TER POORTEN, Hein (1887-   )
Jan. 26, 1942
TERESA, Mother (1910-   )
Dec. 29, 1975
TESLA, Nikola (1857-1943)
July 20, 1931
THACH, John (1905-   )
Sept. 1, 1958
THIEU, Nguyen Van (1923-   )
Sept. 15, 1967; Mar. 28, 1969; Aug. 15, 1969;
Jan. 29, 1973; Apr. 7, 1975
THOM, Jean (1935-   )
June 16, 1958
THOMAS, Elmer (1876-1965)
Jan. 15, 1934
THOMAS, Norman Mattoon (1884-1968)
Aug. 8, 1932
THOMPSON, Dorothy (1894-1961)
June 12, 1939
THOMSON, James E. (1905-   )
Aug. 19, 1966
THOREZ, Maurice (1900-1964)
June 3, 1946
THORNTON, Charles (1914-   )
May 31, 1963; Oct. 4, 1963
THURBER, James Grover (1894-1961)
July 9, 1951
THURMOND, J. Strom (1902-   )
Oct. 11, 1948; Aug. 15, 1969
THUY, Xuan (1913-   )
May 10, 1968
TIBBETT, Lawrence Melvil (1896-1960)
Jan. 16, 1933
TILLICH, Paul (1886-1965)
Mar. 16, 1959
TILLINGHAST, Charles (1911-   )
July 22, 1966
TIMOSHENKO, Semyon K. (1895-1970)
June 30, 1941; July 27, 1942
TIRPITZ, Alfred von (1849-1930)
June 22, 1924
TITO, Josip Broz (1892-   )
Oct. 9, 1944; Sept. 16, 1946; June 6, 1955;
Oct. 3, 1960; June 13, 1969
TOGLIATTI, Palmiro (1893-1964)
May 5, 1947
TOGO, Heihachiro (1847-1934)
Nov. 8, 1926
TOJO, Hideki (1885-1948)
Nov. 3, 1941
TOMSKI, Mikhail Pavlovich (1880-1936)
June 9, 1930
TOSCANINI, Arturo (1867-1957)
Jan. 25, 1926; Apr. 2, 1934; Apr. 26, 1948
TOURE, Sekou (1922-   )
Feb. 16, 1959

TOWERS, John Henry (1885-1955)
June 23, 1941
TOWNES, Charles Hard (1915-   )
Jan. 2, 1961
TOWNSEND, Lynn A. (1919-   )
Dec. 28, 1962
TOYNBEE, Arnold Joseph (1889-1975)
Mar. 24, 1947
TRAUBEL, Helen (1903-1972)
Nov. 11, 1946
TRAYLOR, Melvin Alvah (1878-1934)
July 30, 1928; Nov. 21, 1932
TREVINO, Lee (1940-   )
July 19, 1971
TRI, Quang (1924-   )
Apr. 22, 1966
TRIPPE, Juan Terry (1899-   )
July 31, 1933; Mar. 28, 1949
TROTSKY, Leon (1877-1940)
May 18, 1925; Nov. 21, 1927; June 9, 1930;
Jan. 25, 1937
TRUJILLO, Rafael (1929-1969)
Oct. 24, 1961
TRUMAN, Harry S (1884-1972)
Mar. 8, 1943; Nov. 6, 1944; Apr. 23, 1945;
Dec. 31, 1945; Nov. 1, 1948; Jan. 3, 1949;
May 22, 1950; Apr. 23, 1951; Aug. 13, 1956
TRUMAN, Margaret (1924-   )
Feb. 26, 1951
TSCHUDY, William Michael (1935-   )
Dec. 7, 1970
TSHOMBE, Moise (1919-1969)
Dec. 22, 1961
TUGWELL, Rexford G. (1891-1979)
June 25, 1934
TUNNER, William H. (1906-   )
Dec. 18, 1950
TUNNEY, James J. (1897-1978)
Aug. 30, 1926
TUNNEY, John (1934-   )
Oct. 26, 1970; Nov. 16, 1970
TURNER, Richmond Kelly (1885-1961)
Feb. 7, 1944
TURNER, Roscoe (1895-1970)
Oct. 29, 1934
TWINING, Nathan (1897-   )
Feb. 8, 1954

U

UCHIDA, Yasuya (1865-1936)
Sept. 5, 1932
UDALL, Morris (1923-   )
Jan. 15, 1973; Mar. 8, 1976
UGALDE, Domingo (1900-   )
Jan. 13, 1930
ULBRICHT, Walter (1893-1973)
July 13, 1953; Aug. 25, 1961
ULLMANN, Liv (1939-   )
Dec. 4, 1972
UMEKI, Miyoski (1929-   )
Dec. 22, 1958
UNITAS, Johnny (1933-   )
Oct. 1, 1972
UPDIKE, John (1932-   )
Apr. 26, 1968

V

VAFIADES, Markos (1906-   )
Apr. 5, 1948
VAN ALLEN, James Alfred (1914-   )
May 4, 1959; Jan. 2, 1961
VANCE, Cyrus (1917-   )
May 10, 1968
VANCE, Harold S. (1891-1959)
Feb. 2, 1953
VANDEGRIFT, Alexander A. (1887-1973)
Nov. 2, 1942
VANDENBERG, Arthur Hendrick (1884-1951)
Oct. 2, 1939; Apr. 30, 1945; May 12, 1947;
Dec. 17, 1951
VANDENBERG, Hoyt (1899-1954)
Jan. 15, 1945; May 12, 1952
VANDERBILT, Harold Stirling (1884-1970)
Sept. 15, 1930
VAN DOREN, Charles (1927-   )
Feb. 11, 1957
VAN DUSEN, Henry Pitney (1897-1975)
Apr. 19, 1954
VAN FLEET, James (1892-   )
May 23, 1949; May 14, 1951
VARGAS, Getulio D. (1883-1945)
Aug. 12, 1940
VASILEVSKY, Alexander (1897-1977)
July 5, 1943
VAUCLAIN, Samuel M. (1856-1940)
Apr. 21, 1923
VENIZELOS, Eleutherios (1864-1936)
Feb. 18, 1924
VERDON, Gwen (1925-   )
June 13, 1955
VERWOERD, Hendrik (1901-1966)
Aug. 26, 1966
VIDAL, Eugene Luther (1895-1969)
Dec. 18, 1933
VIDAL, Gore (1925-   )
Mar. 1, 1976
VINES, Henry Ellsworth (1912-   )
Aug. 1, 1932
VINSON, Fred Moore (1890-1953)
July 9, 1945
VISHINSKY, Andrei Y. (1884-1954)
Sept. 29, 1947
VISSER t'HOOFT, Willem (1900-   )
Dec. 8, 1961
VITTORIO EMMANUEL III, King of Italy
(1869-1947)
June 15, 1925
VIVIANI, Rene Raphael (1863-1925)
May 19, 1923
VOLSTEAD, Andrew J. (1860-1947)
Mar. 29, 1926
VON BRAUN, Wernher (1912-1977)
Feb. 17, 1958
VORONOV, Nikolai (1899-1968)
Mar. 20, 1944
VOROSHILOV, Kliment E. (1881-1969)
Feb. 12, 1934

W

WADE, Wallace (1892-   )
Oct. 25, 1937

WADSWORTH, James Wolcott (1877-1952)
Dec. 28, 1925
WAGNER, Robert Ferdinand (1877-1953)
Mar. 19, 1934
WAGNER, Robert Ferdinand (1910-   )
Oct. 1, 1956; Mar. 23, 1962; Oct. 3, 1969
WAINWRIGHT, Jonathan M. (1883-1953)
May 8, 1944
WAKSMAN, Selman Abraham (1888-1973)
Nov. 7, 1949
WALD, George (1907-   )
May 6, 1966
WALDRON, Frank (1905-   )
Apr. 25, 1949
WALKER, George William (1896-   )
Nov. 4, 1957
WALKER, James John (1881-1946)
Jan. 11, 1926; May 20, 1929
WALKER, Walton (1889-1950)
July 31, 1950
WALLACE, DeWitt (1889-   )
Dec. 10, 1951
WALLACE, Edgar (1875-1932)
Apr. 15, 1929
WALLACE, George (1919-   )
Sept. 27, 1963; Oct. 18, 1968; Mar. 27, 1972;
Mar. 8, 1976
WALLACE, Henry A. (1888-1965)
Apr. 10, 1933; Dec. 19, 1938; Sept. 23, 1940;
Sept. 30, 1946; Aug. 9, 1948
WALLACE, Lila Bell (1889-   )
Dec. 10, 1951
WALSH, Thomas (1859-1933)
May 4, 1925
WANG, Ching-wei (1884-1944)
Mar. 18, 1935
WARREN, Charles Beecher (1870-1936)
Jan. 26, 1925
WARREN, Earl (1891-1971)
Jan. 31, 1944; Sept. 27, 1948; Dec. 21, 1953;
July 1, 1957; Jan. 27, 1961
WARREN, George F. (1874-1938)
Nov. 27, 1933
WASHINGTON, George (1732-1799)
Oct. 18, 1948; July 6, 1953; Aug. 6, 1973;
Dec. 14, 1970; Special Bicentennial Issue,
1976
WATKINS, Arthur V. (1886-1973)
Oct. 4, 1954
WATSON, Thomas J. (1914-   )
Mar. 28, 1955
WAVELL, Archibald P. (1883-1950)
Oct. 14, 1940; July 16, 1945
WAYNE, John (1907-1979)
Mar. 3, 1952; Aug. 8, 1969
WEAVER, Henry Grady (1889-1949)
Nov. 14, 1938
WEAVER, Robert C. (1907-   )
Mar. 4, 1966
WEBB, Delbert Eugene (1899-1974)
Aug. 3, 1962
WEBB, Jack Randolph (1921-   )
Mar. 15, 1954
WEBSTER, Harold Tucker (1885-1952)
Nov. 26, 1945
WEDEMEYER, Albert C. (1897-   )
June 4, 1945

WEEKS, John Wingate (1890-1926)
Oct. 22, 1923
WEIL, Miriam (1950-)
Apr. 10, 1972
WEISS, Brian (1947-)
June 7, 1968
WELCH, Raquel (1940-)
Nov. 28, 1969
WELCH, William Henry (1850-1934)
Apr. 14, 1930
WELLES, Orson (1915-)
May 9, 1938
WELLES, Sumner (1892-1961)
Aug. 11, 1941
WELLS, Herbert George (1866-1946)
Sept. 20, 1926
WESLEY, John (1703-1791)
May 8, 1964
WESSIN y WESSIN, Elias (1925-)
May 7, 1965
WEST, James E. (1876-1948)
July 12, 1937
WEST, Rebecca (1892-)
Dec. 8, 1947
WESTMORELAND, William Childs
(1914-)
Feb. 19, 1965; Jan. 7, 1966; May 5, 1967
WEYGAND, Maxime (1867-1965)
Oct. 30, 1933; June 3, 1940; June 17, 1940
WHALEN, Grover A. (1886-1962)
May 1, 1939
WHEELER, Burton Kendall (1882-1975)
June 18, 1923; Apr. 15, 1940
WHEELER, Earle Gilmore (1908-1975)
Feb. 5, 1965
WHITE, Byron R. (1917-)
July 22, 1974
WHITE, Dwight (1949-)
Dec. 8, 1975
WHITE, Edward Higgins (1931-1967)
June 11, 1965; Feb. 3, 1967
WHITE, Harry Dexter (1892-1948)
Nov. 23, 1953
WHITE, Thomas Dresser (1901-1965)
Nov. 25, 1957
WHITE, Walter F. (1893-1955)
Jan. 24, 1938
WHITE, William Allen (1868-1944)
Oct. 6, 1924; Aug. 19, 1940
WHITMAN, Charles Joseph (1941-)
Aug. 12, 1966
WHITNEY, John Hay (1904-)
Mar. 27, 1933
WHITNEY, Richard (1888-1974)
Feb. 26, 1934
WICKARD, Claude R. (1893-1967)
July 21, 1941
WICKERSHAM, George (1858-1936)
Feb. 2, 1931
WIGGIN, Albert Henry (1868-1951)
Aug. 24, 1931
WIGGINS, Charles (1928-)
July 29, 1974
WILBUR, Ray Lyman (1875-1949)
Feb. 28, 1927; Feb. 10, 1930
WILDER, Thornton (1897-1975)
Jan. 12, 1953

WILHELM II, Emperor of Germany (1859-
1941)
June 28, 1926
WILHELMINA, Queen of the Netherlands
(1890-1962)
Aug. 5, 1935; Nov. 22, 1939; May 13, 1946
WILKINS, Roy (1901-)
Aug. 30, 1963
WILLARD, Daniel (1861-1942)
Jan. 11, 1932
WILLEBRANDT, Mabel Walker (1889-1963)
Aug. 26, 1929
WILLIAMS, Gerhard Mennen (1911-)
Sept. 15, 1952
WILLIAMS, John James (1904-)
Oct. 13, 1952
WILLIAMS, Samuel Clay (1884-1949)
Feb. 25, 1935
WILLIAMS, Ted (1919-)
Apr. 10, 1950
WILLIAMS, Tennessee (1911-)
Mar. 9, 1962
WILLIAMSON, Hugh (1735-1819)
Aug. 6, 1973
WILLKIE, Wendell L. (1892-1944)
July 31, 1939; Oct. 21, 1940
WILLS, Helen Newington (1906-)
July 26, 1926; July 1, 1929
WILLSON, Meredith (1902-)
July 21, 1958
WILSON, Brian (1946-)
May 21, 1965
WILSON, Carl Dean (1945-)
May 21, 1965
WILSON, Charles Edward (1886-1972)
Dec. 13, 1943; Feb. 19, 1951
WILSON, Charles Erwin (1890-1961)
Jan. 24, 1949; June 1, 1953; Apr. 16, 1956;
June 4, 1956
WILSON, Dennis (1944-)
May 21, 1965
WILSON, Flip (1933-)
Jan. 31, 1972
WILSON, Gary William (1943-)
June 3, 1966
WILSON, Harold (1916-)
Oct. 11, 1963; Oct. 23, 1964; Apr. 30, 1965;
Nov. 24, 1967
WILSON, Henry Maitland (1881-1964)
Feb. 28, 1944
WILSON, Jerry Vernon (1928-)
July 13, 1970
WILSON, Kemmons (1913-)
June 12, 1972
WILSON, Mary (1944-)
May 21, 1965
WILSON, Woodrow (1856-1924)
Nov. 12, 1923
WINCHELL, Walter (1897-1972)
July 11, 1938
WINDSOR, Duchess of (1896-)
Jan. 4, 1937
WINDSOR, Duke of, Edward (1894-1972)
Aug. 8, 1927; Apr. 1, 1929
WINN, Matt (1861-1949)
May 10, 1937

WOOD, Barry (1910-)
Nov. 23, 1931
WOOD, Leonard (1860-1927)
Apr. 19, 1926
WOOD, Robert Elkington (1879-1969)
Oct. 6, 1941; Feb. 25, 1952
WOOD, Robert Williams (1868-1955)
June 20, 1938
WOODIN, William Hartman (1868-1934)
Mar. 20, 1933
WOODS, Robert Evans (1920-)
June 11, 1945
WOODS, Rose Mary (1918-)
Dec. 10, 1973
WOODWARD, Robert Burns (1917-1979)
Jan. 2, 1961
WOODWARD, William (1876-1953)
Aug. 7, 1939
WOOLDRIDGE, Dean (1913-)
Apr. 29, 1957
WOOLF, Virginia (1882-1941)
Apr. 12, 1937
WOOLTON, Frederick James M. (1883-1964)
Mar. 26, 1945
WORDEN, Alfred M. (1932-)
Aug. 9, 1971
WORTH, Jean Phillippe (1885-)
Aug. 13, 1928
WOUK, Herman (1915-)
Sept. 5, 1955
WRIGHT, Frank Lloyd (1869-1959)
Jan. 17, 1938
WRIGHT, Orville (1871-1948)
Dec. 3, 1928
WRIGLEY, William (1861-1932)
Oct. 14, 1929
WU, Kuo-cheng (1903-)
Aug. 7, 1950
WU, Pei-fu (1878-1939)
Sept. 8, 1924
WYATT, Addie (1924-)
Jan. 5, 1976
WYETH, Andrew (1917-)
Dec. 27, 1963
WYSZNYSKI, Stefan (1901-)
May 20, 1957

Y

YAHYA, Khan (1917-)
Dec. 6, 1971
YAMAMOTO, Isoroku (1884-1943)
Dec. 22, 1941
YAMASAKI, Minoru (1912-)
Jan. 18, 1963

YAMASHITA, Tomyuki (1885-1946)
Mar. 2, 1942
YEAGER, Charles (1923-)
Apr. 18, 1949
YEN, Hsi-shan (1883-1960)
May 19, 1930
YONAI, Mitsumasa (1880-1948)
Aug. 30, 1937; Mar. 4, 1940
YORTY, Samuel William (1910-)
Mar. 23, 1962; Sept. 2, 1966
YOUNG, Clarence Marshall (1889-1973)
Mar. 14, 1932
YOUNG, Clement Calhoun (1869-1947)
June 10, 1929
YOUNG, James (1936-)
Dec. 7, 1970
YOUNG, Owen D. (1874-1962)
Feb. 23, 1925; Jan. 6, 1930
YOUNG, Robert Ralph (1897-1958)
Feb. 3, 1947
YOUNG, Whitney M. (1921-1971)
Aug. 11, 1967

Z

ZAMORA y TORRES, Niceto Alcalá
(1877-1949)
May 4, 1931
ZANGWILL, Israel (1864-1926)
Sept. 17, 1923
ZANUCK, Darryl F. (1902-1979)
June 12, 1950
ZEELAND, Paul von (1893-1973)
June 14, 1937
ZHDANOV, Andrei A. (1896-1948)
Dec. 9, 1946
ZHIVKOV, Todor (1911-)
Oct. 3, 1960
ZHUKOV, Georgi K. (1896-1974)
Dec. 14, 1942; May 9, 1955
ZIEGFIELD, Florenz (1867-1932)
May 14, 1928
ZIMBALIST, Efrem (1923-)
Oct. 26, 1959
ZINOVIEV, Grigori (1883-1936)
June 9, 1930
ZOMOSA, Maximiliano (1937-)
Mar. 15, 1968
ZOOK, George Frederick (1885-1951)
Sept. 18, 1933
ZORIN, Valerian (1902-)
Feb. 24, 1961
ZUKOR, Adolph (1873-1976)
Jan. 14, 1929
ZUMWALT, Elmo (1920-)
Dec. 21, 1970

APPENDIX II

PROFESSIONS OF THE PERSONS WHO HAVE APPEARED ON THE COVERS OF TIME

The persons who. have appeared on the covers of TIME are grouped here by the professions into which they were categorized for the study. The groupings follow the order given in Tables 7 and 8. Many individuals are listed more than once because they were classified according to the profession or position held at the time of each portrayal. Some categories have fewer names than the number indicated in Tables 7 and 8 because of the fact that many individuals appeared two or more times while in the same profession or while holding the same office. See Appendix I for the number of times each individual appeared and the dates of the covers of the portrayals.

POLITICIANS— UNITED STATES

Presidents

Coolidge, Calvin
Eisenhower, Dwight D.
Ford, Gerald R.
Harding, Warren G.
Johnson, Lyndon B.
Kennedy, John F.
Nixon, Richard M.
Roosevelt, Franklin D.
Truman, Harry S

Ex-Presidents

Cleveland, Grover
Eisenhower, Dwight D.
Hoover, Herbert
Jefferson, Thomas
Lincoln, Abraham
Madison, James
Monroe, James
Nixon, Richard M.
Roosevelt, Theodore
Truman, Harry S
Washington, George
Wilson, Woodrow

Vice-Presidents

Agnew, Spiro
Barkley, Alben
Curtis, Charles
Dawes, Charles G.
Ford, Gerald R.
Garner, John N.
Humphrey, Hubert H.
Johnson, Lyndon B.
Nixon, Richard M.
Rockefeller, Nelson

Senators

Aiken, George
Baker, Howard
Ball, Joseph H.
Barkley, Alben
Benston, Lloyd
Borah, William E.
Brock, William
Brooke, Edward
Buckley, James
Bulkley, Robert J.
Bumpers, Dale
Byrd, Harry F.
Capper, Arthur
Case, Clifford
Chiles, Lawton
Connally, Thomas ·
Cooper, John S.
Cormier, Lucia Marie
Couzens, James
Cummins, Albert B.
Curtis, Charles
Dirksen, Everett
Dole, Robert
Douglas, Paul H.
Downey, Sheridan
Eagleton, Thomas
Eastland, James O.
Erwin, Sam
Fulbright, William
George, Walter
Glass, Carter
Glenn, John
Goldwater, Barry
Goodell, Charles
Gore, Albert
Harrison, Pat

Senators (Cont'd)

Hart, Gary
Hatfield, Mark
Hull, Cordell
Humphrey, Hubert H.
Jackson, Henry M.
Javits, Jacob
Johnson, Hiram W.
Johnson, Lyndon B.
Keating, Kenneth B.
Kefauver, Estes
Kennedy, Edward M.
Kennedy, John F.
Kennedy, Robert F.
Knowland, William
Lafollette, Robert M.
Lodge, Henry Cabot, Sr.
Lodge, Henry Cabot, Jr.
Long, Huey P.
McCarthy, Eugene
McCarthy, Joseph R.
McClellan, John Little
McGovern, George
Mansfield, Mike
Mathias, Charles
Metzenbaum, Howard
Morse, Wayne L.
Mondale, Walter
Murphy, Goerge
Muskie, Edmund
Neuberger, Richard
Nixon, Richard M.
Norris, George W.
Ottinger, Richard
Packwood, Bob
Pepper, Claude
Percy, Charles H.

Governors (Cont'd)

Earle, George Howard
Emerson, Frank Collins
Evans, Daniel J.
Farrington, Wallace R.
Faubus, Orval
Fine, John Sydney
Grasso, Ella
Gruening, Ernest
Harriman, William Averell
Heil, Julius P.
Herring, Clyde L.
Herter, Christian A.
Hoegh, Leo
Holloway, William J.
Judd, Lawrence M.
Knight, Goodwin
Landon, Alfred
Langlie, Arthur
Lausche, Frank John
Leader, George M.
Long, Earl
Long, Huey P.
Martin, Ed
Meyner, Robert B.
Moody, Dan
Murray, William H.
Parnell, Harvey
Patterson, John
Pinchot, Gifford
Poindexter, Joseph Boyd
Quinn, William Francis
Reagan, Ronald
Reed, Clyde M.
Ritchie, Albert Cabell
Rockefeller, Nelson
Rockefeller, Winthrop
Romney, George
Roosevelt, Franklin D.
Scranton, William
Shivers, Allan
Smith, Alfred E.
Stepovich, Michael
Sterling, Ross S.
Stevenson, Adlai E.
Talmadge, Eugene
Talmadge, Herman E.
Thurmond, Strom
Wallace, George
Williams, G. Mennen
Young, Clement C.

Mayors

Beame, Abraham D.
Bowron, Fletcher
Collins, John F.
Curter, Lewis W.
Daley, Richard J.
Hoan, Daniel W.
Kelly, Edward J.
LaGuardia, Fiorello
Lapham, Roger D.
Levi, John H.
Lindsay, John V.

Mayors (Cont'd)

Morrison, DeLesseps S.
O'Brien, John P.
O'Dwyer, William
Stokes, Carl
Wagner, Robert F.
Walker, James J.
Yorty, Samuel W.

First Ladies

Coolidge, Grace
Eisenhower, Mamie
Ford, Betty
Hoover, Lou Henry
Johnson, Lady Bird
Kennedy, Jacqueline
Nixon, Pat
Roosevelt, Eleanor

Miscellaneous Politicians and Members of Politicians' Families

Adams, Sherman
Allen, George F.
Andrews, Elmer F.
Andrews, Lincoln C.
Baker, Bobby
Baker, Newton Diehl
Baruch, Bernard M.
Beck, James M.
Bedford, Gunning
Blair, John
Blount, William
Bowles, Chester B.
Boyle, William M.
Breasley, David
Brennan, George E.
Broom, Jacob
Browder, Earl
Brown, Harold
Bundy, McGeorge
Burch, Dean
Butler, Pierce
Butler, William M.
Byrnes, James F.
Califano, Joseph A.
Caplin, Mortimer M.
Carter, Amy
Carter, Jimmy
Carter, Rosalynn
Chandler, Dorothy
Clay, Lucius
Clifford, Clark
Clymer, George
Cohen, Benjamin V.
Cohn, Roy
Colby, William E.
Connally, John B.
Corcoran, Thomas G.
Cox, Archibald
Cox, Eddie
Cox, Tricia Nixon
Crump, Edward H.
Curry, John Francis

Miscellaneous (Cont'd)

Davis, Dwight F.
Davis, Norman H.
Davison, F. Trubee
Dean, Gordon
Dean, John Wesley
Dennis, Eugene
Depew, Chauncey M.
DeSapio, Carmine
Dickinson, John
DiSalle, Michael
Dodge, Joseph M.
Dryden, Franklin B.
Dulles, Allen W.
Dulles, John Foster
Early, Stephen Tyree
Eccles, Marriner S.
Ehrlichman, John
Eisenhower, Dwight D.
Elstein, Kenneth
Farley, James A.
Fechner, Robert
Fitzgerald, John F.
Fitzsimmons, Thomas
Fletcher, Henry P.
Flynn, Edward J.
Ford, Betty
Ford, Gayle
Ford, Jack
Ford, Mike
Ford, Steve
Ford, Susan
Frank, Jerome N.
Franklin, Benjamin
Gilbert S. Parker
Gilman, Nicholas
Good, James W.
Hagerty, James C.
Haldeman, Harry R.
Hall, Leonard W.
Hamilton, John D. M.
Haynes, Roy Asa
Helms, Richard M.
Hoffman, Paul G.
Hoover, Herbert C., Jr.
Hoover, Lou Henry
Hopkins, Harry L.
House, Edward M.
Howe, Louis M.
Hughes, Rowland R.
Hunt, E. Howard
Hurja, Emil E.
Ingalls, David S.
Ingersoll, Jared
Jackson, William
Johnson, Hugh S.
Johnson, Luci B.
Johnson, William Samuel
Jones, Jesse H.
Jordan, Hamilton
Kennedy, Ethel
Kennedy, Joan
Kennedy, Joseph P.
Kennedy, Rose F.
Kennedy, Rosemary

Miscellaneous (Cont'd)

Kennedy, Robert F.
Keppel, Francis
Kissinger, Henry
Klein, Julius
Knight, Carolyn
Knight, Marilyn
LaFollette, Philip Fox
LaFollette, Robert M.
Langdon, John
Lawford, Patricia K.
LeHand, Marguerite
LeMay, Curtis
Liddy, G. Gordon
Lilienthal, David E.
Livingston, William
Longworth, Alice Roosevelt
Lovett, Robert A.
Lowden, Florence
Lowden, Frank O.
McAdoo, William G.
McBride, Francis S.
McCord, James W.
McCormick, Ruth H.
McGovern, Eleanor
McIntyre, Marvin H.
McHenry, James
McKee, Joseph V.
McKelvie, Samuel R.
McNinch, Frank R.
McNutt, Paul V.
Magruder, Jeb Stuart
Meyer, Eugene
Mifflin, Thomas
Mills, Ogden L.
Mitchell, Martha
Mondale, Joan
Morris, Gouveneur
Morrow, Dwight W.
Moses, Robert
Moyers, Bill Don
Nixon, Pat
Nixon, Richard M.
Nugent, Patrick
O'Brien, Lawrence
Paterson, William
Peek, George N.
Percy, Charles H.
Phillips, William
Pinckney, Charles C.
Procaccino, Mario
Quesada, Pete
Reagan, Ronald
Richberg, Donald R.
Rockefeller, Abby
Rockefeller, Nelson
Roosevelt, Eleanor
Roosevelt, Franklin, Jr.
Roosevelt, James
Roosevelt, Sara Delano
Sabin, Pauline M.
Salinger, Pierre
Schine, David
Sherman, Roger
Shouse, Jouett
Shriver, Eunice K.
Shriver, Sargent

Miscellaneous (Cont'd)

Simon, William E.
Smith, Harold Dewey
Smith, Jean K.
Spaight, Richard D.
Spangler, Harrison E.
Sparkman, Ivo Hall
Stans, Maurice
Stassen, Harold
Stevenson, Adlai
Strauss, Lewis L.
Thomas, Norman M.
Wagner, Robert F.
Waldron, Frank
Wallace, George
Welles, Sumner
Whalen, Grover A.
White, Harry Dexter
Willebrandt, Mabel W.
Williams, Samuel Clay
Williamson, Hugh
Willkie, Wendell L.
Wilson, Charles Edward
Wood, Robert Elkington
Woods, Rose Mary
Young, Owen D.

**POLITICIANS—
FOREIGN**

Albania

Shehu, Mehmet

Algeria

Abbas, Ferhat
Benkhedda, Ben Youssef

Argentina

Aramburu, Pedro E.
Castillo, Ramón S.
Frondizi, Arturo
Guevara, Che
Perón, Eva
Perón, Juan Domingo

Australia

Curtin, John
Lyons, Joseph A.
Menzies, Robert G.

Austria

Dollfuss, Engelbert
Schuschnigg, Kurt von

Belgium

Albert I, King
Baudouin I, King
Leopold III, King
Mary Liliane de Rethy, Queen
Spaak, Paul Henri
Zeeland, Paul von

Brazil

Aranha, Oswaldo
Cafe Filho, João
Costa e Silva, Arthur da
Kubitschek, Juscelino
Prestes, Julio
Quadros, Janio
Vargas, Getulio D.

Bulgaria

Boris III, King
Zhivkov, Todor

Burma

Nu, U

Cambodia

Sihanouk, Prince

Canada

Bennett, Richard B.
Bennett, William
Diefenbaker, John G.
Hepburn, Mitchell F.
Houde, Camillien
Howe, Clarence Decatur
King, William M.
Pearson, Lester B.
St. Laurent, Louis

Chile

Allende, Salvador
Dávila, Carlos G.

China

Chen, Li-fu
Chen, Yi
Chiang, Mei-ling
Chiang, Kai-shek
Chou, En-lai
Feng, Yu-hsiang
Li, Fu-chun
Lin, Piao
Liu, Shao-chi
Mao, Tse-tung
Pu Yi, Henry
Soong, Tse-ven
Teng, Hsiao-ping
Wang, Ching-wei
Wu, Kuo-cheng

Cuba

Batista, Fulgencio
Castro, Fidel
Machado, Gerardo
Miró-Cardona, José
Roca, Blas

Czechoslovakia

Benes, Eduard
Dubcek, Alexander
Masaryk, Jan
Masaryk, Thomas G.
Novotny, Antonin

Denmark

Anne-Marie, Princess
Christian X, King
Margrethe, Queen

Dominican Republic

Trujillo, Rafael, Jr.

Egypt

Farouk I, King
Fuad I, King
Nasser, Gamal Abdel
Sadat, Anwar

Ethiopia

Haile Selassie, Emperor

France

Auriol, Jules Vincent
Barthou, Louis
Baudouin, Paul
Bergenger, Victor H.
Blum, Leon
Briand, Aristide
Caillaux, Joseph
Claudel, Paul
Clemenceau, Georges
Couve de Murville, Maurice
Daladier, Edouard
Doumergue, Gaston
Faure, Edgar
Flandin, Pierre E.
Gaulle, Charles de
Henry-Haye, Gaston
Herriot, Edouard
Joan of Arc
Laval, Pierre
Louis XIV, King
Mendes-France, Pierre
Napoleon Bonaparte
Painleve, Paul
Petain, Henri P.
Pinay, Antoine
Poincare, Raymond
Pompidou, Georges
Poujade, Pierre
Reynaud, Paul
Salan, Raoul
Schuman, Robert
Soustelle, Jacques

France (Cont'd)

Tardieu, Andre
Thorez, Maurice
Viviani, Rene R.

Germany

Adenauer, Konrad
Brandt, Willy
Bruning, Heinrich
Erhard, Ludwig
Goebbels, Joseph P.
Goring, Hermann
Hess, Rudolf
Himmler, Heinrich
Hindenburg, Paul von
Hitler, Adolf
Kiesinger, Kurt Georg
Marx, Karl Henrich
Papen, Franz von
Reuter, Ernst
Ribbentrop, Joachim von
Schleicher, Kurt von
Schumacher, Kurt
Strauss, Franz Joseph
Ulbricht, Walter
Wilhelm II, Emperor

Ghana

Nkrumah, Kwame

Great Britain

Amery, Leopold
Asquith, Herbert H.
Astor, Nancy Langhorne
Athlone, Alexander
Athlone, Alice
Attlee, Clement
Baldwin, Stanley
Balfour, Arthur
Beaverbrook, William
Bessborough, Roberte de
Bessborough, Vere Brabazon
Bevan, Aneurin
Buchan, John
Butler, Richard A.
Chamberlain, Austen
Chamberlain, Neville
Charles, Prince
Churchill, Winston
Cripps, Stafford
Douglas, Lewis W.
Douglas-Home, Alec
Eden, Anthony
Elizabeth II, Queen
Elizabeth, Queen Mother
Franks, Oliver
George V, King
George VI, King
Gloucester, Duke of
Halifax, Edward

Great Britain (Cont'd)

Hastings, Patrick
Heath, Edward R.
Hoare, Samuel
Hope, Victor Alexander
Isaacs, Rufus D.
Kent, Duke of
Kerr, Philip Henry
Lang, Cosmo Gordon
Lloyd-George, David
MacDonald, Ramsay
McGarel, Douglas
McKenna, Reginald
Macmillan, Harold
Margaret Rose, Princess
Mary of Teck, Queen
Morrison, Herbert Stanley
Mosley, Oswald E.
Philip, Prince
Portal, Charles
Runciman, Walter
Simon, John A.
Smith, Frederick E.
Snowden, Philip
Stanley, Edward
Wilson, Harold
Windsor, Duchess of
Windsor, Duke of
Woolton, Frederick

Greece

Constantine, King
Damaskinos, Archbishop
Frederika, Queen
George II, King
Vafiades, Markos
Venizelos, Eleutherios

Guatemala

Arbenz, Jacobo
Arevalo, Juan José

Guinea

Toure, Sekou

Haiti

Magloire, Paul Eugene

Hungary

Kadar, Janos

India

Bose, Subhas C.
Gandhi, Indira
Gandi, Mahatma
Jinnah, Mohammed Ali

India (Cont'd)

Krishna Menon, V. L.
Nehru, Jawaharlal
Osman Ali, Nizam of
  Hyderabad
Patel, Vallabhbhai
Shastri, Lal Bahadur

Indonesia

Suharto
Sukarno

Iran

Mohamed Reza Pahlevi, Shah
Mossadeq, Mohamed
Riza Shah Phalevie, Shah

Iraq

Kassem, Abdul Karim
Nuri-al-Said

Ireland

Craig, James
De Valera, Eamon
Lemass, Sean

Israel

Ben-Gurion, David
Eshkol, Levi
Meir, Golda
Rabin, Yitzhak

Italy

Berlinguer, Enrico
Caetani, Gelasio
Ciano, Edda
De Gasperi, Alcide
Grandi, Dino
Mussolini, Benito
Mussolini, Bruno
Mussolini, Vittorio
Togliatti, Palmiro
Vittorio Emmanuel III, King

Japan

Hatoyama, Ichiro
Hirohito, Emperor
Hirota, Koki
Inukai, Ki
Kishi, Nobsuke
Konoye, Prince
Matsuoka, Yosuke
Nomura, Kichisaburo
Saito, Hiroshi
Sato, Eisaku
Shidehara, Kijuro
Shoda, Michiko
Tojo, Hideki

Japan (Cont'd)

Uchida, Yasuya
Yonai, Mitsumasa

Jordan

Abdullah ibn Hussein, King
Hussein, King

Kenya

Mboya, Tom

Korea

Rhee, Syngman

Laos

Savang Vatthana, King

Libya

Gaddafi, Muammar

Malaysia

Rahman, Abdul

Mexico

Alemán, Miguel
Calles, Plutarco
Camacho, Manuel Avila
Cardenas, Lazaro
Lóez-Mateos, Adolfo
Ortíz-Rubio, Pascual
Padilla, Ezequiel
Ruíz-Cortines, Adolfo

Morocco

Abd-el-Krim
Aisha Lalla, Princess
Mohammed V, Sultan

Netherlands

Bernhard, Prince
Juliana, Queen
Mook, Hubertus Johannes von
Wilhelmina, Queen

Nicaragua

Somoza, Anastasio

Nigeria

Balewa, Abubakar
Ojukwu, C. Odemugwu

Norway

Haakon VII, King
Lie, Trygve
Olaf V, King

Pakistan

Ayub Khan
Yahya Khan

Palestine

Arafat, Yasser

Peru

Belaunde-Terry, Fernando
Leguía, Augusto Bernardino

Philippines

Magsaysay, Ramon
Marcos, Ferdinand E.
Quezon, Manuel L.
Roxas, Manuel A.

Poland

Beck, Josef
Gomulka, Wladyslaw
Mikolajczyk, Stanislaw
Pilsudski, Josef

Portugal

Costa Gomes, Francisco da
Gonçalves, Vasco dos Santos
Salazar, Antonio
Saraiva de Carvalho, Otelo

Puerto Rico

Muñoz-Marín, Luis

Rhodesia

Smith, Ian Douglas

Romania

Bratiano, Jon
Carol II, King
Ceausescu, Nicolae
Gheorghiu-Dej, Gheorghe
Marie, Queen
Michael, King
Pauker, Ana

Saudi Arabia

Abdul Aziz ibn Saud, King
Faisal, King
Saud, King

South Africa

Hertzog, James B.
Malan, Daniel F.
Verwoerd, Hendrik

Soviet Union

Beria, Lavrenty
Brezhnev, Leonid
Bulganin, Nikolai
Gromyko, Andrei
Kalinin, Michael
Kalinin (son of Michael)
Kalinin, Yekaterina
Kamenev, Lev B.
Katushev, Lonstanin
Khrushchev, Nikita
Kosygin, Aleksei
Kozlov, Frol R.
Lenin, Nokolai
Litvinov, Maxim
Malenkov, Georgi
Malik, Jacob
Malinkovsky, Rodion
Mazurov, Kirill
Menzhinsky, Viacheslav
Mikoyan, Anastas I.
Milotov, Viacheslav
Morozov, Platon
Nesterenko, Alexei
Podgorny, Nikolai
Poliansky, Dimitry
Rykov, Alexis I.
Shelepin, Aleksandr
Stalin, Joseph
Tomski, Mikhail P.
Trotsky, Leon
Vishinsky, Andrei Y.
Zhdanov, Andrei A.
Zinoviev, Grigori
Zorin, Alerian

Spain

Alfonso XIII, King
Azaña, Manuel
Franco, Francisco
Juan Carlos, King
Juan de Borbón y Battenberg
Rivera, Miguel Primo de
Zamora y Torres, Niceto
  Alcala

Sweden

Carl XVI Gustaf, King
Gustaf V, King
Gustaf VI, King
Hammarskjold, Dag
Martha, Princess

Syria

Assad, Hafez

Tanzania

Nyerere, Julius K.

Thailand

Bhumibol Adulyadej, King
Prajadhipok, King
Sirikit, Queen

Tunisia

Slim, Mongi

Turkey

Ataturk, Kemal
Inonu, Ismet
Menderes, Adnan
Saracoglu, Sukru

Venezuela

Betancourt, Romulo
Pérez-Jimenez, Marcos

Vietnam

Bao Dai, Emperor
Bo, Mai Van
Diem, Ngo Dinh
Ho, Chi Minh
Khanh, Hguyen
Ky, Nguyen Cao
Le, Duc Tho
Nhu, Tran Le Xuan
Thieu, Nguyen Van
Thuy, Xuan
Tri, Quang

Yugoslavia

Alexander, King
Paul, Prince
Simovitch, Dusan
Tito, Josip Broz

Zaire

Tshombe, Moise

**MILITARY—
UNITED STATES**

Abbott, Joan
Abbott, Joe
Abrams, Creighton
Allen, Terry
Almond, Edward M.
Anderson, George
Andrews, Frank M.
Arnold, Henry
Bradley, Omar N.
Brereton, Lewis
Brown, Clide
Bucher, Lloyd M.
Buckman, Simon B.
Burke, Arleigh A.
Butler, Smedley D.
Byerly, Kathleen
Calley, William L.
Chennault, Claire L.
Chidlaw, Benjamin W.
Clark, Mark
Clay, Lucius

Military, U.S. (Cont'd)

Craig, Eddie
Dean, William F.
Doolittle, James H.
Eaker, Ira C.
Eberle, Edward W.
Eichelberger, Robert L.
Eisenhower, Dwight D.
Felt, Harry D.
George, Harold Lee
Ghormley, Robert Lee
Greene, Wallace M.
Gruenther, Alfred M.
Halsey, William F.
Harkins, Paul D.
Hart, Thomas
Hobby, Oveta Culp
Hodges, Courtney H.
Holcomb, Thomas
Holloway, James L.
Hughes, Charles F.
Hutton, James
Johnson, Harold K.
Kenney, George C.
Kimmel, Husband E.
King, Ernest J.
Krueger, Walter
Land, Emory S.
Leahy, William D.
Lee, John C. H.
Lee, Robert E.
Leigh, Richard H.
LeMay, Curtis E.
Lemnitzer, Lyman
Lengyel, Margaret
McAfee, Mildred H.
MacArthur, Douglas
McConnell, John P.
McDonald, David Lamar
McKone, John
McNair, Lesley James
Marshall, George
Neville, Wendell C.
Nimitz, Chester W.
Norstad, Lauris
Olmstead, Bruce
Patch, Alexander M.
Patrick, Mason M.
Patton, George
Pershing, John
Pride, Alfred
Radford, Arthur
Reeves, Joseph M.
Richardson, James O.
Rickover, Hyman
Ridgway, Matthew B.
Risner, Robbie
Schriever, Ben
Sharp, Grant
Shepherd, Lemuel
Sherman, Forrest
Simpson, William H.
Sims, William S.
Smith, Holland M.
Smith, Oliver P.
Somervell, Brehon

Military U.S. (Cont'd)

Spaatz, Carl
Spruance, Raymond A.
Stilwell, Joseph W.
Tanner, Charles
Taylor, Maxwell
Thach, John
Towers, John H.
Tschudy, William M.
Tunner, William H.
Turner, Richmond K.
Twining, Nathan
Vandegrift, Alexander A.
Vandenberg, Hoyt S.
Van Fleet, James
Wainwright, Jonathan M.
Walker, Walton H.
Wedemeyer, Albert C.
Westmoreland, William C.
Wheeler, Earle G.
White, Thomas D.
Wilson, Gary W.
Wood, Leonard
Woods, Robert Evans
Young, James
Zumwalt, Elmo

MILITARY—FOREIGN

Canada

Crerar, Henry Duncan
McNaughton, Andrew

China

Cheng, Chen
Lo, Jui-ching
Wu, Pei-fu
Yen, Hsi-shan

Dominican Republic

Wessin y Wessin, Elias

Egypt

Naguib, Mohammed

Finland

Mannerheim, Carl Gustav
Emil von

France

Darlan, Alain
Foch, Ferdinand
Fonck, Rene
Gamelin, Maurice G.
Gaulle, Charles de
Giraud, Henri
Lyautey, Hubert
Navarre, Henri Eugene
Tassigny, Jean Lafitte de
Weygand, Maxime

Germany

Bock, Fedor von
Brauchitsch, Heinrich von
Doenitz, Karl
Falkenhorst, Nickolaus von
Guderian, Heinz
Halder, Franz
Heydrick, Reinhard
Keitel, Wilhelm
List, Siegmund
Ludendorff, Erich
Manstein, Fritz Erich von
Milch, Erhard
Raeder, Erich
Rommel, Erwin
Rundstedt, Karl von
Tirpitz, Alfred von

Great Britain

Alexander, Harold
Anderson, Kenneth A. N.
Auchinleck, Claude
Barratt, Arthur S.
Bowhill, Frederick
Brooke, Alan F.
Byng, Julian H. G.
Coningham, Arthur
Cunningham, Andrew
Dempsey, Miles C.
Gort, John S.
Harris, Arthur T.
Montgomery, Bernard L.
Mountbatten, Louis
Newall, Cyril
Noble, Percy
Playfair, Patrick H. L.
Pound, Dudley
Pownall, Henry R.
Tedder, Arthur
Templer, Gerald
Wavell, Archibald P.
Wilson, Henry M.

Greece

Papagos, Alexander

Israel

Dayan, Moshe

Italy

Badoglio, Pietro

Japan

Araki, Sadao
Itagaki, Seishiro
Koga, Mineichi
Nagano, Osami
Shimada, Shigetaro
Togo, Heihachiro
Yamamoto, Isoroku
Yamashita, Tomyuki
Yonai, Mitsumasa

Laos

Le, Kong

Netherlands

Helfrich, Conrad
Poorten, Hein ter

Poland

Smigly-Rydz, Edward

South Africa

Smuts, Jan. C.

Soviet Union

Budenny, Semion
Golikov, Filip I
Gorshkov, Sergei
Novikov, Alexander
Rokossovsky, Konstantin
Shaposhnikov, Boris
Stalin, Vasily
Timoshenko, Semyon K.
Vasilevsky, Aleksandr
Voronov, Nikolai
Voroshilov, Klimentiy
Zhukov, Georgi K.

Spain

Mola, Emilio
Pozas, Sebastian

Vietnam

Giap, Vo Nguyen
Minh, Van Duong

Yugoslavia

Mihailovich, Draja

BUSINESS

Automobile Industry

Angelli, Giovanni
Bluhdorn, Charles
Chrysler, Walter Percy
Colbert, Lester Lum
Cole, Edward N.
Cord, Errett Lobban
Curtice, Harlow H.
Donner, Frederic G.
Ford, Benson
Ford, Henry, Sr.
Ford, Henry, II
Ford, William
Gordon, John F.
Iacocca, Lee
Keller, Kauman Thuma
Kettering, Charles Franklin
Knudsen, William S.

Automobile Industry (Cont'd)

Macauley, Alvan
Moran, James Martin
Nordhoff, Heinz
Roche, James M.
Romney, George W.
Sloan, Alfred Pritchard
Townsend, Lynn A.
Vance, Harold S.
Walker, George William
Weaver, Henry Grady
Wilson, Charles Erwin

Banking

Adams, Charles Francis
Aldrich, Winthrop W.
Alexander, Henry C.
Baker, George Fisher
Black, Eugene R.
Dawes, Rufus Cutler
Giannini, Amadeo P.
Kahn, Otto H.
Lamont, Thomas W.
Martin, William McChesney
Mellon, Richard King
Morgan, John Pierpont
Norman, Montagu Collett
Peterson, Rudolph A.
Rockefeller, David
Rothschild, Guy de
Schacht, Hjalmar
Schweitzer, Pierre-Paul
Traylor, Melvin Alvah
Wiggin, Albert Henry

Aerospace Industry

Allen, William McPherson
Douglas, Donald W.
Emanuel, Victor
Fleet, Reuben Hollis
Fokker, Anthony H. G.
Gross, Courtlandt S.
Gross, Robert E.
Grumman, Leroy Randle
Hughes, Howard
Jones, Thomas Victor
Kindelberger, James H.
McDonnell, James Smith
Martin, Glenn L.
Pace, Frank, Jr.
Rentschler, Frederick Brant

Oil Industry

Getty, J. Paul
Haider, Michael Lawrence
Holman, Eugene
Jacobsen, Alfred
Jamieson, John Kenneth
Loudon, John Hugo
McCarthy, Glenn
Pew, Joseph N.

Oil Industry (Cont'd)

Pratt, Herbert Lee
Rathbone, Monroe Jackson
Rieber, Torkild
Rockefeller, John D., Sr.
Rockefeller, John D., Jr.
Sinclair, Harry Ford
Teagle, Walter Clark

Advertising

Batten, Harry Albert
Brower, Charles H.
Burnett, Leo
Cone, Fairfax M.
Cunningham, John Philip
Ganger, Robert M.
Gribbin, George H.
Harper, Marion
Little, Henry Guy
Lusk, Robert Emmett
Ogilvy, David M.
Strouse, Norman H.

Railroads

Atterbury, William W.
Clement, Martin W.
Jeffers, William M.
Pelley, John Jeremiah
Russell, Donald J. M.
Saunders, Stuart Thomas
Schiff, Mortimer Leo
Shoup, Paul
Sproule, William
Vauclain, Samuel M.
Willard, Daniel
Young, Robert Ralph

Food Industry

Busch, August A.
Chester, Colby M.
Gallo, Ernest
Gallo, Julio
Hartford, George Ludlum
Hartford, John Augustine
Lipton, Thomas
Mortimer, Charles Greenough
Post, Marjorie Merriweather
Simon, Norton
Wrigley, William

Stock Market

Cutten, Arthur W.
Funston, Keith
Housser, Harry B.
McCarthy, Mitchell W.
Martin, William McChesney
Murchison, Clint W., Jr.
Robinson, Dwight P.
Stein, Howard
Thomson, James E.
Whitney, Richard

Retail Stores

Ferkauf, Eugene
Lazarus, Ralph
Nelson, Donald Marr
Simpson, James
Straus, Jack Isidor
Straus, Percy Selden
Wood, Robert Elkington

Air Travel

Halaby, Najeeb E.
Grosvenor, Graham B.
Patterson, William A.
Rickenbacker, Edward V.
Smith, Cyrus Rowlett
Tillinghast, Charles
Trippe, Juan Terry

Steel Industry

Block, Joseph L.
Blough, Roger Miles
Fairless, Benjamin F.
Farrell, James Augustine
Gary, Elbert Henry
Krupp, Alfried
Schwab, Charles M.
Taylor, Myron Charles

Miscellaneous

Adams, Edward Dean
Arden, Elizabeth
Barnes, Julius Howland
Bates, John Grenville
Blumenthal, W. Michael
Brown, Lewis H.
Carlsberg, Arthur
Chalkley, Otway H.
Clayton, William L.
Copeland, Lammot DuPont
Cordimer, Ralph J.
Costello, Frank
Cresap, Mark
Decio, Arthur Julius
Diebold, John
Dollar, Robert
Duke, Nanaline
DuPont, Ethel
DuPont, Pierre S.
Eaton, Cyrus Stephen
Estes, Billie Sol
Fairchild, Sherman Mills
Fitzhugh, Gilbert
Franklin, Philip A. S.
Geneen, Harold S.
Gibbs, William Francis
Gray, Bowman
Greenwalt, Crawford H.
Hefner, Hugh
Hilton, Conrad N.
Insull, Samuel
Kagami, Kenkichi
Kappel, Frederick R.
Kintner, Robert Edmonds
Kreuger, Ivar

Miscellaneous (Cont'd)

Land, Edwin Herbert
Legge, Alexander
Levitt, William J.
Ling, James Joseph
Litchfield, Paul Weeks
Luckman, Charles
McElroy, Neil Hosler
Marx, Louis
Matsushita, Konosuke
Mickelson, Merlyn Francis
Miller, George William
Mond, Alfred Moritz
Morita, Akio
Morrison, Harry W.
Murchison, Clinton W., Sr.
Murchison, John Dabney
Niarchos, Starvos
Onassis, Aristotle
Onassis, Jacqueline
Paley, William S.
Pfeiffer, Jane Cahil
Porter, Seton
Price, Gwilym Alexander
Procter, William Cooper
Reed, Ralph Thomas
Sarnoff, David
Shanks, Carrol Meteer
Smith, Alfred E.
Smith, Harsen A.
Stanton, Frank Nicholas
Stinnes, Hugo
Thornton, Charles
Watson, Thomas J.
Webb, Delbert Eugene
Wilson, Kemmons

PUBLIC ENTERTAINMENT

Actors

Allen, Fred
Allen, Woody
Arkin, Alan
Arliss, George
Arness, James
Balieff, Nikita
Barrymore, John
Barrymore, Lionel
Beatty, Warren
Bergen, Edgar
Berle, Milton
Bogart, Humphrey
Bond, Ward
Boone, Richard
Boyd, William
Brando, Marlon
Burr, Raymond
Burton, Richard
Carey, Philip
Carson, Johnny
Cavett, Dick
Chaplin, Charlie
Cooper, Gary

Actors (Cont'd)

Crosby, Bing
Durante, Jimmy
Eisen, Louis
Falk, Peter
Fenholt, Jeff
Fonda, Henry
Fonda, Peter
Foxx, Redd
Francis, Alec B.
Gable, Clark
Garner, James
Gleason, Jackie
Godfrey, Arthur
Gould, Elliott
Guinness, Alec
Hampden, Walter
Harrison, Rex
Harrison, Richard Berry
Hayes, Bill
Hoffman, Dustin
Holden, William
Hope, Bob
Janssen, David
Johnson, Arte
Kaye, Danny
Lahr, Bert
Lang, Alois
Lang, Anton
Laughton, Charles
Lunt, Alfred
Martin, Dick
Marx, Chico
Marx, Groucho
Marx, Harpo
Marx, Zeppo
Mauch, Billy
Mauch, Bobby
Muni, Paul
Nicholson, Jack
O'Brian, Hugh
O'Connor, Carroll
Olivier, Laurence
Paar, Jack
Peck, Gregory
Preston, Robert
Reagan, Ronald
Redford, Robert
Robertson, Dale
Rogers, Will
Rooney, Mickey
Rowan, Dan
Sahl, Mort
Scott, George C.
Stevens, Craig
Sullivan, Ed
Wayne, John
Webb, Jack Randolph
Wilson, Flip
Zimbalist, Efrem

Actresses

Anderson, Judith
Andrews, Julie

Actresses (Cont'd)

Arthur, Bea
Bacall, Lauren
Ball, Lucille
Bancroft, Anne
Bankhead, Tallulah
Barrymore, Ethel
Berenson, Marisa
Bergman, Ingrid
Bloom, Claire
Bono, Cher
Booth, Shirley
Carne, Judy
Channing, Carol
Claire, Ina
Cook, Barbara
Cornell, Katherine
Davis, Bette
DeHavilland, Olivia
Dennis, Sandy
Dietrich, Marlene
Dressler, Marie
Dunaway, Faye
Duse, Eleanora
Farrow, Mia
Fawcett-Majors, Farrah
Fonda, Jane
Fontaine, Joan
Fontanne, Lynn
Gardner, Ava
Garson, Greer
Geddes, Barbara Bel
Gordon, Ruth
Grable, Betty
Harlow, Jean
Harper, Valerie
Harris, Julie
Hayes, Helen
Hayes, Susan Seaforth
Hayworth, Rita
Henry, Charlotte
Hepburn, Audrey
Hepburn, Katharine
Hopkins, Miriam
Hutton, Betty
Jackson, Kate
Jones, Jennifer
Kelly, Grace
Kerr, Deborah
Lang, Jessica
Lawrence, Gertrude
LeGallienne, Eva
Leigh, Vivien
Lollobrigida, Gina
Loren, Sophia
MacGraw, Ali
McGuire, Dorothy
MacLaine, Shirley
Manners, Diana
Merman, Ethel
Minnelli, Liza
Monroe, Marilyn
Moore, Mary Tyler
Moreau, Jeanne
Novak, Kim
Redgrave, Lynn

Actresses (Cont'd)

Redgrave, Vanessa
Riefenstahl, Leni
Rogers, Ginger
Russell, Rosalind
Schell, Maria
Simmons, Jean
Smith, Alexis
Smith, Jaclyn
Taylor, Elizabeth
Temple, Shirley
Ullman, Liv
Verdon, Gwen
Welch, Raquel

Producers and Directors of Stage and Screen

Bergman, Ingmar
Capra, Frank
Colby, Anita
DeMille, Cecil B.
Disney, Walt
Harris, Jed
Hays, William Harrison
Merrick, David
Nichols, Mike
Prince, Harold Smith
Rank, J. Arthur
Reinhardt, Max
Welles, Orson
Zanuck, Darryl F.
Ziegfield, Florenz
Zukor, Adolph

Circus

Beatty, Clyde
Ringling, John T.

SPORTS

Baseball

Bauer, Hank
Bench, Johnny
Blue, Vida
Campanella, Roy
Cochrane, Mickey
Colavito, Rocky
Dean, Dizzy
DiMaggio, Joe
Durocher, Leo
Feller, Bob
Finley, Charles O.
Foxx, Jimmy
Gehrig, Lou
Gomez, Vernon
Hornsby, Rogers
Hubbell, Carl
Jackson, Reggie
McGraw, John Joseph
Mack, Connie

Baseball (Cont'd)

McLain, Denny
Mantle, Mickey
Marichal, Juan
Mays, Willie
Musial, Stan
O'Malley, Walter
Ott, Mel
Rickey, Branch
Roberts, Robin E.
Robinson, Jackie R.
Robinson, Wilbert
Ruppert, Jacob
Ruth, Babe
Sisler, George Harold
Stanky, Eddie
Stengel, Casey
Street, Gabby
Tebbetts, Birdie
Williams, Ted

Football

Blanchard, Felix
Bradshaw, Terry
Brown, Jimmy
Cagle, Christian K.
Chappius, Robert R.
Daugherty, Duffy
Davis, Glenn
Edwards, William Hanford
Grange, Red
Greene, Joe
Greenwood, L. C.
Griese, Bob
Hanratty, Terry
Harmon, Tom
Holmes, Ernie
Huff, Sam
Jones, Howard H.
Kazmaier, Richard W.
Landry, Greg
Lattner, John
Layne, Bobby
Leahy, Frank
Lombardi, Vince
Namath, Joe
Parseghian, Ara R.
Plunkett, Jim
Rockne, Knute
Seymour, Jim
Shula, Don
Stagg, Amos Alonzo
Staubach, Roger T.
Unitas, Johnny
Wade, Wallace
White, Dwight
Wood, Barry

Tennis

Betz, Pauline
Budge, Donald

Tennis (Cont'd)

Connors, Jimmy
Cramm, Gottfried von
Crawford, Jack
Gibson, Althea
Jacobs, Helen Hull
King, Billie Jean
Kramer, Jake
Nuthall, Betty
Perry, Frederick J.
Riggs, Bobby
Savitt, Dick
Vines, Ellsworth
Wills, Helen Newington

Ping-pong

Bochenski, Judy
Boggan, Tim
Braithwaite, George
Cowan, Glenn
Harrison, Rufford
Howard, Jack
Resek, Erroll
Resek, Mrs. Erroll
Soltesz, Olga
Steenhoven, Graham B.
Sweeris, Connie
Tannehill, John

Boxing

Ali, Muhammad
Carnera, Primo
Dempsey, Jack
Frazier, Joe
Louis, Joe
Robinson, Sugar Ray
Schmeling, Max
Tunney, James J.

Golf

Cummings, Edith
Goodman, Johnny
Hogan, Ben
Jones, Robert Tyre
Nicklaus, Jack
Palmer, Arnold
Snead, Sam
Trevino, Lee

Horse Racing

Arcaro, Eddie
Bradley, Edward Riley
Hartack, Willie
Jones, Ben
Sanford, Stephen
Winn, Matt
Woodward, William

Track and Field
Eastman, Ben
Johnson, Rafer
Matthias, Bob
O'Brien, Perry
Patton, Melvin E.

Boating, Canoeing
Rockefeller, James S.
Mosbacher, Bus
Shields, Cornelius
Vanderbilt, Harold s.

Hockey
Chabot, Lorne
Hull, Bobby
Kerr, Dave
Parent, Bernie

Chess
Capablanca, José R.
Fischer, Bobby
Spassky, Boris

Ice Skating
Hamill, Dorothy
Henie, Sonja
Scott, Barbara Ann

Skiing
Agustsson, Linda
Cushing, Alexander
Lawrence, Andrea M.

Swimming
Holm, Eleanor
Spitz, Mark
Weil, Miriam

Auto Racing
Clark, Jim
Cunningham, Briggs

Polo
Hitchcock, Louise Eustis
Milburn, Devereux

Acrobatics
Comaneci, Nadia

Basketball
Robertson, Oscar

Bullfighting
Belmonte, Juan

Card Playing
Goren, Charles H.

Jai-Alai
Ugalde, Domingo

RELIGION
Religious Leaders, Ministers, Rabbis and Priests
Adams, Theodore F.
Arrupe, Pedro
Barth, Karl
Berggrav, Eivind J.
Blake, Eugene Carson
Brent, Charles Henry
Buchanan, Frank N. D.
Caspary, Anita
Cheek, Alison
Coffin, Henry Sloane
Coughlin, Charles E.
Cushing, Richard
Dalai Lama
Dibelius, Otto
Dougherty, Denis Joseph
Finkelstein, Louis
Fisher, Geoffrey F.
Fosdick, Harry E.
Freeman, James E.
Fry, Franklin Clark
Garbett, Cyril F.
Graham, Billy
Grant, Heber J.
Harvard, John
Hayes, Patrick Joseph
Inge, William Ralph
Kennedy, Gerald H.
Lawrence, William
Luther, Martin
Mindszenty, Jozsef
Mundelein, George W.
Murray, John C.
Niebuhr, Reinhold
Niemoller, Martin
O'Connell, William H.
Oxnam, Bromley
Pacelli, Eugenio
Perry, James D.
Pike, James A.
Pugmire, Ernest I.
Ramsey, Arthur M.
Sergei, Ivan
Sheen, Fulton J.
Sherrill, Henry Knox
Smith, George Albert
Spellman, Francis Joseph
Tillich, Paul
Van Dusen, Henry P.
Visser t'Hooft, Willem
Wesley, John
Wyszynski, Stefan

Biblical Personages
Balthazar, wise man of the
  Three Magi
Eve, first woman in the Bible
Gaspar, wise man of the
  Three Magi
Jesus Christ

Biblical Personages (Cont'd)
Joseph, husband of the
  Virgin Mary
Mary, mother of Jesus
Melchior, wise man of the
  Three Magi
Paul, Saint

Popes
John XXIII (Roncalli, Angelo
  Giuseppe)
Paul VI (Montini, Giovanni
  Battista)
Pius XI (Ratti, Achille)
Pius XII (Pacelli, Eugenio)

Miscellaneous
Bhave, Vinoba
Mahesh, Maharrishi
Shannon, James P.
Teresa, Mother of Calcutta

MUSIC
Popular Singers
Anderson, Ian
Anderson, Marian
Baez, Joan
Ballard, Florence
Belafonte, Harry
Clark, Petula
Clooney, Rosemary
Danko, Rick
Downey, Morton
Flack, Roberta
Franklin, Aretha
Haggard, Merle
Harrison, George
Hatfield, Bob
Helm, Levon
Herman
Hudson, Garth
Jardine, Alan
John, Elton
King, Carole
Lennon, John
Lopez, Trini
Love, Mike
McCartney, Paul
Manuel, Richard
Medley, Bill
Meller, Raquel
Mitchell, Joni
Nilsson, Harry
Noone, Peter
Robertson, Jaime
Ross, Diana
Sinatra, Frank
Springsteen, Bruce
Starr, Ringo
Streisand, Barbra
Suzuki, Pat

Popular Singers (Cont'd)

Taylor, James
Truman, Margaret
Umeki, Miyoshi
Wilson, Brian
Wilson, Carl Dean
Wilson, Dennis
Wilson, Mary

Opera Singers

Bori, Lucrezia
Callas, Maria
Farrar, Geraldine
Flagstad, Kirsten
Garden, Mary
Jeritza, Maria
Johnson, Edward
Lanza, Mario
Lehmann, Lotte
Melba, Nellie
Melchior, Lauritz
Munsel, Patrice
Pons, Lily
Ponselle, Rosa
Price, Leontyne
Sills, Beverly
Talley, Marion N.
Tebaldi, Renata
Tibbett, Lawrence M.
Traubel, Helen

Composers

Bach, Johann Sebastian
Berlin, Irving
Britten, Benjamin
Cohan, George M.
Gershwin, George
Hart, Lorenz
Kahn, Roger Wolfe
Loewe, Frederick
Mascagni, Pietro
Menotti, Gian-Carlo
Porter, Cole
Prokofiev, Sergei
Rodgers, Richard
Shostakovich, Dmitri
Sibelius, Jean
Strauss, Richard
Stravinsky, Igor
Taylor, Joseph Deems
Willson, Meredith

Conductors

Beecham, Thomas
Bernstein, Leonard
Caldwell, Sarah
Hertz, Alfred
Koussevitzky, Sergei
Mehta, Zubin
Munch, Charles
Rodzinski, Artur
Solti, Georg

Conductors (Cont'd)

Stokowski, Leopold
Szell, George
Toscanini, Arturo

Instrumentalists

Armstrong, Louis
Brubeck, Dave
Cliburn, Van
Ellington, Duke
Kreisler, Fritz
Menuhin, Yehudi
Monk, Thelonius
Paderewski, Ignace Jan
Rubinstein, Artur

Opera Managers

Bing, Rudolf
Gatti-Casazza, Giulio

WRITERS

Novelists

Bach, Richard
Baldwin, James
Cary, Joyce
Cather, Willa
Cheever, John
Conrad, Joseph
Cozzens, James G.
Dos Passos, John R.
Faulkner, William
Grass, Gunter
Greene, Graham
Hemingway, Ernest
Irving, Washington
Joyce, James
Lewis, Sinclair
Mailer, Norman
Malraux, Andre
Mann, Thomas
Marquand, John P.
Nabokov, Vladimir
Norris, Kathleen
Oppenheim, Edward Phillips
Pasternak, Boris
Rice, Craig
Roberts, Kenneth
Salinger, J. D.
Sinclair, Upton
Solzhenitsyn, Alexander
Tarkington, Booth
Updike, John
Vidal, Gore
Wallace, Edgar
Wells, Herbert George
West, Rebecca
Woolf, Virginia
Wouk, Herman
Zangwill, Israel

Playwrights

Anderson, Maxwell
Barry, Philip
Coward, Noel
Fry, Christopher
Hammerstein, Oscar
Howard, Sidney Coe
Kaufman, George S.
Kerr, Jean
Lerner, Alan Jay
Odets, Clifford
O'Neill, Eugene
Shakespeare, William
Shaw, George Bernard
Wilder, Thornton
Williams, Tennessee

Poets

Bridges, Robert
Eliot, T. S.
Evtushenko, Evgeny
Frost, Robert
Homer
Jeffers, Robinson
Kipling, Rudyard
Lowell, Amy
Lowell, Robert
McGinley, Phyllis
Sandburg, Carl

Historians

Freeman, Douglas S.
Schlesinger, Arthur
Toynbee, Arnold Joseph

Miscellaneous

Arlen, Michael
Breasted, James Henry
Brooks, Van Wyck
Buckley, William F.
Canby, Henry Seidel
Castaneda, Carlos
Cerf, Bennett
Curie, Eve
Fielding, Temple H.
Gunther, John
Irving, Clifford
Lawrence, T. E.
Lewis, Clive Staples
Mumford, Lewis
Stein, Gertrude

SCIENTISTS

Physicists

Bragg, William L.
Compton, Arthur H.
Draper, Charles S.

Physicist (Cont'd)

Einstein, Albert
Einstein, Elsa
Glaser, Donald R.
Lawrence, Ernest O.
Millikan, Robert A.
Ogle, William E.
Oppenheimer, Robert
Pickering, William H.
Purcell, Edward M.
Rabi, Isidor Isaac
Schockley, William
Segre, Emilio G.
Teller, Edward
Townes, Charles Hard
Van Allen, James A.
Von Braun, Wernher
Wood, Robert Williams

Biologists

Andrews, Roy Chapman
Beadle, George W.
Commoner, Barry
Conklin, Edwin G.
Enders, John F.
Lederberg, Joshua
Little, Clarence Cook
Perkins, Marlin
Riddle, Oscar
Siple, Paul-Allman
Waksman, Selman A.

Chemists

Baekeland, Leo H.
Langmuir, Irving
Libby, Willard
Nesmeyanov, Aleksandr
Pauling, Linus Paul
Seaborg, Glenn T.
Woodward, Robert Burns

Astronomers

Eddington, Arthur S.
Hubble, Edwin P.
Schmidt, Maarten
Shapley, Harlow

Miscellaneous

Byrd, Richard E.
Cousteau, Jacques-Yves
Eastman, George
Edison, Thomas A.
Glueck, Nelson
Iselin, Columbus, O.
Lull, Richard S.
Osborn, Henry Fairchild
Ramo, Simon
Rossby, Carl-Gustaf
Tesla, Nikola
Wooldridge, Dean

EDUCATORS

Adler, Mortimer
Alington, Cyril
Angell, James R.
Arons, Arnold
Athos, Anthony
Aydelotte, Frank
Barzun, Jacques
Bohnenblust, H. Frederick
Bowman, Isaiah
Brewster, Kingman
Bunting, Mary I.
Butler, Nicholas M.
Chandor, Valentine
Clapp, Margaret
Conant, James Bryant
Conway, Jill Ker
Copeland, Charles Townsend
Diamond, Martin
Dodds, Harold W.
DuBridge, Lee Alvin
Duffield, Edward Dickinson
Eisenhower, Dwight D.
Eisenhower, Milton S.
Ellsberg, Daniel
Farrand, Livingston
Gould, Samuel B.
Gildersleeve, Virginia C.
Griswold, A. Whitney
Gross, Calvin E.
Hutchins, Robert Maynard
Hardison, Osborne B.
Harvard, John
Heald, Henry T.
Hesburgh, Theodore
Jansen, William
Jordan, David Starr
Kaplan, Abraham
Kemper, John Mason
Kerr, Clark
Lowell, Abbott Lawrence
MacCracken, Henry Noble
Meiklejohn, Alexander
Miner, Dwight
Montessori, Maria
Moynihan, Daniel Patrick
Oberholtzer, Kenneth E.
Pusey, Nathan M.
Redefer, Frederick L.
Schorske, Carl
Scully, Vincent
Sproul, Robert G.
Stearns, Alfred E.
Tead, Clara
Wald, George
Wilbur, Ray Lyman
Zook, George F.

NEWS MEDIA

Anderson, Jack N.
Beaverbrook, William
Blythe, Samuel George
Brinkley, David

News Media (Cont'd)

Brisbane, Arthur
Chandler, Norman
Cowles, John
Cronkite, Walter
Davis, Elmer Holmes
Graham, Philip L.
Grant, Harry J.
Harvey, George B. M.
Hearst, William Randolph, Sr.
Hearst, William Randolph, Jr.
Hopper, Hedda
Howard, Roy Wilson
Huntley, Chester
Kent, Frank Richarson
Lippmann, Walter
Luce, Henry Robinson
McCormick, Robert Rutherford
McNamee, Graham
Moley, Raymond
Murrow, Edward R.
Newhouse, Samuel I.
Ochs, Adolph S.
Patterson, Alicia
Patterson, Joseph Medill
Pearson, Drew
Pyle, Ernie
Reid, Helen
Reston, James B.
Reynolds, Frank
Roberts, Roy Allison
Rose, Billy
Scripps, Ellen Browning
Stout, Wesley W.
Streit, Clarence K.
Sullivan, Mark
Sulzburger, Arthur H.
Sutton, Carol
Swope, Herbert B.
Thompson, Dorothy
Van Doren, Charles
Wallace, DeWitt
Wallace, Henry A.
Wallace, Lila Bell
White, William Allen
Whitney, John Hay
Winchell, Walter

LAWYERS AND JUDGES

Bailey, F. Lee
Baker, Newton Diehl
Black, Hugo L.
Blackmun, Harry A.
Bok, Curtis
Brandeis, Louis D.
Brennan, William J.
Browning, James R.
Burger, Warren
Cardozo, Benjamin N.
Clarke, John Hessin
Davis, J. Mason
Davis, June
Dewey, Thomas E.

Lawyers & Judges (Cont'd)

Douglas, William Orville
Fortas, Abe
Hogan, Frank J.
Holmes, Oliver Wendell, Jr.
Hughes, Charles Evans
Jaworski, Leon
Jenkins, Ray Howard
Johnson, Frank J.
Kennedy, Edward
Lehman, Herbert H.
Lincoln, Robert Todd
McAdoo, William Gibbs
Marshall, Thurgood
Medina, Harold
Neylan, John Francis
Pecora, Ferdinand
Powell, Lewis, Jr.
Rehnquist, William
Rhyne, Charles S.
Roosevelt, Franklin D.
St. Clair, James
Seabury, Samuel
Sharp, Susie Marshall
Sirica, John J.
Stewart, Potter
Stone, Harlan Fiske
Taft, Charles Phelps
Taft, William Howard
Warren, Earl
White, Byron R.
Wickersham, George

MEDICINE

Amaral, Afranio do
Bailey, Charles P.
Banting, Frederick G.
Barnard, Christiaan
Carlson, Anton Julius
Carlson, Paul Earle
Carrel, Alexis
Coffey, Walter Bernard
Dawson, Bertrand
DeBakey, Michael
DeLee, Joseph
Enders, John Franklin
Ewing, James
Fishbein, Morris
Fleming, Alexander
Good, Robert Alan
Heller, John R.
Humber, John Davis
Johnson, Virginia
Keys, Ancel
Laragh, John Henry
Larson, Leonard W.
Libman, Emanuel
Masters, William H.
Mayo, Charles H.
Merck, George W.
Miner, Leroy
Moore, Francis D.
Page, Irvine H.
Parran, Thomas

Medicine (Cont'd)

Rhoads, Cornelius P.
Salk, Jonas E.
Schweitzer, Albert
Sigerist, Henry E.
Stapp, John Paul
Welch, William Henry

LABOR LEADERS

Beck, David
Bevin, Ernest
Bridges, Harry
Chavez, Cesar
Curran, Joe
Dubinsky, David
Gilbert, H. Edward
Gompers, Samuel
Green, William
Hillman, Sidney
Hoffa, James Riddle
Lewis, John L.
McDonald, David John
Meany, George
Murray, Philip
Petrillo, James Caesar
Powers, Bertram A.
Reuther, Walter
Stone, Warren Sanford
Wyatt, Addie

ARTISTS

Benton, Thomas Hart
Cahill, Holger
Caniff, Milton
Capp, Al
Chagall, Marc
Cortissoz, Royal
Dalí, Salvador
Davidson, Jo
Disney, Walt
Gibson, Charles Dana
Hopper, Edward
John, Augustus Edwin
Matisse, Henri
Mauldin, Bill
Moore, Henry
Moses, Grandma
Picasso, Pablo
Rauschenberg, Robert
Rivera, Diego
St. Gaudens, Homer
Smith, Tony
Taylor, Francis Henry
Thurber, James Grover
Webster, Harold Tucker
Wyeth, Andrew

ASTRONAUTS

Anders, William A.
Armstrong, Neil
Borman, Frank
Chaffee, Roger

Astronauts (Cont'd)

Cooper, Gordon
Gagarin, Yuri
Glenn, John H.
Grissom, Virgil
Haise, Fred W.
Irwin, James B.
Leonov, Aleksei A.
Lovell, James A.
McDivitt, James A.
Nikolayev, Andrian G.
Popovich, Pavel R.
Scott, David R.
Shepard, Alan B.
Swigert, John L.
White, Edward H.
Worden, Alfred M.

CIVIC LEADERS

Alphand, Nicole
Astor, Vincent
Brownmiller, Susan
Catt, Carrie C.
Conners, Grace Isabell
Guest, Lucy
Jackson, Jesse
King, Martin Luther
Matlovich, Leonard
Mesta, Perle
Millett, Kate
Nader, Ralph
Payne, John Barton
Rockefeller, Nelson A.
Smith, Guy
Smith, Peggy
West, James E.
White, Walter F.
Wilkins, Roy
Young, Whitney M.

ECONOMISTS

Burns, Arthur F.
Dunlop, John T.
Friedman, Milton
Galbraith, John Kenneth
Heller, Walter W.
Henderson, Leon
Keynes, John Maynard
Liberman, Evsei G.
Monnet, Jean
Porter, Sylvia Field
Schmitt, Kurt
Schultz, George Pratt
Schultze, Charles L.
Smith, Adam
Tugwell, Rexford G.
Warren, George F.

PILOTS

Balbo, Italo
Bellanca, Giuseppe
Bridgeman, Bill

Pilots (Cont'd)
Curtiss, Glenn H.
Eckener, Hugo
Hughes, Howard
Lansdowne, Zachary
Lindbergh, Charles A.
Musick, Edwin C.
Powers, Gary Francis
Turner, Roscoe
Vidal, Eugene L.
Wright, Orville
Yeager, Charles

ARCHITECTS

Bacon, Edmund N.
Cram, Ralph Adams
Delano, William Adams
Fuller, R. Buckminster
Harrison, Wallace K.
Le Corbusier
Neutra, Richard J.
Owings, Alexander
Pereira, William Leonard
Saarinen, Eero
Stone, Edward D.
Wright, Frank Lloyd
Yamasaki, Minoru

DANCERS

Balanchine, George
Baryshnikov, Mikhail
Fonteyn, Margot
Nureyev, Rudolf
Shindig Dancers
Singleton, Trinette
Zomosa, Maximiliano

CRIMINALS

Berrigan, Daniel
Berrigan, Philip
Capone, Alphonse
Chessman, Caryl
Colombo, Joe
Escobedo, Danny
Fromme, Lynette
Hearst, Patricia
Oswald, Lee Harvey
Whitman, Charles Joseph

FASHION DESIGNERS AND MODELS

Dior, Christian
Fairchild, John Burr
Fonssagrives, Lisa
Gernreich, Rudi
Gimbel, Sophie
Gustafson, Carol
Hemingway, Margaux
McCardell, Claire
Schiaparelli, Elsa
Thom, Jean
Worth, Jean Phillippe

LAW ENFORCEMENT AND PENOLOGISTS

Gray, L. Patrick
Hoover, J. Edgar
Kennedy, Stephen Patrick
Lawes, Lewis Edward
Reddin, Tom
Wilson, Jerry Vernon

ENGINEERS

Bush, Vannever
Hammond, John Hays
Holmes, Dyer Brainerd
Kraft, Christopher Columbus
Loewy, Raymond F.
Marconi, Guglielmo
Sikorsky, Igor

PHILOSOPHERS

Aristotle
Buddha
Confucius
Dewey, John
Malraux, Andre
Santayana, George

PSYCHOLOGISTS

Coles, Robert
Freud, Sigmund
Jung, Carl
Menninger, William C.
Skinner, B. F.

AGRICULTURISTS

Campbell, Tom Donald
Kleberg, Robert J.
Kuester, Gustav T.
Moore, Joe
North, Warren
Schuman, Charles Baker

SOCIOLOGISTS

Boas, Franz
Kinsey, Alfred C.
Riesman, David

MISCELLANEOUS

Abbott, Charles
Abbott, Daniel
Abbott, Dorothy
Abbott, Elizabeth
Abbott, Joan
Abbott, Joseph
Abbott, Matthew
Anderson, Michael
Briard, Barbara
Briard, William
Child, Julia
Davis, Jay
Davis, Karen
Dayan, Yael
Dionne, Annette
Dionne, Cecile
Dionne, Emilie
Dionne, Marie
Dionne, Yvonne
Evans, Hiram Wesley
Gallup, George
Grzebyk, Anthony
Illingworth, Cyril G.
Kennedy, John Joseph
Langle, Eugenie
Lindbergh, Charles A., Jr.
Lloyd, Harold
Manning, Harry
Margulis, Gordon
Nabokov, Helene R.
Oswald, Marina
Righter, Carroll
Rijn, Titus van
Rogers, Mrs. (Will Rogers' aunt)
Savage, Howard Paul
Smith, John William
Stakhanov, Alexei
Stevens, Henry Leonidas
Taylor, John Thomas
Temple, Gertrude
Weiss, Brian

PERSONAL NAME INDEX

A

Abbott, Joe, 30

Abbott, Matthew, 30

Abdul Aziz ibn Saud, King of Saudi Arabia, 70

Abdullah ibn Hussein, King of Jordan, 70

Adenauer, Konrad, 65

Agnew, Spiro T., 32, 36, 47, 78

Aisha Lalla, Princess of Morocco, 69

Albert I, King of Belgium, 67

Albert, Carl Bert, 33

Alexander, King of Yugoslavia, 69

Alfonso XIII, King of Spain, 69

Ali, Muhammad, 64

Allen, George E., 77

Allende, Salvador, 55

Alonso, Mateo, 76

Anders, William A., 42

Anderson, Marian, 64

Anderson, Robert B., 76

Anne-Marie, Princess of Denmark, 67

Aristotle, 51, 75, 80

Armstrong, Louis, 64

B

Bach, Johann Sebastian, 51

Baldovinetti, Alesso, 73

Baldwin, James, 64

Baldwin, Stanley, 33

Ballard, Florence, 64

Balthazar, wise man of the Three Magi, 33, 54, 74

Barkley, Alben W., 47

Barrymore, Ethel, 27

Bartholdi, Frederic, 77

Baudouin I, King of Belgium, 67

Beadle, George W., 42

Beatty, Clyde, 81

Bedford, Gunning, 53

Belafonte, Harry, 64

Bernhard, Prince of the Netherlands, 68

Bhumibol, King of Thailand, 70

Blair, John, 53

Blount, William, 53

Blue, Vida, 64

Boris III, King of Bulgaria, 67

Borman, Frank, 42

Bradley, Omar Nelson, 33

Braithwaite, George, 64

Brandt, Willy, 42

Breasley, David, 53

Brezhnev, Leonid I., 31, 36, 37

Briard, Barbara, 20

Briard, William, 20

Bridges, Robert Seymour, 30

Brinkley, David, 78

Brock, William, 78

Brooke, Edward, 64

Broom, Jacob, 53

Brown, Clide, 64

Brown, James "Jimmy" N., 64

Brownmiller, Susan, 42

Buckley, James, 78

Buddha, 51

Bulganin, Nikolai, 83

Burch, Dean, 78

Butler, Pierce, 53

Byerly, Kathleen, 42

Byrnes, Jimmy F., 42

C

Campanella, Roy, 64

Cannon, Joseph Gurney, 2, 3, 5, 30, 56, 57

Capone, Al, 39

SUBJECT INDEX

A

A & P (Great Atlantic and Pacific Tea Company), 94

Acrobatics, 22, 158

Actors and actresses, 19, 21, 23, 63, 104, 156, 157

Advertising, 21, 155

Aerospace industry, 21, 155

Aerospace technology, 88, 92

Africa, 16, 17, 28, 69, 70, 71, 103, 104 *see also* individual countries

Afro-Americans, 59-65, 105, 106

Age of cover subjects, 29, 30, 63, 104

Aged persons, 30

Agriculturists, 19, 25, 162

Air travel, 21, 155

Airplanes, 84, 106

Alaska, 90

Albania, 15, 150

Algeria, 15, 150

Ambassadors (United States), 20, 148

American, *see also* United States

American Express Company, 94

American Indians, 59-62, 86

American society, 85-87, 91, 93, 94

Americans, 13, 14, 16, 17, 57, 91, 93, 94, 103, 105, 147-150, 153, 154

Animals, 81-84, 91-93, 106

Ants, 82

Architects, 19, 25, 104, 162

Argentina, 14, 76, 150

Art works, 53, 54, 73-80, 106

Artists, 19, 25, 53, 104, 161

Asia, *see* Far East; Near East

Astronauts, 19, 24, 25, 41, 161

Astronomers, 23, 160

Australia, 14, 16, 28, 83, 150

Austria, 14, 150

Auto racing, 22, 23, 158

Automobile industry, 21, 154, 155

Automobiles, 80, 84, 88, 106

B

Ballet, *see* Dancers

Bangladesh, 17, 90

Banking, 21, 155

Baseball, 22, 23, 63, 90, 157

Basketball, 22, 23, 63, 158

Bears, 81-83

Bees, 81, 82, 106

Belgium, 14, 67, 150

Biafra, 90

Biblical personages, 13, 15, 16, 19, 21, 24, 25, 28, 29, 51, 54, 57, 158

Bicycles, 84

Biologists, 23, 160

Birds, 82, 83, 106

Black Americans, 59-65, 105, 106

Boating, 22, 158

Boats, 84, 106

Borden Company, 94

Boxing, 22, 23, 63, 157

Brazil, 14, 17, 150

Budweiser, 95

Bulgaria, 15, 67, 150

Bullfighting, 22, 158

Bulls, 81-83

Burma, 15, 150

Business persons, 19, 21, 23, 25, 41, 154-156

Butterflies, 82

C

California, 90

Cambodia, 15, 70, 150